PowerScore®
LSAT
READING
COMPREHENSION
BIBLE
WORKBOOK

The best resource for practicing PowerScore's
famous Reading Comprehension methods!

POWERSCORE®
TEST PREPARATION

Published by
PowerScore Publishing, a division of PowerScore Incorporated
57 Hasell Street
Charleston, SC 29401

Author: David M. Killoran
        Steven G. Stein
        Nicolay I. Siclunov

Manufactured in Canada
06 08 20 18

ISBN: 978-0-9846583-5-0

MIX
Paper from
responsible sources
FSC® C004071

Guess what?
We offer **LSAT Prep Courses** too!

In Person, Online, and On Demand options available.

Planning to study on your

own for the LSAT?

on your own schedule and at your own pace!

POWERSCORE
TEST PREPARATION

CONTENTS

INTRODUCTION

CHAPTER ONE: PRACTICE DRILLS

CHAPTER TWO: INDIVIDUAL PASSAGES

CHAPTER THREE: PREPTEST 69 READING COMPREHENSION SECTION

CHAPTER FOUR: PREPTEST 70 READING COMPREHENSION SECTION

GLOSSARY

About PowerScore

PowerScore is one of the nation's fastest growing test preparation companies. Founded in 1997, PowerScore offers LSAT, GMAT, GRE, SAT, and ACT preparation classes in over 150 locations in the U.S. and abroad. Preparation options include In Person courses, Accelerated courses, Live Online courses, On Demand courses, and private tutoring. For more information, please visit our website at powerscore.com or call us at (800) 545-1750.

For supplemental information about this book, please visit the *Reading Comprehension Bible Workbook* website at powerscore.com/lsatbibles.

About the Author

Dave Killoran, a graduate of Duke University, is an expert in test preparation with over 25 years of teaching experience and a 99th percentile score on a LSAC-administered LSAT. In addition to having written PowerScore's legendary LSAT Bible Series, and many other popular publications, Dave has overseen the preparation of thousands of students and founded two national LSAT preparation companies.

Introduction

Welcome to *The PowerScore LSAT Reading Comprehension Bible Workbook*. This book is designed to be used in conjunction with the *PowerScore LSAT Reading Comprehension Bible*; its purpose is to help you better understand the ideas presented in the *Reading Comprehension Bible*, and to allow you to practice the application of our methods and techniques. This is not a how-to manual, but rather a traditional workbook designed to reinforce the skills and approaches that will enable you to master the Reading Comprehension section of the LSAT.

If you are looking for a how-to guide, please refer to the *PowerScore LSAT Reading Comprehension Bible*, which provides the conceptual basis for the general strategies you will be practicing here. In the discussions of passage approaches and techniques in this workbook, we will assume that you have read the *Reading Comprehension Bible* and are familiar with its basic terminology.

To help you practice the application of your Reading Comprehension skills, this book is divided into three sections:

Section One: Practice Drills

The first section of this workbook contains drills which test isolated analytical abilities, designed to reinforce and improve the specific skills necessary to successfully attack the Reading Comprehension section. The set of drills is followed by an answer key explaining each item.

Section Two: Individual Passages

The second section of this workbook contains ten individual Reading Comprehension passages. While they have been designed to approximate the style and general difficulty level of LSAT passages, in some cases you may find them even more challenging, which is by design. At the end of the section is a comprehensive explanation of each passage, including an expansive breakdown of each passage, a VIEWSTAMP analysis, and a complete explanation of every question and answer choice.

Section Three: Full Reading Comprehension Sections

The third section of the book includes two complete, recently released LSAT Reading Comprehension sections. Each section can be taken as a timed exercise and is followed by full passage discussions, VIEWSTAMP analyses, and explanations of each question and answer choice.

Each portion of the book is easily located using the black sidebars that mark each section.

As you finish each item, we suggest that you carefully read the corresponding explanation. Examine the correct answer choice, but also study the incorrect answer choices. Look again at the problem and determine which elements led to the correct answer. Study the explanations provided in the book and check them against your own work; by doing so you will greatly increase your chances of performing well on the Reading Comprehension section of the LSAT.

Finally, in our LSAT courses, in our admissions counseling programs, and in our publications, we always strive to present the most accurate and up-to-date information available. Consequently, we have devoted a section of our website to *Reading Comprehension Bible Workbook* students. This free online resource area offers supplements to the book material and provides updates as needed. There is also an official book evaluation form that we strongly encourage you to use. The exclusive *LSAT Reading Comprehension Bible Workbook* online area can be accessed at:

 powerscore.com/lsatbibles

If you would like to discuss the LSAT with our experts, please visit our free LSAT discussion forum at:

 forum.powerscore.com/lsat

If we can assist you in your LSAT preparation in any way, or if you have any questions or comments, please do not hesitate to email us at:

 lsatbibles@powerscore.com

We are happy to assist you in your LSAT preparation in any way, and we look forward to hearing from you!

Chapter One:
Practice Drills

Chapter One: Practice Drills

POWERSCORE
TEST PREPARATION

Chapter Notes ▮▮▮▮▮▮▮▮▮▮▮▮

This section contains a set of drills designed to achieve the following goals:

1. Reacquaint you with the type of language used in LSAT Reading Comprehension passages.

2. Isolate, test, and reinforce certain skills that are used in Reading Comprehension, and refine your ability to apply those skills.

We believe the best approach is to complete each drill, and then check the answer key in the back, examining both the questions you answered correctly and the ones you answered incorrectly.

These drills have no timing restrictions. Instead of worrying about speed, focus on a complete understanding of the idea under examination. Later in this book, there will be passages and sections that can be taken as timed exercises.

Active Reading Drill I

The following drill is presented to reinforce the valuable habit of reacting to important verbal cues. You are undoubtedly familiar with such transitional words as "furthermore" and "however." Now, your job is to pay attention to your reaction to these verbal cues, and attempt to predict the future development of the ideas in the passage. After each excerpt, take a moment to consider what is likely to come next in the passage, and then write down your predictions. *Answers on page 82*

1. Issues with the construction of the massive structure were numerous. Furthermore...

   _____

   _____

   _____

   _____

2. Not everyone who learned of the program was in favor of the proposed changes; as a matter of fact, several...

   _____

   _____

   _____

   _____

3. The crossing of the mountain range in the dead of winter was considered an incredible feat. When one considers the significant portion of the army that was lost to freezing and drowning, though,...

   _____

   _____

   _____

   _____

4. While almost everyone present had been trained extensively in the building's emergency response procedures,...

   _____

   _____

   _____

   _____

Active Reading Drill I

5. Following its initial publication, the physicist's controversial work was met with many different reactions. Some were quick to adopt his new theories, but many critics were immediately dismissive. Still others...

    _____

    _____

    _____

    _____

    _____

6. Jackson found these challenges nearly insurmountable. In fact...

    _____

    _____

    _____

    _____

7. Despite strong objections to the proposed legislation...

    _____

    _____

    _____

    _____

    _____

8. Although the movement had encountered resistance at first, eventually...

    _____

    _____

    _____

    _____

9. It was indeed true that many of the men had volunteered for the difficult mission, but...

    _____

    _____

    _____

    _____

    _____

Active Reading Drill I

10. Unlike the complex language that pervaded the writer's first three novellas...

_____

_____

_____

_____

_____

11. The general mood at the conference was lighthearted. However...

_____

_____

_____

_____

_____

12. On one side of the debate were those who had been directly affected by the storm...

_____

_____

_____

_____

_____

_____

13. As the journey progressed, unfortunately for all those involved, conditions did not improve...

_____

_____

_____

_____

_____

14. Since the corporation rescinded its proposal to build a distribution center on the edge of town, the zoning commission's sole reason for approving the variance required by the proposal was gone. With this in mind,...

_____

_____

_____

_____

_____

Active Reading Drill I

15. The cold case detective assigned to review the investigation file began to notice several inconsistencies between the crime scene photographs and the original investigator's notes describing the scene. For instance,...

_____

_____

_____

_____

_____

16. On one hand, the non-profit's treasurer was relieved to discover that it was not the organization's charismatic president who had embezzled the $125,000 missing from the organization's bank account. On the other hand,...

_____

_____

_____

_____

17. Last year, the school board wasted valuable tax dollars buying the football team new uniforms and equipment. Meanwhile,...

_____

_____

_____

_____

18. While it may be true that the government's newly announced passenger car fuel economy standards will enable vehicles meeting those standards to travel farther on a tank of gas,...

_____

_____

_____

_____

Active Reading Drill I

19. Early in the 20th century, astronomers discovered that the light emitted from nearly all observable stars was shifted into the red part of the color spectrum, meaning that the stars were moving away from Earth. In other words,...

_____

_____

_____

_____

_____

20. Historical data suggests that no one-term representative of the minority party will be able to successfully sponsor important legislation during the representative's first term in office. Even so,...

_____

_____

_____

_____

_____

_____

Active Reading Drill II

The following drill is intended to further reinforce your active reading skills. In particular, note the different directions that can be taken with subtle shifts in the language. After each of the following examples, write down your predictions about what is likely to come next. *Answers on page 86*

1. The small army suffered through a brutal winter; supplies had been extremely limited, and many of the men neared starvation. Their condition was not ideal for the battle that was to come...

    (A)   , and, predictably,...

    _____

    _____

    _____

    _____

    _____

    _____

    (B)   , but even so...

    _____

    _____

    _____

    _____

    (C)   To the enemy's amazement, however,

    _____

    _____

    _____

    _____

    _____

    _____

Active Reading Drill II

2. It was to be one of the tallest buildings in the world, and the size and scope of the project would present many unique challenges. As the building continued, issues with the construction of the massive structure were numerous...

(A)   Incredibly, though...

_____

_____

_____

_____

_____

(C)   As a result...

_____

_____

_____

_____

_____

(B)   Challenges included...

_____

_____

_____

_____

_____

Active Reading Drill II

3. Having planned extensively for a variety of different emergency situations, including both hurricanes and flash floods, city officials had considered themselves well-prepared for just such an emergency.

(A)   Thankfully...

_____

_____

_____

_____

_____

(C)   Some, however, were not quite so confident;

_____

_____

_____

_____

_____

(B)   Unfortunately...

_____

_____

_____

_____

_____

Active Reading Drill II

4. At the time of its publication, McMillan's first novel
    was lauded by many as one of the most important
    literary works of the era,

    (A)   but in retrospect...

    _____

    _____

    _____

    _____

    _____

    (C)   and although several of McMillan's
           contemporaries took issue with this
           characterization...

    _____

    _____

    _____

    _____

    _____

    (B)   and critics continue to praise the work's
           insights;

    _____

    _____

    _____

    _____

    _____

Active Reading Drill II

5.   The proposal was intended to provide a compromise
     that would be considered equitable by all concerned
     parties, but some who learned of the changes opposed
     the new plan;

(A)   regardless,...

_____

_____

_____

_____

_____

_____

(C)   these opponents claimed...

_____

_____

_____

_____

_____

_____

(B)   indeed,...

_____

_____

_____

_____

_____

_____

Active Reading Drill II

6. The strike went on for months, and some wondered whether it would go on indefinitely. Management seemed completely intractable, and the union had no intention of giving up on what the group considered to be very reasonable demands...

(A) Making matters worse,...

_____

_____

_____

_____

_____

(C) , such as...

_____

_____

_____

_____

_____

(B) Eventually, though...

_____

_____

_____

_____

_____

Active Reading Drill III: Viewpoint Prediction

In addition to noting important transitional terms and phrases, effective readers can often predict an author's perspective on a topic before it has been stated explicitly. Read each of the following excerpts and write down your predictions regarding the author's viewpoint on the given topic. *Answers on page 90*

1. For years, health officials have argued that a diet high in saturated fat contributes to an elevated risk of heart disease...

    _____

    _____

    _____

    _____

    _____

    _____

    _____

2. Stevens rejected the student's application for a seat on the school's steering committee, based in part on the debatable assertion that no student who has been enrolled in school for less than two years can have sufficient knowledge of the school and its issues to make a real contribution to the committee's work...

    _____

    _____

    _____

    _____

    _____

    _____

3. While the journalist maintains that she should be entitled to withhold the identity of her confidential source, citing the need to protect her reputation for integrity as an investigative reporter...

    _____

    _____

    _____

    _____

    _____

    _____

    _____

    _____

Active Reading Drill III: Viewpoint Prediction

4. A recent proposal by the federal government to establish a ratings system for colleges and universities has garnered the approval of several public universities, which urge the government to tie federal grants and subsidies to the proposed ratings. Private universities argue that the proposed ratings system is unnecessary, since market forces already in place set the value of these institutions of higher learning...

    _____

    _____

    _____

    _____

    _____

    _____

5. At a conference held last year, representatives from several traditional brokerage institutions expressed lingering doubts that the surprising growth of "in-app" purchases, in which consumers using applications on mobile communication devices can purchase ancillary products and services, will generate significant revenue streams in the near term...

    _____

    _____

    _____

    _____

    _____

    _____

6. Debate concerning the proposed 2021 manned Mars flyby mission has focused both on cost and astronaut safety. Some lawmakers publicly signaling support for the mission have indicated to administration officials during closed-door sessions that their support is limited to a privately funded mission...

    _____

    _____

    _____

    _____

    _____

    _____

Active Reading Drill III: Viewpoint Prediction

7. A recent survey of tenured university faculty indicates that most rate as poor their students' ability to write a well-researched and cogent paper on an assigned topic within each individual student's primary field of study. Despite the data referenced by the respondents,...

_____

_____

_____

_____

_____

_____

8. Many automobile safety experts have lobbied intently for the passage of legislation that would criminalize the use of any electronic device while driving. The theory is that a broadly stated usage ban of this nature will reduce accidents caused by distracted drivers. However,...

_____

_____

_____

_____

_____

_____

Language Simplification Drill I

Read each of the following sentences, and in the space that follows, paraphrase each using a simpler, more efficient writing style. *Answers on page 93*

Example: The law protects executives from incurring personal liability for their conduct while working for their companies, but such indemnification rights are not unlimited.

Basic Translation: *The law protects executives for their conduct, but only up to a point.*

1. The jurors will probably not be inclined to acquiesce to the defendant's plea for mercy.

   Basic Translation: _____

   _____

   _____

   _____

   _____

   _____

3. While there is some wisdom behind prohibiting the use of non-renewable resources, such an injunction does not preclude the use of renewable resources.

   Basic Translation: _____

   _____

   _____

   _____

   _____

   _____

   _____

2. Expensive machinery is rarely, if ever, a necessary precondition for facilitation and enhancement of the manufacturing process.

   Basic Translation: _____

   _____

   _____

   _____

   _____

   _____

4. The Prime Minister's recent announcement reaffirms his party's long-standing belief that a policy of nuclear deterrence is generally incompatible with long-lasting peace.

   Basic Translation: _____

   _____

   _____

   _____

   _____

   _____

Language Simplification Drill I

5. The requirement to document all tax-deductible expenses imposes a heavy burden on some taxpayers, though it does not obviate the need for compliance with all other provisions of the tax code as well.

    Basic Translation: _____

    _____

    _____

    _____

    _____

    _____

7. Unless the candidate clarifies his recent statements, his position on several integral issues will likely be the subject of widespread misinterpretation.

    Basic Translation: _____

    _____

    _____

    _____

    _____

    _____

    _____

6. We strongly oppose the allocation of healthcare spending from the public to the private sector, which not only contradicts the government's alleged reluctance to increased private sector spending, but also threatens to disrupt continuity of care and deprive the public of medical services.

    Basic Translation: _____

    _____

    _____

    _____

    _____

    _____

8. The use of complicated wording as an overall literary technique does not always detract from the intended meaning of the text, though the ironic prevalence of this approach in some lowbrow literary journals raises important questions about the degree to which complexity of language may correlate with simplicity of thought.

    Basic Translation: _____

    _____

    _____

    _____

    _____

    _____

Language Simplification Drill II

Read each of the following short excerpts, and in the space that follows, try to relay the same basic ideas in a more straightforward manner. *Answers on page 95*

Example: Many of the notably acerbic comments regarding the author's latest work were made by critics who sadly lacked the intellectual wherewithal necessary to understand the nuanced message of the beautifully written, epic tome. Unfortunately, the efforts of many of these purported sophisticates to break through the esoteric language often used by the academic writer were met, evidently, with limited success.

Basic Translation: *Some critics were harsh, because they tried but couldn't understand the author's big book.*

1. Recent scholarship on the role of Eskimo women in ritual practice often relies on the dubious assumption that female participation in this activity simply supported the male role. Such interpretations of mere complementarity not only undervalue the distinctly unique and indispensable role of women in ritual practice, but also impose a decidedly patriarchal viewpoint upon its subject.

    Basic Translation: _____

    Recent scholarship imposed patriarchal views on the interp. of role of Eskimo women in rituals.

2. Comprehensive plans are statements of local governments' objectives and standards for future land development, including distribution of population, density, and infrastructure. Because such plans are usually prepared by experts, the standards they set are often overly technocratic for the complex and ever-changing area of urban planning. As a result, the practical enforceability of these standards remains somewhat dubious in some of the fastest-growing municipalities.

    Basic Translation: _____

    Comprehensive plans are difficult to enforce by local gov'ts in fastest growing municipalities

Language Simplification Drill II

3. Professor Lavin's simplistic interpretation of Hieronymus Bosch's disquieting religious paintings is more revealing of the professor's own inadequacies than of those that allegedly plagued the subject of his critique. Indeed, Lavin's attempts to explain Bosch's style as the result of a mental illness are as hackneyed as they are predictable, symptomatic of the cultural conventions to which many contemporary historians inadvertently cling.

Basic Translation: _____

Professor Lavin's critique of Bosch, that he had a mental illness, is simplistic & a result of stupid cultural conventions historians cling to.

4. The recently introduced city tax on cigarettes seeks to curb smoking by imposing a significant financial disincentive on people who choose to continue smoking. Some critics have contended that the tax can inadvertently lead to a counterproductive effect, because many residents resort to buying cigarettes in bulk from vendors outside the city. Studies show, however, that smoking trends correlate rather poorly with smokers' perception of the quantity of cigarettes available to them at any given time. These critics' fears are therefore unwarranted.

Basic Translation: _____

Critics of new

Language Simplification Drill II

5. One of Bertolt Brecht's major critiques of Western theater targets its dialogue as a text-bound performance whose compulsory repetition is devoid of spontaneity and therefore lacking in true meaning. The compulsion to repeat the text, however, can yield different interpretations, as the dialogue through which characters convey their versions of the written text can itself be a source of spontaneity in the performance of that text.

    Basic Translation: _____

    _____

    _____

    _____

    _____

6. Under some common law jurisdictions, for an offer and acceptance to constitute a valid contract, the acceptance of the offer must meet and correspond with the offer in every respect, including the manner in which each is made. Not every variance between offer and acceptance, however, should render the intended acceptance ineffective or preclude formation of a contract, because acceptance can assume a variety of forms.

    Basic Translation: _____

    _____

    _____

    _____

    _____

7. One of the main goals of a criminal justice system is to optimize the control of crime by devising a set of punishments whose magnitude is sufficient to deter a reasonable person from committing any given crime. Although deterrence is an intuitively compelling strategic goal, there is a growing skepticism about the deterrent effect of criminal law itself. For instance, rather than imposing draconian sentencing guidelines for illegal drug users, there is a strong deterrence argument in favor of a public health doctrine that depicts the consequences of using such substances in order to discourage their use.

    Basic Translation: _____

    _____

    _____

    _____

    _____

8. Lawmakers argue that governance results from a fundamentally normative project of deliberation and consent. However, the modalities of deliberation and contractual obligation depend not upon the stability of civil government but rather on its occasional failure to deliver upon the promise it creates. Granted, such failures can be rightfully viewed as temporary setbacks, but they eventually occasion the discourse that is a hallmark of a well-functioning democracy.

    Basic Translation: _____

    _____

    _____

    _____

    _____

Language Simplification Drill II

9. In the absence of a statute providing otherwise, the admitting physician at McLean Hospital was under no legal obligation to render professional services to Jack Johnson, who was not a patient of the hospital at the time he arrived there. Regardless of whether one finds doctrinal or moral grounds for establishing a duty to treat, neither the existence of a license law nor the possession of a license to practice medicine can be construed as instruments that enlarge a physician's duty in regard to accepting an offered patient, because such laws are essentially a preventive, rather than compulsory, measure.

Basic Translation: _____

_____

_____

_____

_____

10. There is little credibility to the claim that even a politically polarized nation can distinguish between legitimate calls to action and the voices of messianic demagoguery. To speak without listening is an exercise in futility, for no matter how informed or erudite the views, they are bound to fall on deaf ears. Unfortunately, the same cannot be said about shouting.

Basic Translation: _____

_____

_____

_____

_____

11. Scholars of Antonin Artaud often argue that the dramatic effects of the satirical genre were not entirely consistent with his philosophy of truth and illusion. Whereas satire uses humor to ridicule the topical issues of the day, for Artaud the only "truths" worth deriding are supposedly those that cannot be proven as such, and may, in fact, be false. It would be too facile to assume, however, that by imbuing his plays with futuristic elements and absurd plot lines, Artaud drew a line between illusion and reality, or—worse—protected the sanctity of politics from satire's corrosive effects. A play need not be credible to be topical. As a skilled dramaturge, Artaud blurred the distinction between the boundaries we take for granted, often staging them as conditions for their mutually assured destruction.

Basic Translation: _____

_____

_____

_____

_____

_____

12. Socrates defines timocracy as the regime closest to, but decidedly inferior to, aristocracy. However, the language used to differentiate them makes such proximity both essential and unsettling. The surprise emerging from the passage on timocracy lies precisely in a dialectic whose attainment of regime derivation and differentiation depends on a certain failure to obliterate difference and faction as constitutive elements of either regime. In seeing both regimes as mutually constitutive and co-extensive, rather than oppositional or mutually exclusive, Socrates inadvertently questions the valorized difference between the two.

Basic Translation: _____

_____

_____

_____

_____

13. Scientists who reject the notion that excessive exposure to sunlight in tropical areas increases the risk of melanoma cannot reliably conclude that their theories cannot be disproved. Granted, none of the studies showing a correlation between ultraviolet radiation and skin cancer were conducted in tropical areas, and many of them failed to control for exposure to other potential carcinogens such as diet and smoking. Nevertheless, lack of evidence for a particular claim should not be interpreted as evidence undermining that claim.

Basic Translation: _____

_____

_____

_____

_____

14. More than a theory of governance proscribing the framework of a rather fragile social contract, Kobe's ideology describes the quintessence of a social contract that rescues us from the vicissitudes of anarchy. By relying upon the modality of retrospection, Kobe achieves his goal from the very vantage point it seeks to address—the vantage point of the modern constitutional state. Admittedly, such an ideology is a work of contradictions that resists a simple explanation, revealing in form as well as content a profound struggle with the contingency of its time. But this is true of most, if not all, doctrinal texts.

Basic Translation: _____

_____

_____

_____

_____

Passage Analysis and Diagramming Drill

Diagram each of the following passages using the appropriate markings and notations, and then summarize the basic structure of each passage. For further guidance on diagramming techniques, please consult *The Reading Comprehension Bible. Answers on page 101*

Passage #1:

(N)

Modern conceptions of the origin of large-scale architecture in the Americas often tend toward the belief that there was no significant construction until after 1700, when a mass immigration of
(5) European settlers began. However, this view ignores the significant contributions of the native peoples who inhabited the continent prior to the arrival of the Europeans. For example, the pyramidal structures built by the Mayans in El
(10) Mirador date back to the pre-Classic era, and represent some of the largest structures in the world to this day. In a more recent example, the pueblo peoples of the American Southwest constructed sprawling cliff dwellings that included unique
(15) apartment-like designs and immense public worship buildings capable of holding over 1000 people. These structures, still standing today, date as far back as 1500 years ago.

(N)

While architectural historians do recognize the
(20) existence of these structures, appreciation for their importance in a historical context has largely been withheld. Historiographers have only recently started to recognize this error, suggesting that a more complete and accurate understanding of the
(25) true history of architecture in the Americas will soon be forthcoming.

Conclusion

Example

Summary: _____

_____

_____

_____

_____

_____

_____

_____

Passage Analysis and Diagramming Drill

Passage #2:

The legal concept of "freedom of the seas" can be traced back to the 17th century Dutch jurist Grotius. Relying on precepts from Roman law, as well as on legal cases from other maritime

(5) countries, Grotius asserted that no one country could rightly claim ownership of the oceans, and that therefore all nations had an inherent right of free passage on the high seas. Although Welwood and Selden would later argue against the notion of freedom of the seas, the concept slowly became

(10) embedded in international law doctrine.

Grotius' initial formulation of the principle stipulated that freedom of passage extended up to the shoreline. However, practical considerations, such as piracy and military aggression, soon

(15) necessitated a policy of local governmental control over shore waters. Although the extent of that control was initially seen as controversial, in the 18th century it was agreed that local governmental control would extend the distance of direct military

(20) control from the shoreline. As cannons had a maximum impact distance of approximately three miles, that became the standard of the time.

While this standard is still in existence today, other significant demarcations are also in use. A

(25) nation's contiguous zone extends out 24 miles from shore, and allows control over all vessels in that zone. Extending outward 200 miles from shore is a nation's exclusive economic zone, largely granting ownership and control over resources in these waters. Beyond 200 miles, general international

(30) maritime laws apply, which can limit, but not necessarily override, national law.

Summary: _____

_____

_____

_____

_____

_____

_____

Passage Analysis and Diagramming Drill

Passage #3:

"Punishment" is the imposition of negative consequences upon perpetrators of intolerable activities, by entities with some type of authority over those who committed these activities.

(5) There are several common justifications for punishment, including deterrence, retribution, and rehabilitation.

First, the threat of punishment is intended to deter future wrongdoers from breaking the law, and

(10) to dissuade those who have been punished from committing further transgressions. Punishment for the sake of retribution seeks to address imbalances of justice by making sure that offenders pay a price for whatever wrongdoing has been committed.

(15) When punishment is imposed in a rehabilitative effort, the purported goal is to improve the character of those who have acted unacceptably.

Summary: _____

_____

_____

_____

_____

_____

_____

_____

_____

Passage Analysis and Diagramming Drill

<u>Passage #4:</u>

The "domino effect" and the "butterfly effect"
both describe causal chains of events, in which
an initial cause leads to an effect, which in turn
(5) leads to another effect. Where one notion is
finite, however, the other is significantly more
open-ended. The domino effect, as its namesake
suggests, refers to a clear and exhaustive sequence
of reactions that take place as a result of an initial
(10) occurrence; typically, these chains of events have
no relative scale of significance (that is, a small
event can be followed by an event of smaller,
greater, or similar magnitude).

In contrast to the domino effect, the butterfly
(15) effect posits more expansive and complex causal
chains, allowing for even a very small change in
initial conditions to have vast and varied "ripple"
effects that often leave the line of causality unclear.
Newton's third law of motion holds that for every
(20) action there is an equal and opposite reaction,
suggesting a potential for infinite butterfly effects in
response to any given occurrence.

Summary: _____

_____

_____

_____

_____

_____

_____

_____

Question Classification I: Location Designation Drill

Each of the following items contains a question stem. In the space provided, categorize each stem using one of the three Location Designations: Specific Reference (SR), Concept Reference (CR), and Global Reference (GR). Understanding the location element of any question will help to ensure that you attack the question efficiently. For a complete discussion of the question types found in the Reading Comprehension section of the LSAT, please consult *Chapter Five* in *The Reading Comprehension Bible. Answers on page 105*

1. The author would be most likely to agree with which one of the following statements?

    Location Designation:

    _____

2. Which one of the following does the author present as an example of 18th century justice?

    Location Designation:

    _____

3. Which one of the following statements is affirmed by the second paragraph of the passage?

    Location Designation:

    _____

4. In discussing "the early efforts of the organization" (line 35), the author seeks primarily to:

    Location Designation:

    _____

5. Which one of the following most accurately describes the organization of the passage?

    Location Designation:

    _____

6. Which one of the following would the author be most likely to characterize as one of the "institutional challenges" discussed in lines 13-14 of the passage?

    Location Designation:

    _____

Question Classification II: Location, Type, and Sub-type Drill

The following is a collection of sample Reading Comprehension questions. In the space provided, categorize each question using one of the three Location Designations: Specific Reference (SR), Concept Reference (CR), and Global Reference (GR). In addition, you need to categorize each question as one of the six Reading Comprehension Question Types: Must Be True, Main Point, Strengthen, Weaken, Parallel Reasoning, or Cannot Be True. Include any relevant sub-type designations, such as Purpose (P), Organization (O), Author's Perspective (AP), Subject Perspective (SP), Passage Expansion (E), Except (X), or Principle (PR). *Answers on page 107*

1. The author of the passage would be most likely to agree with which one of the following statements?

    Location, Type, Sub-type:

    _____

2. Which one of the following, if true, would most undermine the claims of Sutton's early critics?

    Location, Type, Sub-type:

    _____

3. Which one of the following, if true, would most strengthen the claims of the critics mentioned in the second paragraph of the passage?

    Location, Type, Sub-type:

    _____

4. Which one of the following statements would provide the most logical continuation of the discussion in the last paragraph of the passage?

    Location, Type, Sub-type:

    _____

5. Which one of the following most accurately expresses the main point of the passage?

    Location, Type, Sub-type:

    _____

6. According to the passage, Harding would most likely agree with which one of the following statements?

    Location, Type, Sub-type:

    _____

7. Which one of the following most accurately describes the organization of the passage?

    Location, Type, Sub-type:

    _____

8. The author mentions each one of the following as an example of early technological innovations, EXCEPT:

    Location, Type, Sub-type:

    _____

Question Classification II: Location, Type, and Sub-type Drill

9. Which one of the following principles most closely conforms to the author's notion of justice, as it is expressed in the passage?

    Location, Type, Sub-type:

    _____

10. Which one of the following most accurately describes the organization of the material presented in the first paragraph of the passage?

    Location, Type, Sub-type:

    _____

11. The author's attitude regarding the early views of the skeptics can most accurately be described as:

    Location, Type, Sub-type:

    _____

12. With which one of the following would the author of the passage be LEAST likely to agree?

    Location, Type, Sub-type:

    _____

13. Which one of the following views can most reasonably be attributed to the experts cited in line 14?

    Location, Type, Sub-type:

    _____

14. Which one of the following relationships would be most closely analogous to the symbiotic business relationship discussed in the passage?

    Location, Type, Sub-type:

    _____

15. Which one of the following most closely expresses the author's intended meaning of the word "compromised," as it is used in line 32 of the passage?

    Location, Type, Sub-type:

    _____

16. Which one of the following, if true, would cast the most doubt on Ellison's argument concerning the role of the American middle-class in the first half of the 20th Century?

    Location, Type, Sub-type:

    _____

Question Classification II: Location, Type, and Sub-type Drill

17. The researcher mentioned in lines 15-16 would be most likely to agree with which one of the following statements?

Location, Type, Sub-type:

_____

19. Which one of the following studies would provide the most support for the claim mentioned in the last paragraph of the passage?

Location, Type, Sub-type:

_____

18. Which one of the following is most closely analogous to the process of automation discussed in lines 23-31?

Location, Type, Sub-type:

_____

20. The author of the passage would be LEAST likely to agree with which one of the following statements about interstate commerce?

Location, Type, Sub-type:

_____

EXCEPT and *LEAST* Identify the Question Stem Mini-Drill

Each of the following items contains a sample question stem. In the space provided, note the Reading Comprehension question type and notate any Except (X) identifier you see. *Answers on page 114*

1. The author provides at least one example of each of the following EXCEPT:

   Question Type: _____

2. The information in the passage provides the LEAST support for which one of the following claims?

   Question Type: _____

3. It can be inferred from the passage that each of the following was achievable before the rise of modern computing EXCEPT:

   Question Type: _____

4. The passage provides information intended to help explain each of the following EXCEPT:

   Question Type: _____

5. Which one of the following, if true, is LEAST consistent with the theory mentioned in the first paragraph of the passage?

   Question Type: _____

6. The author mentions each of the following as a potential detriment associated with fracking EXCEPT:

   Question Type: _____

VIEWSTAMP Element Drills

On the following pages, you will find five drills, each focusing on one of the five VIEWSTAMP elements integral to Reading Comprehension passages.

There are five passages in each drill. After each passage, analyze the relevant VIEWSTAMP element in the space provided, and then answer the multiple-choice question testing your understanding of that element.

VIEWSTAMP Analysis: Viewpoint Identification Drill

This drill focuses on the VIEW in VIEWSTAMP: consideration of the various perspectives presented is essential if you wish to fully understand any given passage. Read each of the following passages, and notate each identifiable viewpoint while reading. In the space that follows each passage, list the featured viewpoints as well as the lines on which they are presented, and then move on to the questions that follow (try to prephrase each answer before even looking at the choices provided).

Answers on page 116

Passage #1:

Psychogeography is the study of how the physical geography of an environment affects human emotion and perception. First articulated in 1953 by French theorist Ivan Chtcheglov, and
(5)   later expanded by fellow Frenchman Guy Debord, psychogeography sought to alter contemporary architecture and to re-imagine the interaction of man and environment. But, the field struggled to find a defining ethic, and the intensely personal
(10)   nature of psychogeography made the creation of a unifying interpretation difficult, if not impossible. In recent years, psychogeography has been repopularized, primarily through performance art and literature.

Number of Viewpoints: _____1_____

Viewpoint Line References:

_____

_____

_____

_____

_____

_____

_____

1. The author would be most likely to agree with which one of the following statements?

    (A)   Recently, psychogeography has repopularized performance art and literature.

    (B)   The intensely personal nature of psychogeography allowed for the creation of a complex unifying interpretation.

    (C)   Psychogeography should be repopularized despite the field's ongoing struggles to find a defining ethic.

    (D)   The creation of a unifying interpretation of psychogeography may have been an impossibility.

    (E)   The repopularization of psychogeography has been a long but well-planned process.

VIEWSTAMP Analysis: Viewpoint Identification Drill

Passage #2:

Research into the physiology of lying has yielded mixed results. Initial research seemed to indicate that individuals engaged in the act of lying have certain immediate and consistent physical
(5) responses, including elevated blood pressure and pupil dilation. Researchers have recently shown that physiological reactions are an unreliable indicator of lying, because some individuals either do not experience such reactions, or else are able
(10) to actively suppress them. Newer studies using magnetic resonance imaging have shown that compulsive liars have more "white matter"—the brain's version of wiring—than individuals who do not lie compulsively. However, the validity of
(15) such studies is clearly questionable because the individuals classified as "liars" were largely self-reported, potentially biasing the study.

Number of Viewpoints: _____3_____

Viewpoint Line References:

_____

_____

_____

_____

_____

_____

_____

_____

2. The author would most likely agree with each of the following statements EXCEPT:

(A) Initial research into the field of lying suggested that certain immediate and consistent physical responses were associated with the act of lying.

(B) The results yielded by research into the psychology of lying have been inconsistent.

(C) Compulsive liars have more "white matter" than individuals who do not lie compulsively.

(D) Some researchers in the field believed physical reactions to be unreliable indicators of the act of lying.

(E) The validity of certain studies in the field of lying is somewhat questionable.

VIEWSTAMP Analysis: Viewpoint Identification Drill

Passage #3:

Patent laws are thought to have originated in Italy, but legal history professors have convincingly shown that the concept of patents existed as far back as the third century in ancient Greece.

(5) Despite the long legal history of patents, recent commentators have suggested that their use should be either abolished or curtailed significantly. They argue that social and technological changes have surpassed the capacities of the patent system,

(10) and instead of being an engine of expansion, patent laws are now more commonly used as a means of suppression.

Number of Viewpoints: _____ *2*

Viewpoint Line References:

_____

_____

_____

_____

_____

_____

_____

3. It can be inferred from the passage that the commentators mentioned in line 6 would be most likely to agree with which one of the following statements regarding patents?

(A) The patent system is now commonly used as an engine of expression.

(B) Changes within the patent system have outpaced technological and social changes.

(C) The use of patents should be abolished or significantly reduced.

(D) Social and technological changes slowed the creation of the patent system that is currently in use.

(E) The concept of patents has traditionally been thought to have originated in ancient Greece.

VIEWSTAMP Analysis: Viewpoint Identification Drill

Passage #4:

Peruvian poet César Vallejo left behind a relatively small body of work, but his poetry has been lauded as uniquely insightful by many commentators. The monk-poet Thomas Merton called him the greatest
(5) poet since Dante, and others praised him as "a sublime wordsmith with no contemporary peer." His notably low level of output excludes him from the group of poets that would later be considered as the best of the 20th century, although he certainly
(10) would have warranted inclusion in that group had he produced a larger body of work.

Number of Viewpoints: _____

Viewpoint Line References:

_____

_____

_____

_____

_____

_____

_____

4. Based on the information provided in the passage, Thomas Merton would be most likely to agree with which one of the following statements?

(A) César Vallejo left behind a large and impressive body of work.

(B) Vallejo's low level of output is one of the reasons why his poetry was so impressive.

(C) Vallejo's work has been lauded by many uniquely brilliant commentators.

(D) Vallejo's level of output was roughly equivalent to that of many of the 20th century's greatest poets.

(E) Dante was a great poet.

VIEWSTAMP Analysis: Viewpoint Identification Drill

Passage #5:

While often maligned by political commentators of the 1970s, the early success of the Five Year Plans for the Soviet economy is indisputable. After languishing for decades economically, in
(5) just 13 years under Plan stewardship the Russian economy produced double-digit growth.

Number of Viewpoints: _____

Viewpoint Line References:

_____

_____

_____

_____

_____

_____

_____

_____

5. The author would most likely agree with which one of the following statements regarding the Five Year Plans?

   (A) The plans were justifiably maligned by political commentators.
   (B) The plans brought the Russian economy double-digit growth for 13 years.
   (C) The plans were intended to stimulate double-digit growth within 13 years.
   (D) The plans, which were criticized by some, were initially successful.
   (E) The Russian economy languished for decades under Plan stewardship.

VIEWSTAMP Analysis: Structure Identification Drill

In this drill, your objective is to distill from each paragraph a condensed understanding of the text that is concise enough for you to remember without writing it down, yet detailed enough to serve as a practical guide when you return to the passage to prephrase your response to a question. Accordingly, each question tests your abstract, structural understanding of the organization of the passage as a whole. In the space provided, describe what the author does in each passage, and then use that prephrase to attack the question. *Answers on page 125*

Passage #1:

When considering the rate of expansion of the Universe, astrophysical theorists have long held that the universe's growth must be slowing due to gravity. However, recent observations from
(5) the Hubble Telescope suggest that the Universe is actually expanding more rapidly today than it has in the past. What, then, would account for this surprising observation? One explanatory model involves vacuum energy, a form of dark energy that
(10) exists in space throughout the Universe. The precise nature of this energy, however, remains unknown. Another explanation allows for the possibility of a cosmological model containing phantom energy that could cause the expansion of the universe to
(15) accelerate beyond the speed of light, and eventually rip it apart. A third hypothesis argues that the accelerating universe could be due to a repulsive gravitational interaction of anti-matter. Of course, it is entirely possible that the rate of expansion is not
(20) homogeneous, and that we are, coincidentally, in a temporary period where expansion is faster than the background. The benefit of this model is that it does not require any new physics such as dark energy, whose fundamental properties are yet to be fully
(25) understood.

1. Which one of the following best describes the organization of the passage?

   (A) A scientific conundrum is described, discrepancies among proposed solutions to it are evaluated, and a course of action is recommended.

   (B) A phenomenon is described, three different theories regarding its effects are presented, and an argument that the phenomenon may be short-lived is defended.

   (C) A commonly held scientific belief is rejected, three explanations for the new belief are evaluated, and a fourth hypothesis is presented as more plausible than the the other three.

   (D) Three solutions to a scientific puzzle are advanced, the implications of a fourth solution are evaluated, and an assumption underlying these solutions is rejected as not yet fully understood.

   (E) A scientific dispute is discussed, the case for one side is made and supported by examples, and a new hypothesis is advocated.

Structure:

_____ general belief

_____

_____

_____

_____

_____

_____

VIEWSTAMP Analysis: Structure Identification Drill

Passage #2:

On War, the posthumously published seminal work of military theorist Carl von Clausewitz (1780-1831), is regarded as an effort, unique in its time, to marry the concepts of political and military
(5)   strategy. Guided by the principle that war is "simply the expression of politics by other means," Clausewitz rejected a succession of preceding works of military theory for being focused too heavily on practical, geometrical, and unilateral
(10) considerations. In short, Clausewitz sought a unified theory of war that encompassed both the practical considerations of conducting war and the constant, reciprocal application of intelligent forces that permit military genius to rise above the fixed
(15) rules of traditional military doctrine.

2. Which one of the following most accurately describes the organization of the passage?

(A) Two strategies are described and a general principle is used to resolve the conflict between them.

(B) A general principle is described and instantiated by two different ways of resolving a conflict.

(C) Two ways of resolving a conflict are introduced, and a principle is used to show that they are not incompatible with each other.

(D) A general principle is described and used to discredit a commonly held belief.

(E) Two theories are outlined and a general principle is applied to decide between them.

Structure:

_____

_____

_____

_____

_____

_____

_____

VIEWSTAMP Analysis: Structure Identification Drill

Passage #3:

Harriet Tubman was born a slave in Maryland in 1819 or 1820. Having suffered vicious beatings as a child, she escaped north to Philadelphia when she was approximately thirty years old. Over the
(5) next several years, Tubman learned the duties of a conductor on the Underground Railroad, a network of people and secret places used to help slaves escape to non-slave-holding territories, and to freedom. During this time she worked tirelessly,
(10) devoid of fear for her personal safety, to help others escape as she had done. Through her work, Tubman became acquainted with other figures whose words and actions would echo down through history, telling both her story and their own.

Structure:

_____

_____

_____

_____

_____

_____

_____

3. The author's discussion proceeds in which one of the following ways?

(A) from a common claim about slavery to an inference regarding a particular individual to whom that claim applies

(B) from an account of an individual's overcoming an obstacle to a recognition of that individual's ability to help others overcome a similar obstacle

(C) from a specific observation about an individual to a more general claim about the applicability of that observation to other, similar individuals

(D) from a depiction of a predicament faced by a particular individual to a more general observation about the extent to which this predicament was shared by other individuals

(E) from general comments about a historical fact to a counterexample to these comments as applied to a particular individual

VIEWSTAMP Analysis: Structure Identification Drill

Passage #4:

Forensic handwriting analysis, a pattern matching discipline in which an examiner compares a "known" handwriting sample to the handwriting on a "questioned" document to determine whether
(5)   the person who created the known sample also wrote the questioned document, has been the subject of ongoing and vigorous debate within the legal community. Granted the status of "expert testimony," such forensic analysis is an infrequently
(10)   used but often powerful evidentiary tool employed by prosecutors to convince juries of a defendant's guilt. But, should such evidence even be admissible at trial? The answer to this question begins with another question: Is forensic handwriting analysis
(15)   a science? Recent federal appeals court decisions are split on this issue, which is critical to the determination of the proper legal standard to be used by trial courts in ruling on the admissibility of forensic handwriting evidence.

Structure:

_____

_____

_____

_____

_____

_____

_____

4.   Which one of the following best describes the organization of the passage as a whole?

(A)   A type of forensic analysis is described as controversial, its value in courtroom proceedings is presented, and questions regarding its admissibility at trial are raised.

(B)   The benefits of using an evidentiary tool are debated, its adoption is criticized as unreliable, and the implications of that adoption are evaluated.

(C)   The value of a particular type of evidence is viewed as theoretically plausible, the practical difficulties of using such evidence at trial are enumerated, and the validity of that evidence is called into question.

(D)   A type of forensic evidence is discussed, two viewpoints regarding its admissibility are outlined, and one of those viewpoints is endorsed at the expense of the other.

(E)   The advantages of using a specific type of forensic analysis are discussed, its fairness is questioned, and a more fundamental question is introduced as controversial.

VIEWSTAMP Analysis: Structure Identification Drill

Passage #5:

In the early 1950s, a diagnosis of autism—a broad
term used to describe developmental brain disorders
resulting in difficulties in social interaction and
communication, both verbal and non-verbal, and
(5) also resulting in repetitive behaviors—almost
always meant a life of institutionalization for the
person diagnosed, beginning in childhood and
lasting throughout the rest of the person's life.
Temple Grandin, born in the late 1940s, was
(10) herself diagnosed with autism in 1950. As a child,
Grandin did not speak until she was more than three
years old, communicating only through screams
and other non-verbal vocalizations. Despite these
disadvantages, Grandin went on to earn a doctorate
(15) in animal science and to invent a livestock restraint
system used for the humane handling of nearly
half of the cattle in North America. One key to Dr.
Grandin's success was a symptom of her autism:
she was a photo-realistic visual thinker able to
(20) construct and examine complex designs in her mind
before they are constructed, just as someone might
examine a photograph of the built object, down to
the last detail.

5.   The primary purpose of the passage is to

   (A)   provide a biographical account of an
accomplished scientist

   (B)   examine the hidden consequences of a
developmental disorder

   (C)   outline the historical understanding and
treatment of a medical condition

   (D)   show that a specific disorder may confer
unique benefits that would otherwise be
unobtainable

   (E)   praise an accomplished inventor for turning an
apparent disadvantage into an advantage

Structure:

_____

_____

_____

_____

_____

_____

_____

VIEWSTAMP Analysis: Tone Identification Drill

Next, we move on to the T in VIEWSTAMP: The Tone of the passage, or the author's attitude as expressed through the choices of language and subject matter. Connecting with the author to understand his or her perspective is vital to a full understanding of any passage. Read each of the following paragraphs, write down the attitude or tone of the author, and then move on to the question that follows. *Answers on page 134*

Passage #1:

Hydraulic fracturing, or "fracking," is the practice of introducing pressurized fluids into rock layers—such as those in shale—in order to assist in the removal of petroleum and natural gas from
(5) the rock strata. While fracking has increased the recovery of oil and gas from U.S. reserves and has provided economic growth in areas of the country that had been depressed, the environmental risks are unquestionably cause for concern. Groundwater
(10) contamination is the primary threat, because fracking fluids can migrate into water supplies. Other threats exist as well, including air pollution and toxic waste. These concerns need to be addressed if fracking is allowed to continue.

Tone:

_____

_____

_____

_____

_____

_____

_____

1. The author's attitude toward fracking can best be described as one of

   (A) admiration
   (B) fascination
   (C) disbelief
   (D) caution
   (E) confusion

VIEWSTAMP Analysis: Tone Identification Drill

Passage #2:

The works of Maya Angelou reflect a passion for living and a breathtaking range of life experience. Her dazzling 1969 autobiographical work, *I Know Why the Caged Bird Sings*, rightly brought her
(5) worldwide recognition and fame, but "author" was just one of many artistic endeavors at which she excelled. Angelou was also an acclaimed poet, playwright, screenwriter, editor, dancer, narrator, journalist, broadcaster, composer, actor, producer,
(10) and director.

Tone:

_____

_____

_____

_____

_____

_____

_____

2. The author would be most likely to agree with which one of the following statements regarding Maya Angelou?

(A) After Angelou wrote *I Know Why the Caged Bird Sings*, she was able to attain her justifiable goal of achieving worldwide recognition and fame.

(B) Angelou's worldwide recognition and fame was probably attributable to her many artistic endeavors.

(C) Angelou would not have been famous had it not been for the success of *I Know Why the Caged Bird Sings*.

(D) The fame that *I Know Why the Caged Bird Sings* brought to Maya Angelou was justified.

(E) Angelou had many talents, but her poetry deserves the most acclaim.

VIEWSTAMP Analysis: Tone Identification Drill

Passage #3:

In the aftermath of the Great Depression, the Glass-Steagall Act of 1933 reformed the American banking system. Later congressional actions weakened Glass-Steagall until, ultimately,
(5) significant sections were repealed in 1999. These developments directly led to the financial meltdown of the late 2000s, an event that affected millions of citizens. However, with the recent shift in voter attitudes, I am certain that changes will
(10) be made to the current banking statutes that will result in greater stability and sustained economic growth.

Tone:

_____

_____

_____

_____

_____

_____

_____

3. Which one of the following most accurately identifies the attitude shown by the author toward future bank regulations?

(A) incensed
(B) ambivalent
(C) cynical
(D) acquiescent
(E) optimistic

VIEWSTAMP Analysis: Tone Identification Drill

Passage #4:

The legal system of Yemen has traditionally been weak and disorganized. Although Sharia (the religious law of Islam) is the constitutionally mandated source of Yemeni law, in practice the
(5) system is administered by the Supreme Judicial Council (SJC). The SJC appoints judges (and can remove them at will), leading to an uncertain system prone to corruption, harassment, and manipulation. While many attempts to reform the
(10) judiciary have been made in recent years, real reform remains unlikely, and Yemen is liable to continue to suffer without genuine rule of law.

Tone:

_____

_____

_____

_____

_____

_____

_____

4. The author's attitude toward the prospect of reforming the Yemeni legal system is best revealed by which one of the following phrases?

(A) "genuine rule of law" (line 12)
(B) "traditionally … weak" (lines 1-2)
(C) "attempts…have been made" (lines 9-10)
(D) "remove them at will" (line 7)
(E) "reform remains unlikely" (line 11)

Passage #5:

West Indian manatees are aquatic mammals that
inhabit the Caribbean and U.S. Southeastern coastal
area. The large, slow-moving manatee has an
inquisitive nature and amiable temperament, and
(5)   presents no threat to humans. For a number of
years, manatee populations have been decreasing,
and encounters with humans or man-made refuse
is often the cause. For example, fast-moving
watercraft regularly strike these gentle mammals,
(10)   sometimes killing them and often inflicting serious
injury. In other instances, discarded fishing gear
such as hooks, sinkers, and monofilament line, is
ingested by the curious manatee, causing distress
and sometimes agonizing death. We should do
(15)   more to save the manatee from this inhumane
treatment.

Tone:

_____

_____

_____

_____

_____

_____

_____

5. The author's attitude toward the manatee can best be
    described as

    (A)   angry
    (B)   hopeless
    (C)   concerned
    (D)   jocular
    (E)   inquisitive

VIEWSTAMP Analysis: Argument Identification Drill

Read each of the following paragraphs, and note any identifiable arguments while reading. In the space provided, identify each argument by the line reference, then move on to the question that follows. *Answers on page 141*

<u>**Passage #1:**</u>

Incentivization has recently become a hotly debated topic. On one side of the debate are theorists who believe that the use of incentives is fraught with dangers, including unintended
(5) side effects that could lead to the distortion of our social values and goals. On the other side of the debate are pragmatists who insist that, while such dangers exist and are legitimate causes for concern, there is no other feasible way to
(10) induce needed social changes.

Number of Arguments: _____

Argument Line References:

_____

_____

_____

_____

_____

_____

_____

1. With which one of the following statements regarding incentivization would the theorists and the pragmatists discussed in the passage be most likely to agree?

(A) The use of incentives is not advisable.
(B) Incentivization is not likely to distort social values and goals.
(C) Incentivization is the only feasible way to induce needed social changes.
(D) There are risks associated with the use of incentives.
(E) The use of incentives will likely distort social values and goals.

VIEWSTAMP Analysis: Argument Identification Drill

Passage #2:

The Universal Declaration of Human Rights, drawn up in 1946 after consultation with leading politicians and philosophers from around the world, was a much needed proclamation of fundamental
(5) human rights. While the opinions of those who supported the Declaration were surprisingly consistent, the practical application of these rights proved much more controversial. An early criticism came from cultural relativists, who argued that
(10) the concept of human rights derived from Western individualism and was thus a form of Western cultural imperialism. These criticisms were ultimately dismissed, and rightly so. As the critics of the cultural relativists noted, no culture
(15) contains a wholly separate set of values, and many of the values that the cultural relativists attributed solely to Western thinking were also present in non-Western cultures. The cultural relativists also assumed, erroneously, that each country possesses a
(20) single uniform "culture," rather than a large number of sub-cultures blended together to create the whole.

Number of Arguments: _____

Argument Line References:

_____

_____

_____

_____

_____

_____

_____

2. The observation that "no culture contains a wholly separate set of values" (lines 14-15) plays which one of the following roles in the passage?

(A) It is a claim that the rest of the passage is designed to establish.

(B) It is a statement serving merely to introduce the critics' objection to the cultural relativists.

(C) It is used to support the conclusion that many of the values that the cultural relativists attributed solely to Western thinking are also present in non-Western cultures.

(D) It is offered to call into question the claim that the concept of rights is a form of Western cultural imperialism.

(E) It is supported by the observation that the cultural relativists were wrong in their criticism of the notion of human rights.

[Handwritten annotations: "Just a premise" near (C); circled (D); "The Conclusion is that the criticisms of the cultural relativists were rightly dismissed"]

VIEWSTAMP Analysis: Argument Identification Drill

Passage #3:

Before creating any of his seminal works, at the
age of 13, Michelangelo was apprenticed to painter
Domenico Ghirlandaio. Many historians believe
that Ghirlandaio played a pivotal role in the
(5)   artistic development of Michelangelo, while others
argue that Michelangelo's inherent talent would
have similarly developed at any of the academies
at that time, and that Ghirlandaio was simply a
stepping stone. According to the latter theory, the
(10)   Medici played a far greater role in Michelangelo's
artistic development than Ghirlandaio, in part
because the Medici were Michelangelo's patrons
and commissioned a number of his works. While
acknowledging the significance of the Medici
(15)   to Michelangelo's career, the opposition
maintains that it was Ghirlandaio who introduced
Michelangelo to the Medici: when asked to
name his two best pupils, Ghirlandaio pointed at
Michelangelo without hesitation, even though
(20)   the young artist's apprenticeship had not yet been
completed.

Number of Arguments: _____

Argument Line References:

_____

_____

_____

_____

_____

_____

_____

3. Which one of the following, if true, would most
    strengthen the contention that Ghirlandaio played
    a pivotal role in the artistic development of
    Michelangelo?

    (A)   The Medici would not have become
          Michelangelo's patrons without Ghirlandaio's
          initial endorsement.
    (B)   Ghirlandaio had many apprentices, none of
          whom were as successful as Michelangelo.
    (C)   Given that patronage by the Medici was
          invariably associated with superb artistic skill,
          it conferred instant status and prestige upon
          the artist.
    (D)   As patrons, the Medici allowed Michelangelo
          more artistic freedom than Ghirlandaio had.
    (E)   Some of the earliest works of Michelangelo,
          created under the guidance of Ghirlandaio,
          were not appreciated by the Medici.

VIEWSTAMP Analysis: Argument Identification Drill

Passage #4:

Neutrinos are subatomic particles, similar to electrons but lacking an electrical charge. In a recent scientific controversy, experimental results indicated that neutrinos were able to travel faster
(5) than the speed of light, a violation of Einstein's theory of special relativity. While some researchers hailed the results as a breakthrough with profound implications for the future, other researchers immediately questioned the credibility of the
(10) reported findings.

Number of Arguments: _____

Argument Line References:

_____

_____

_____

_____

_____

_____

_____

4. Based on the information presented in the passage, it can be inferred that Einstein would probably agree with which one of the following assertions?

(A) Electrons lack an electrical charge.
(B) Neutrinos are able to travel at speeds faster than the speed of light.
(C) The findings reported from recent neutrino experiments lack credibility.
(D) The results of recent experiments involving neutrinos represent a breakthrough with profound implications for the future.
(E) Neutrinos cannot travel faster than the speed of light.

This expresses beliefs specific to Einstein

VIEWSTAMP Analysis: Argument Identification Drill

Passage #5:

Bitcoin, a peer-to-peer digital currency that permits
electronic payments between strangers without
third-party intervention, has left state, national, and
international governmental organizations
(5)   grasping to understand the technology and predict
its potential impact on monetary policy. To
some, bitcoin is simply a novelty that is entirely
independent of the traditional banking system, and
without effect on the process by which the
(10)   monetary authority of a country controls the supply
of money. Others, however, argue that bitcoin's
independence and potential for nearly instantaneous
geometric expansion could seriously threaten a
nation's financial security.

Number of Arguments: ____2____

Argument Line References:

_____

_____

_____

_____

_____

_____

_____

_____

5.   The two groups discussed in the passage would
most likely disagree over which one of the following
statements?

(A)   Bitcoin can simplify large, international
monetary transactions.

(B)   Bitcoin is a form of peer-to-peer, digital
currency.

(C)   Bitcoin has the potential for nearly
instantaneous geometric expansion.

(D)   Bitcoin's potential impact might be difficult to
predict.

(E)   Bitcoin represents a serious threat to the
nation's financial security.

VIEWSTAMP Analysis: Main Point Identification Drill

In Reading Comprehension as well as Logical Reasoning, identifying the main point of a passage or argument is critical. Identify the main point in each of the following five passages, and write it down in the space provided. Use that prephrase to attack the Main Point question that follows. *Answers on page 151*

Passage #1:

Several members of the Appropriations Committee have taken the stance that public funds should only be given to projects that have proven successful in the past. Such a position does not actually serve
(5) the public good, however. This criterion, though intended to help ensure that public funding is provided for projects with the greatest chances of success, unfortunately also precludes consideration of new and potentially beneficial uses of those
(10) funds.

Main Point:

_____

_____

_____

_____

_____

_____

_____

1. Which one of the following best states the main idea of the passage?

    (A) Public funds should be limited to projects that have proven successful in the past.

    (B) The strategy of limiting public funding to projects that have proven successful is intended to ensure that funding is provided to projects with the greatest chance of success.

    (C) The public good is not well-served by the stance that public funding should be limited to projects that have proven successful in the past.

    (D) Several Appropriations Committee members have taken the stance that public funds should only be given to projects that have proven successful in the past.

    (E) Funding only projects that have proven successful in the past would preclude consideration of new uses of those funds.

VIEWSTAMP Analysis: Main Point Identification Drill

Passage #2:

Although the eagle became the national emblem of the United States in 1782, according to Benjamin Franklin the turkey would have been a more suitable symbol. In a letter he wrote to his daughter,
(5)   he described the eagle as "a bird of bad moral character" and "a rank coward." He felt that the bald eagle lacked many positive attributes of the turkey, which he described in the letter as a "much more respectable bird, and withal a true original
(10)   native of America."

Main Point:

_____

_____

_____

_____

_____

_____

_____

2.   Which one of the following most completely and accurately reflects the main point of the passage?

(A)   The eagle became the national emblem of the United States in 1782.

(B)   Benjamin Franklin believed that the turkey was less suitable as a national symbol than the eagle would have been.

(C)   Benjamin Franklin saw the eagle as "a bird of bad moral character."

(D)   Benjamin Franklin believed that the bald eagle lacked many of the positive attributes of the turkey.

(E)   Benjamin Franklin regarded the eagle as a less suitable emblem than the turkey.

VIEWSTAMP Analysis: Main Point Identification Drill

<u>**Passage #3:**</u>

Since corporations are driven, in large part, by the motivation to increase profits, they cannot always be relied upon to make morally or ethically sound decisions. This is especially true if there are no

(5) legal disincentives for making unethical decisions. While the practices of some companies are beyond reproach, many corporations act in a manner that is clearly devoid of ethical or moral fortitude.

Main Point:

_____

_____

_____

_____

_____

_____

_____

_____

3. Which one of the following statements best expresses the main idea of the passage?

   (A)   Corporations are driven by their motivation to increase profits.

   (B)   The actions of many corporations are driven exclusively by moral and ethical considerations.

   (C)   The law allows corporations to make morally or ethically questionable decisions.

   (D)   Corporations cannot always be relied upon to make morally or ethically sound decisions.

   (E)   Some companies' practices are beyond reproach.

VIEWSTAMP Analysis: Main Point Identification Drill

Passage #4:

People should not be surprised that the number of
movie tickets sold annually nationwide has been
decreasing precipitously for several years. Even as
the prices of movie tickets—and the various
(5) concessions sold at those theaters—have continued
to increase year after year, the public has been
provided access to a vast and ever-increasing array
of other entertainment options. While some theaters
have continued to draw crowds on a regular basis,
(10) sales numbers have dropped steadily as a result
of rising ticket prices, coupled with an increased
competition for the public's attention.

Main Point:

_____

_____

_____

_____

_____

_____

_____

4. Which one of the following best states the main idea
    of the passage?

(A) The decreasing sales of movie tickets should
    have been expected.
(B) Some theaters have continued to draw crowds
    on a regular basis.
(C) Movie ticket sales have increased steadily as a
    result of falling ticket prices.
(D) Prices of movie tickets and concessions have
    continued to rise year after year.
(E) In recent years the public has been provided
    access to a vast and ever-increasing array of
    entertainment options.

VIEWSTAMP Analysis: Main Point Identification Drill

Passage #5:

Zoologist: Despite their size, honey badgers are well-equipped for survival, with large, strong claws and skin thick enough to ward off attacks by almost any predator. They have been known to challenge

(5) animals much bigger than themselves, including lions, horses, cattle, and buffalo. In addition to their fighting prowess, honey badgers are also extremely intelligent, as members of one of the few species on earth with a documented capacity to

(10) utilize basic tools.

Main Point:

_____

_____

_____

_____

_____

_____

_____

5. Which one of the following most accurately states the author's main point?

(A) Honey badgers are extremely intelligent, as reflected in their ability to use basic tools.

(B) Honey badgers are skilled fighters and are also extremely intelligent.

(C) Honey badgers are well equipped for survival despite their size.

(D) Honey badgers are able to use basic tools to protect themselves from predators.

(E) Honey badgers have many natural predators, including lions, horses, cattle, and buffalo.

Passage Elements and Formations Recognition Drill

Read each of the following paragraphs, and identify any notable passage elements, formations, or sources of difficulty as discussed in Chapter Three of the *Reading Comprehension Bible*. In the space that follows each paragraph, briefly list each item (note that examples may contain more than one identifiable element). *Answers on page 158*

<u>Passage #1:</u>

Mozart composed his first musical piece in 1761, at age 5. The following year, he and his sister performed at the court of Maximilian III. Mozart spent much of his youth traveling throughout Europe and performing. By 1773, he had gained a
(5) number of admirers in his hometown of Salzburg, and secured a position as court musician to Count Colloredo. However, financial concerns and artistic limitations caused Mozart to resign the Salzburg
(10) court position in 1777.

Analysis: _____

_____

_____

_____

_____

_____

_____

<u>Passage #2:</u>

Antiquities law addresses the ownership, sale, and protection of cultural items of value. While these laws are clear in their protective intent, they remain, to some extent, open to interpretation,
(5) and consequently, in some cases the public good is not protected as intended. What priorities, then, should a jurist consider when overseeing a case that involves antiquities?

Analysis: _____

_____

_____

_____

_____

_____

Passage Elements and Formations Recognition Drill

Passage #3:

About 5,000 years ago, the Harappan civilization sprawled over nearly 400,000 square miles (1 million square kilometers) on the plains of the Indus River in modern-day India and Pakistan.
(5)   At its peak, this civilization accounted for nearly 10 percent of the world population. Only recently have scientists determined why this civilization disappeared, and climate change was a key ingredient in this collapse. As weather patterns
(10) shifted, the monsoons that fed the Indus River plain began to move eastward, and many of the rivers coursing through the region began to dry up. The resulting population shift deprived the Harappans of vital economic resources, which led to the
(15) civilization's eventual demise.

Analysis: _____

_____

_____

_____

_____

_____

_____

Passage #4:

Polychlorinated biphenyls (PCBs), which were once widely used in coolants and insulators, have been banned by Congress because of the severe danger they presented to the public.
(5)   Epidemiological studies of the effects of PCBs on humans revealed potential carcinogenicity and significant long-term persistence in the environment. Non-carcinogenic effects include damage to the immune system, reproductive
(10) system, nervous system, and endocrine system.

Analysis: _____

_____

_____

_____

_____

_____

_____

Passage Elements and Formations Recognition Drill

Passage #5:

"Jazz poetry" largely blossomed during the Harlem Renaissance of the 1920s and 1930s. In general, jazz poetry attempted to mimic several aspects of the jazz music that was then in vogue.
(5) First, the poetry spoke in a uniquely African American voice. Second, the structure within individual poems often varied, much like the music improvised by jazz musicians. Finally, the writing style and word usage mirrored the
(10) rhythms and pacing of jazz music.

Analysis: _____

_____

_____

_____

_____

_____

_____

_____

Passage #6:

Recently, the International Court of Justice in The Hague ruled that Japan breached international law when it captured and killed thousands of whales of certain types and issued permits for the killing of
(5) other types in an area designated as the Southern Ocean Whale Sanctuary. The ruling, identified by many court observers as unprecedented in its unequivocal rebuke and injunction of whaling activities by a sovereign nation, was lauded by
(10) environmentalists. However, many Japanese fishermen urged their government to fight the ruling, arguing that whaling is a cultural tradition that deserves respect. Yet one observer of Japanese politics noted that the banned whaling activities
(15) were no longer financially viable, requiring government subsidies anticipated to soon reach $50 million per year, and that this need for subsidies explains the Japanese government's almost immediate decision to abide by the Court's ruling.

Analysis: _____

_____

_____

_____

_____

_____

_____

Passage Elements and Formations Recognition Drill

Passage #7:

Physicists studying super-heavy atomic nuclei conducted experiments in which they bombarded a thin layer of americium, an artificial radioactive metal created when plutonium atoms absorb

(5)   neutrons during nuclear reactions, with calcium ions. This collision produced a new element that has 115 protons at its center. If approved by an international committee of physicists and chemists, this new element will be placed on the periodic

(10) table with the atomic number 115. Temporarily named "ununpentium," this artificial element would be the latest super-heavy element to be created through accelerator based experimentation. Of the elements found naturally occurring on Earth,

(15) the heaviest is uranium, which has 92 protons in its nucleus, although the heaviest stable element, meaning an element that does not decay, is lead, which has 82 protons in its nucleus.

Analysis: _____

_____

_____

_____

_____

_____

_____

Passage #8:

Immediately after pleadings are filed, or at some other time during the pendency of the suit, a trial court may appoint a Guardian ad Litem (GAL) to represent a child in matters of custody and

(5)   visitation. GALs are appointed under the theory that the child's parents, embroiled in difficult litigation, may put their own needs above those of the child when making strategic and tactical decisions related to the contest. The decision

(10) regarding whether and when to appoint a GAL for a child is almost universally a matter within the plenary discretion of the trial court, and that decision is given considerable deference by the appellate courts. This wide-ranging discretion

(15) has produced great disparity in how trial judges appoint and use GALs. Some judges appoint them by default, even when the parties are sophisticated and represented by counsel, a situation in which GALs are commonly considered to be unnecessary.

(20) Other judges will appoint a GAL only upon formal motion by a party, and even then only when a party has demonstrated a particularized need for the child to have independent counsel. A new survey indicates that this disparity in appointment results

(25) in substantial practical implications for family law practitioners.

Analysis: _____

_____

_____

_____

_____

_____

_____

Passage Elements and Formations Recognition Drill

Passage #9:

Fearing the emergence of a new, pandemic zoonotic disease—a contagious disease transmitted from animals to humans and caused by bacteria, viruses, parasites and fungi carried by animals and insects—
(5) scientists recently created a new pathogen (i.e., a bacterium, virus, or other microorganism that can cause disease) that is 97 percent similar to the 1918 Spanish Flu, which is thought to have originated in birds and which killed approximately 50 million
(10) people. The scientists constructed the new virus by cobbling together wild bird flu fragments. To make the pathogen easier to spread from one animal to another, the scientists mutated it, making it airborne. Some have labeled the project "insane,"
(15) stressing the tremendous danger involved in intentionally creating a virus that could potentially kill millions of people if released into the general population, either accidentally, or deliberately, as a terrorist act, for example. Moreover, the threat of
(20) such a virus emerging naturally from the animal population is too low to justify the risk posed by the research. The researchers have defended their work by pointing to the possibility that a disease similar to the Spanish Flu could spontaneously emerge
(25) without warning from the animal population. By creating such a pathogen in a secure, laboratory environment, they argue, health officials can better prepare to detect and treat a naturally occurring outbreak.

Analysis: _____

_____

_____

_____

_____

_____

_____

_____

Passage #10:

In an era of corporate downsizing, large law firms have renewed their insistence that law schools focus less on academia and more on the production of the "practice-ready lawyer." However, some law
(5) professors argue that their institutions should reject what they view as a misguided and short-sighted attempt by the firms to shift their training expenses to the law schools. While firms urge law schools to offer more clinics, externships, and practitioner-
(10) specific courses, these professors argue that such an approach is impractical. The first hurdle involves identifying the proper standard for determining what a practice-ready lawyer is. If the standard is minimal competence, professors argue, then
(15) the state-level bar examination already ensures that level of preparedness. Next is the issue of specialization: should law students try to determine a field of practice prior to graduation, the professors ask? If they do not, then the scope of the private
(20) legal market would be too broad for law schools to provide significant practical experience in even the major sub-categories of legal work. Finally, law professors point out that much of what makes legal practice unique is the confluence of institutional
(25) structures, power dynamics, economic incentives, and complex ethical obligations that is impossible to replicate in the law school setting.

Analysis: _____

_____

_____

_____

_____

_____

_____

_____

Science Mini-Passage Drill

To most students, science topics appear at least a bit intimidating. However, keep in mind that the LSAT will not assume that you know anything about advanced technical or scientific ideas: key terms and concepts will always be defined and explained. The following two mini-passages are intended to reinforce your facility with dense, scientific text. Pay particular attention of Passage Elements and Formations that could generate questions. After each passage, you will find a set of three multiple-choice questions. Try to prephrase your answers whenever possible. For more information on how to tackle Science Passages, please consult the Chapter Eight of *The Reading Comprehension Bible. Answers on page 165*

Science Mini-Passage Drill

<u>Passage #1:</u>

Systemic lupus eythematosus (SLE) is an autoimmune disease characterized by the aberrant and chronic stimulation of the innate immune system—our first line of defense against infection.
(5) Under normal circumstances, immune cells are recruited to sites of infection through the production of chemical factors called cytokines. In patients with SLE, cytokines recruit cells to attack normal, healthy tissues without the presence of an
(10) infectious pathogen. This results in the proliferation of antibody-immune complexes that cause inflammation and damage to the kidneys, blood vessels, and skin.

Patients with SLE are often treated with courses
(15) of strong immunosuppressive drugs, such as cytotoxic drugs, antimalarial compounds and glucocorticoids. While glucocorticoid therapy is considered the most effective course of treatment, it is regrettably transient, requiring more aggressive
(20) (and potentially more harmful) treatments such as high-dose methylprednisolone pulse therapy. Discovering why glucocorticoid therapy fails to provide lasting relief has been the subject of numerous studies. The main culprit seems to be
(25) the plasmacytoid dendritic cells (pDC)—innate immune cells that circulate in the blood and are found in peripheral lymphoid organs. While pDCs are normally susceptible to treatment with glucocorticoids, they are resistant to such
(30) treatment in patients with SLE. And, since pDCs are responsible for producing the key cytokines involved in SLE pathogenesis, the level of these cytokines does not substantially decrease with treatment, and symptoms quickly relapse. The
(35) precise mechanism by which pDC resistance occurs is still unknown.

1. In the passage the author is primarily concerned with doing which one of the following?

    (A) outlining the mechanisms by which immune cells attack healthy tissues in patients with SLE
    (B) demonstrating the difficulties that must be overcome if a satisfactory cure for SLE is to be found
    (C) describing how SLE originates and explaining why it is difficult to treat
    (D) showing why one explanation of the difficulties involved in treating SLE falls short in explaining these difficulties
    (E) evaluating the evidence supporting the explanation as to why SLE is difficult to treat

2. Which one of the following is most strongly supported by the passage?

    (A) Identifying a cure for SLE requires understanding the precise mechanism by which pDC resistance occurs.
    (B) Infection is not necessary for the innate immune system to be stimulated.
    (C) Successful treatment of SLE does not require reducing the harmful effects of antibody-immune complexes on healthy tissues.
    (D) In patients with SLE, the risks associated with high-dose methylprednisolone pulse therapy outweigh the benefits of such a therapy.
    (E) Cytokines do not cause inflammation unless an infection is detected.

3. The author mentions that pDCs are responsible for producing the key cytokines involved in SLE pathogenesis (lines 30-32) primarily in order to

    (A) explain how pDCs develop resistance to glucocorticoid therapy
    (B) help distinguish pDCs from other innate immune cells that circulate in the blood
    (C) emphasize the importance of pDCs in fighting infection
    (D) indicate why pDC resistance to glucocorticoid therapy interferes with our ability to treat SLE
    (E) explain why glucocorticoid therapy fails to provide lasting relief

Science Mini-Passage Drill

Passage #2:

Biologists have long suspected that cancer elicits a cell-mediated antitumor immune response in humans, and their suspicion has finally been confirmed. Unlike humoral immunity, which is
(5) mediated not by cells but by antibodies, cell-mediated immunity refers to the activation of antigen-specific T-cells, macrophages and natural killer cells that destroy invading pathogens. Although cell-mediated immunity is directed
(10) primarily at microbes and is most effective in removing virus-infected cells, research conducted in the 1990s offers definitive proof that most tumors contain tumor-infiltrating T-cells. Although the prognostic significance of infiltration varies
(15) among tumor type, the mere presence of such cells suggests that tumors express antigens capable of eliciting cell-mediated immunological responses. Similar studies have replicated these findings using experimental rodent models.
(20) Why antitumor T-cells ultimately fail to eliminate the tumor represents a major paradox of tumor immunology. Some scientists hypothesize that tumor cells are able to escape T-cell surveillance entirely. Dr. Genart, however, has recently shown
(25) that while tumor-specific T-cells can infiltrate tumors, they are inhibited from performing their lytic function—the ability of T-cells to destroy target cells. This lytic defect is probably an acquired characteristic exclusive to T-cells residing
(30) in the tumor microenvironment, since similar cells that reside elsewhere in the body do not exhibit the same defect. The defect is also transient: upon purifying tumor-infiltrating T-cells from the tumor, Genart has shown that their lytic function is rapidly
(35) restored. These observations support the hypothesis that the lytic function of tumor-infiltrating T-cells is inhibited by the tumor itself.

1. The passage mentions each of the following as support for the hypothesis that cancer elicits a cell-mediated antitumor immune response in humans EXCEPT:

   (A) the occurrence of an apparently similar immune response in other species
   (B) the presence of tumor-infiltrating T-cells in the tumor microenvironment
   (C) the ability of tumors to express certain antigens
   (D) the inability of T-cells to destroy the tumor
   (E) the results of scientific studies conducted in the 20th century

2. The author would be most likely to agree with which one of the following statements about the lytic function of tumor-infiltrating T-cells?

   (A) It is inhibited by the ability of tumor cells to escape T-cell surveillance.
   (B) It is disrupted by tumor-specific antigens.
   (C) It is a critical component of cell-mediated immunity.
   (D) It is directed primarily at microbes.
   (E) It is dependent upon the environment in which the T-cell resides.

3. Which one of the following, if true, would most seriously challenge the hypothesis mentioned in lines 28-30?

   (A) Many tumors are caused by viruses that can also disrupt the normal function of T-cells.
   (B) Tumor-infiltrating T-cells have other important, nonlytic functions that are also disrupted at the tumor site.
   (C) Some tumors avoid T-cell recognition by mimicking healthy cells.
   (D) T-cells are not always capable of destroying their target cells completely, even if the target cells are not cancerous.
   (E) Some pathogens inhibit the lytic function of T-cells by integrating into the cell's genome.

...lowing Comparative Reading mini-passage sets, noting similarities and
...the passages in each set before attacking the questions. *Answers on page 169*

Passage Set #1:

Passage A

Bacteria are a type of prokaryotic organism
present in most habitats on Earth. In fact, their
total biomass exceeds that of all plants and animals
combined. In a single milliliter of fresh water, for
(5)   instance, there could be as many as one million
bacterial cells, most of which are perfectly harmless
to humans or other animals. Some waterborne
bacteria, however, can be pathogenic. Waterborne
diarrheal disease, for instance, annually causes
(10) about 1.8 million human deaths, most of them
a direct result of bacterial infections with any
number of disease-causing pathogens, including
Campylobacter, E. coli, V. cholerae, Salmonella,
and *C. botulism.* Proper hygiene and water
(15) sanitation are crucial in protecting the public from
waterborne diseases, especially in developing
countries where the risk of infection and the
potential socioeconomic costs are particularly high.

Passage B

All animals, including humans, live in close
(20) association with microbial organisms. Until
recently, this interaction has been defined mostly
in the context of disease-causing pathogens and a
relatively small number of symbiotic case studies.
Organisms, however, do not live in isolation—they
(25) evolve in the context of complex communities.
In a new five-year federal endeavor, the Human
Microbiome Project, researchers have discovered
that the human body contains as many as 100
trillion "good" bacteria which are essential for
(30) life, including digestion, vitamin synthesis, and
the regulation of the immune system. Even more
surprising is the discovery that there are disease-
causing bacteria in each of us. Instead of making
us ill, however, they coexist peacefully with their
(35) hosts.

1. Each of the passages contains information sufficient
    to answer which one of the following questions?

    (A) Approximately how many human deaths result
         from bacterial infections each year?
    (B) What proportion of the bacteria contained in
         the human body is essential for life?
    (C) Are harmful pathogens sometimes present in
         the human body?
    (D) Approximately how many prokaryotic
         organisms are contained in a single milliliter
         of fresh water?
    (E) What are some of the disease-causing
         pathogens that live inside the human body
         without harming it?

2. It can be inferred that both authors would be most
    likely to agree with which one of the following
    statements regarding bacteria?

    (A) Some of them are essential for life.
    (B) Some of them are harmless to humans.
    (C) They can cause diseases whose socioeconomic
         costs are particularly high.
    (D) Their biomass exceeds that of all other living
         organisms.
    (E) They evolved in the context of complex
         communities.

Comparative Reading Mini-Passages

Passage Set #2:

Passage A

(1)   To avoid consuming sugar and thus lower their
total caloric intake, many people resort to artificial
sweeteners—a $1.5 billion-a-year market in the
United States alone. Some still worry that the
(5)   potential long-term side effects are yet unknown.
However, despite some early warnings that certain
types of sugar substitutes cause bladder cancer
in rats, the scientific community is confident
that sugar substitutes are generally safe. Having
(10)   adequately tested for potential toxicities in doses
that were hundreds of times higher than the typical
amounts humans consume (artificial sweeteners are
much sweeter than sugar, so people consume very
little of them), the Federal Drug Administration
(15)   has issued a definitive statement endorsing their
consumption, because the health benefits of
consuming less sugar far outweigh the potential
theoretical costs.

Passage B

(20)   Nutritionists and obesity experts welcome the
newly issued ban on the sale of large sugary drinks
at restaurants and movie theaters in New York City,
but many argue that the ban imposes a draconian
rule that is unlikely to have any significant health
benefits. The New York City Beverage Association,
(25)   for instance, complains that the city has unfairly
singled out soda, calling the city's concern for the
health of its residents an "unhealthy obsession"
that avoids seeking real solutions to curb obesity.
Others claim that the ban is an infringement on
(30)   personal freedom preventing people from making
real choices about the food they eat. Nevertheless,
the city's ban is a step in the right direction. In
New York City, more than half of adults are obese
or overweight, and about a third drink at least one
(35)   sugary drink a day. Neighborhoods where soda
consumption is more common have even higher
obesity rates, suggesting that sweetened drinks are
directly responsible, at least in part, for the increase
in citywide obesity rates. The ban would not apply
(40)   to drinks with fewer than 25 calories per 8-ounce
serving, such as unsweetened iced teas or diet sodas
that use artificial sweeteners instead of sugar.

1. The passages have which one of the following aims in
    common?

    (A) Illustrating the difficulty of reaching scientific
         consensus on controversial nutritional issues.
    (B) Describing certain scientific studies concerned
         with nutritional safety.
    (C) Analyzing the effects of sugar consumption on
         obesity.
    (D) Defending a policy that aims to decrease sugar
         consumption.
    (E) Questioning the feasibility of any policy that
         aims to curb obesity.

2. Which of the following statements most accurately
    characterizes a difference between the two passages?

    (A) Passage A provides evidence corroborating the
         safety of making certain nutritional choices,
         whereas passage B attests to the dangers of
         not making similar choices.
    (B) Passage A is concerned solely with identifying
         what are seen as obstacles to the adoption
         of a particular nutritional strategy, whereas
         passage B is not concerned with any such
         obstacles.
    (C) Passage A discusses evidence adduced by
         scientists in support of a particular nutritional
         strategy, whereas passage B assumes that this
         strategy is beneficial without discussing the
         support that has been adduced for it.
    (D) Passage A considers the potential costs of
         making a recommended nutritional choice,
         whereas passage B does not consider the costs
         of making a similar choice.
    (E) Passage A explains why people make bad
         nutritional choices, whereas passage B
         examines the consequences of making such
         choices.

Comparative Reading Mini-Passages

Passage Set #3:

Passage A

Because they ensure equivalent content and testing conditions for all students without the possibility of subjective bias, standardized tests are reliable and objective measures of student
(5) achievement. The use of frequent, standardized testing to monitor student progress is strongly associated with significant and sustained gains on national and international assessments of cognitive ability. China, for instance, with its long tradition of
(10) standardized testing, leads the world in educational achievement. Despite some recent criticism that learning to "ace the test" narrows student curriculum and replaces good teaching practices, standardized tests provide a much needed incentive
(15) for teachers to focus on important basic skills that all students should master. Additionally, because a 50-item standardized test can be given in under an hour at a cost of $15—$33 per student, such tests provide educators with a lot of useful information
(20) at a comparatively low cost.

Passage B

Despite using standardized tests for several decades, policymakers and educators do not yet know how to use such tests to consistently generate positive effects on student achievement.
(25) Proponents tout a correlation between student testing and test score improvements, but fail to recognize that such progress is temporary and has little to do with long-term changes in learning. Indeed, standardized tests measure only a small
(30) portion of what makes education meaningful, ignoring important personal qualities such as creativity, critical thinking, curiosity, empathy, and motivation. Even the seemingly unquestionable "fairness" of standardized testing is a myth.
(35) Most standardized tests unwittingly discriminate against students with diverse backgrounds who are expected to answer questions predominantly written for the white, abled majority. More than merely ineffective, student testing detracts from teaching
(40) higher-order thinking, lowers the cognitive content of the curriculum, and causes severe stress among even the brightest of students, often making young children vomit, cry, or both.

1. Passage A differs from passage B in that passage A is more

(A) skeptical towards the possibility of quantifying student achievement by means of standardized testing.
(B) supportive of ongoing research related to the reliability of standardized testing.
(C) optimistic regarding the ability of standardized testing to monitor student progress.
(D) open-minded in its willingness to accept a variety of metrics in assessing cognitive ability.
(E) circumspect in its refusal to acknowledge that standardized tests are inherently biased.

2. Which one of the following, if true, would cast doubt on the argument in passage B but bolster the argument in passage A?

(A) Standardized tests are just as likely to cause severe stress among students as other forms of testing, such as final exams.
(B) The importance of test scores in college admissions is not as high as many students, parents and teachers suspect.
(C) Chinese students, on average, spend more time preparing for standardized tests than most other students.
(D) A curriculum designed to improve student performance on standardized tests can be just as challenging as a curriculum whose purported objectives are more holistic in nature.
(E) Standardized tests, when combined with other metrics, have an unusually high level of predictive validity in estimating the academic potential of most students.

Comparative Reading Mini-Passages

Passage Set #4:

Passage A

More than half of all video games sold in the United States include violent content and carry a "Mature" rating recommended for persons aged 17 and older. Considering the sheer number of
(5) video games sold every year—between 300 and 600 million annually—the popularity of violent video games should be a cause for concern among parents, teachers, and policy makers nationwide. Since most video games reward players for
(10) exhibiting violent behavior, it is not surprising that playing such games correlates with reports of school bullying and animal abuse. By teaching players to associate pleasure with the ability to cause pain in others, they not only desensitize
(15) players to real-life violence, but also encourage aggressive behavior. In fact, a 2000 FBI report includes playing violent video games in a list of behaviors associated with school shootings.

Passage B

Many of the studies looking for a correlation
(20) between violent video games and violent behavior suffer from design flaws and use unreliable measures of aggression. They confuse thoughts about aggression with actual behavior, and fail to follow children over long periods of time.
(25) Nevertheless, although a causal link between violent video games and violent behavior has not been definitively proven, the design flaws in these studies should not be interpreted as a validation of safety. More extensive and reliable studies are
(30) clearly needed to determine if a correlation between video games and violence actually exists. If it does, we must also acknowledge the equally plausible hypothesis that violent youth simply seek out violent entertainment in the form of video games.

1. Which one of the following most accurately describes the attitude expressed by the author of passage B toward the argument presented in passage A?

   (A) tacit agreement
   (B) pure neutrality
   (C) cautious reservation
   (D) outright rejection
   (E) moral outrage

2. The author of passage B mentions the possibility that violent youth may seek out violent entertainment in the form of video games (lines 33-34) primarily in order to

   (A) highlight the potentially addictive nature of video games
   (B) question the factual accuracy of the evidence relied upon in passage A
   (C) raise the possibility that a particular correlation does not exist
   (D) offer an alternative interpretation of the evidence cited in passage A
   (E) provide additional evidence supporting the causal relationship described in passage A

Comparative Reading Mini-Passages

Passage A

Although John Locke wrote his *Second Treatise of Civil Government* as a self-professed attempt to justify a particular constitutional revolution in late seventeenth-century England, his work is now
(5) without doubt part of the transatlantic canon of Western constitutional democracy. History itself may have occasioned this rapid transformation. As the second half of the 20th century witnessed a relentless communist attack upon the liberal state,
(10) Locke's treatises were quickly summoned to its defense. This dubious deployment of a scholarly work that bears no direct relevance to modern-day political discourse reveals something unique about the nature of canonical works: rather than
(15) historically or geographically-bound, they are timeless classics that offer the means to interpret and understand a wide range of seemingly disparate issues.

Passage B

The modern constitutional state is widely
(20) regarded as the ultimate arbiter of social dispute. For John Locke, however, author of the widely acclaimed *Second Treatise of Civil Government*, that arbiter was the private man. Indeed, Locke saw preserving mankind and maintaining private
(25) property as co-extensive and, indeed, co-constitutive of liberalism. This is not surprising: the *Second Treatise* was written at a time when the forced extraction of goods, services, and money was becoming particularly oppressive in Europe.
(30) It was especially so in England, where the Crown habitually seized private property in the name of supporting the military. Locke's intention therefore was to redefine private property as broadly as he could, affording it maximum immunity. To
(35) extrapolate a broader social implication from his stance, or interpret it as a rejection of state power in general, would be both intellectually dishonest and politically dangerous.

1. The approaches toward John Locke's *Second Treatise of Civil Government* exhibited by the two authors differ in which one of the following ways?

   (A) The author of passage A is more interested in the historical context of John Locke's treatise than the author of passage B is.

   (B) The author of passage A is more committed to the principles of liberalism espoused by John Locke than the author of passage B is.

   (C) The author of passage B is more intent on explaining how John Locke's work became part of the transatlantic canon of Western constitutional democracy than the author of passage A is.

   (D) The author of passage B is more inclined to extrapolate broader social implications from John Locke's treatise than the author of passage A is.

   (E) The author of passage B is more circumspect in its willingness to view John Locke's treatise as a timeless classic than the author of passage A is.

2. Which of the following is discussed in passage B but not in passage A?

   (A) The political motivations behind some of the arguments contained in Locke's *Second Treatise of Civil Government*.

   (B) The role of history in transforming Locke's work into a canonical treatise.

   (C) The historical events that gave rise to a particular viewpoint that is no longer relevant.

   (D) The potential of some scholarly works to provide the means of interpreting a wide range of seemingly disparate issues.

   (E) The implications of communism for the liberal state.

Comparative Reading Mini-Passages

Passage Set #6:

Passage A

The popularity of social networking sites such as Facebook has quadrupled in the last 5 years. Today, social networking accounts for 17% of all time spent on the Internet, nearly three times as

(5) much as in 2008. Despite what may appear to be a concomitant decrease in face-to-face interactions, social networking allows people to create new relationships, maintain old ones, and bring people with common interests together. People who have

(10) difficulty communicating in person are typically much more comfortable interacting via the Internet, which lowers inhibitions to overcome social anxiety.

Passage B

Cyberbullying is a form of harassment

(15) that occurs on the Internet. It differs from the more traditional forms of bullying in that it can occur at any time, and take many forms. Embarrassing e-mails or videos can be distributed instantaneously worldwide while the perpetrator

(20) remains anonymous, which increases the potential harm to the victim while lowering the risk that the perpetrator would face retribution. Social networking sites make cyberbullying particularly easy to do, as they lower social inhibitions and incite ever more insidious forms of cyberbullying.

(25) A 2009 study found that 17.3% of middle school students have been victims of cyberbullying, which leads to a drop in grades, decreased self-esteem, and other symptoms of depression.

1. With which of the following statements regarding social networking sites would the two authors be most likely to agree?

   (A) They facilitate a particular form of harassment on the Internet.
   (B) They lead to a decrease in face-to-face interactions.
   (C) They lower social inhibitions.
   (D) They are more popular today than in the past.
   (E) Their benefits do not always outweigh their costs.

2. How does the purpose of passage B relate to the content of passage A?

   (A) The author of passage B criticizes the argument made in passage A directly by illustrating the dangers inherent in any social interaction on the Internet.
   (B) The author of passage B examines a particular downside to a phenomenon that the author of passage A sees in a predominantly positive light.
   (C) The author of passage B argues that the type of evidence used in passage A is frequently derived from inaccurate observations.
   (D) The author of passage B undermines the value of a technological innovation described in passage A by showing that its costs outweigh the benefits.
   (E) The author of passage B seeks to undermine the type of argument made in passage A by suggesting that it relies on questionable reasoning.

THE POWERSCORE LSAT READING COMPREHENSION BIBLE WORKBOOK

Prephrasing Drill

The following drill is designed to help you develop the habit of prephrasing—an exceptionally valuable skill for attacking both Logical Reasoning and Reading Comprehension questions on the test. Essentially, it involves quickly speculating on what you think the correct answer will be *before* examining the answer choices. The precision with which a prephrase can be formed varies significantly from question to question, and depends on the question type. Do not worry if your prephrase does not have an exact match in any of the answers; it can still help you narrow down the range of possible contenders.

Each of the following passages is followed by several questions that test your understanding of key elements in that passage. In the space provided after each question stem, write down your own response to that question before examining the five answer choices. Do NOT look at the answer choices until you have formulated a suitable prephrase to the question. *Answers on page 178*

Prephasing:
Spec answer b4 choice

Prephrasing Drill

<u>Passage #1:</u>

A carbon footprint is historically defined as the total set of greenhouse gas emissions caused by an organization, event, product, or person. A common misconception about our carbon footprint

(5) is the belief that it is only a measurement of direct energy usage, such as cooking with natural gas or refueling at the gas station. However, a person's carbon footprint includes a plethora of other, far less obvious, activities. Whenever we purchase out-

(10) of-season produce at the grocery store, for instance, we increase our carbon footprint by consuming a product that is often shipped long distances and not infrequently via air. Nearly half of all fruit sold in the United States is imported, and produce grown

(15) in North America travels on average of 2,000 km from source to point of sale. Even eating local food out of season may leave a large footprint, because growing fruits and vegetables in a non-native climate often requires a hothouse, which uses

(20) power.

Taking small steps to reduce our carbon footprint is not terribly difficult. For instance, to live a more environmentally healthy lifestyle, we can choose to limit our consumption of bottled water.

(25) Bottled water requires the combustion of fossil fuels to make the bottle, transport it, and dispose of it (if not recycled), whereas in-house filtration systems provide a relatively affordable and energy-efficient alternative. We can also choose to unplug

(30) appliances that are not frequently in use, many of which are often left on standby and waste energy.

Despite the relatively low cost of creating an energy-efficient home, the average U.S. citizen is still responsible for almost 20 metric tons of carbon

(35) dioxide each year—a world record that is five times the world average. Without a comprehensive regulatory framework for the adoption and implementation of environmental policies aimed at curbing greenhouse gas emissions, the U.S. has

(40) quickly become the second largest source of total greenhouse emissions in the world after China. Given the current political climate, this dubious distinction is unlikely to change anytime soon.

1. The author mentions the distance that produce grown in North America travels from source to point of sale (lines 13-16) primarily in order to

Prephrase: _____

_____

_____

_____

_____

(A) explain how certain activities can leave an unexpectedly large carbon footprint
(B) compare the carbon footprint of imported produce to that of produce grown in North America
(C) estimate the degree to which our carbon footprint can be reduced by taking certain precautionary measures
(D) advocate reducing our carbon footprint by consuming locally grown produce
(E) argue that we often underestimate the degree to which our activities contribute to global warming

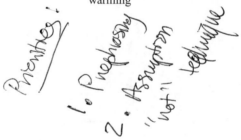

Prephrasing Drill

2. The author's attitude regarding the prospect of reducing our carbon footprint can most accurately be described as

Prephrase: _____

(A) concerned that it is not technologically feasible
(B) certain that it is achievable in the foreseeable future
(C) skeptical that its realization is economically unrealistic
(D) doubtful that such a prospect can ever become a political priority
(E) disappointed that its realization is delayed for political, rather than practical, reasons

3. It can be inferred from the passage that the author would be most likely to agree with which one of the following statements about consumers today?

Prephrase: _____

(A) Their carbon footprint can never be eliminated.
(B) They probably underestimate the size of their carbon footprint.
(C) The carbon footprint of the average U.S. consumer is second only to that of the average Chinese consumer.
(D) They misunderstand the steps they need to take in order to reduce their carbon footprint.
(E) They are largely oblivious to the environmental damage caused by their lifestyle.

4. Of the following, which one would the author most likely say is the most troublesome barrier facing countries that aim to reduce their carbon footprint?

Prephrase: _____

(A) the reluctance of their populations to adopt an environmentally healthy lifestyle
(B) the economic cost of implementing technological innovations that can curb greenhouse emissions
(C) the assumption that the government cannot be trusted to adopt and implement environmental policies aimed at curbing greenhouse gas emissions
(D) the apparent lack of political will to enact the necessary environmental reforms
(E) the belief that taking small steps to reduce greenhouse emissions is not terribly effective

5. According to the passage, any of the following types of decisions would be an effective step towards reducing one's carbon footprint EXCEPT

Prephrase: _____

(A) eating local, rather than imported, produce that is out of season
(B) disconnecting electrical appliances when not in use
(C) drinking filtered water instead of bottled water
(D) refusing to purchase produce that is not in season
(E) doing less nonessential driving

Prephrasing Drill

Passage #2:

① In Caledonia, voters elect trial or appellate judges at the polls, requiring costly election campaigns. But even when they come to the bench by way of the ballot, judges are not politicians. Unlike

(5) a politician, who is expected to be appropriately responsive to the preferences of supporters, a judge may not follow the preferences of his supporters or provide any special consideration to his campaign donors. To preserve public confidence

(10) in the integrity of its judicial system, Caledonia has justifiably decided to prohibit judges (and any judicial candidates) from personally soliciting funds for their campaigns.

② The solicitation ban aims squarely at the conduct
(15) most likely to undermine public confidence in the integrity of the judiciary: personal requests for money by judges and judicial candidates. It applies evenhandedly to all judges and judicial candidates, regardless of viewpoint or means of solicitation.

(20) The ban does not extend, however, to solicitations by a candidate's campaign committee. Proponents of the exception argue that committees do not place the judge's name and reputation behind the request, because the person signing the fundraising letter

(25) is not the same person who might one day sign the judgment.

③ Their reasoning is absurd. A campaign committee is not an impartial third party: it acts solely on behalf of the candidate. The two solicitations are

(30) similar in form as well as substance, presenting disturbingly similar appearances to the public. Any appeal for money by a judicial candidate, whether direct or through an intermediary, may create an appearance of impropriety that causes the public

(35) to lose confidence in the integrity of the judiciary. That interest may be implicated to varying degrees in particular contexts, but the interest remains whenever the public perceives the judge to be beholden to a specific individual or corporation,

(40) regardless of the manner in which the solicitation was made.

1. Which one of the following most accurately expresses the main point of the passage?

Prephrase: _exception_

_to campaign
donations is
harmful to
judges public
appearance_

(A) To preserve the public's confidence in the integrity of the judiciary, neither the judicial candidates, nor their campaign committees, should be allowed to solicit individuals for funds during a campaign.

(B) To avoid a conflict of interest, campaign committees should act solely on behalf of the candidates they represent.

(C) Since campaign committees do not place the judge's name and reputation behind the request for solicitation, such solicitations should not be banned.

(D) Because judges are not politicians, they should not act in a manner that creates an appearance of impropriety.

(E) Caledonia is justified in prohibiting judges and judicial candidates from personally soliciting funds for their campaigns.

Prephrasing Drill

2. The author would be most likely to agree with which one of the following statements about a campaign committee working on behalf of a judicial candidate?

Prephrase: _____

_____

_____

_____

_____

(A) It should act independently of the candidate it represents.
(B) It can solicit campaign donations without undermining the public's confidence in the integrity of the judiciary.
(C) Its main objective is to raise money without compromising the candidate's reputation.
(D) Its actions can damage the reputation of the candidate.
(E) Its actions are indistinguishable from those of the candidate.

3. The main function of the second paragraph is to

Prephrase: _____

_____

_____

_____

_____

_____

(A) raise a possible objection to the author's views regarding campaign solicitations
(B) evaluate the scope of a legal doctrine regarding campaign solicitations
(C) argue that solicitations made on behalf of a judicial candidate do not implicate the candidate's name or reputation
(D) highlight the circumstances that make solicitations by campaign committees particularly problematic
(E) present the rationale for allowing an exception to the legal doctrine regarding campaign solicitations

4. It can most reasonably be inferred from the passage that the author would be LEAST likely to object to which one of the following solicitation requests?

Prephrase: _____

_____

_____

_____

_____

_____

(A) A judicial candidate's campaign committee launches a TV ad encouraging supporters to make small donations to the campaign.
(B) A judge personally solicits donors for campaign contributions, but fully discloses the amount of each donation.
(C) A campaign committee invites auto industry executives to a fundraiser event hosted by the judicial candidate.
(D) An incumbent judge running for reelection solicits a major donor who helped fund the judge's previous election campaign.
(E) A judicial candidate asks a wealthy donor to fundraise on behalf of the candidate.

*correct answer is A. Answer C is a targeted event to auto industry executives, making then focused on the interests of a specific group. The TV ad is general, not focused on a group.

*B is the correct answer. first part of the second paragraph discusses the legal doctrine, while the second half discusses its scope. NOT just about the exception to the legal doctrine

Active Reading Drill I Answer Key—page 6

Do not be concerned if your predictions fail to perfectly match those discussed below; the most important function of this exercise is to reinforce the habit of using context clues to your advantage while reading the passage.

1. Issues with the construction of the massive structure were numerous. Furthermore...

   "Furthermore" indicates that the next thought will build upon the last; here, the author will likely turn to discussing more challenges associated with the project.

---

2. Not everyone who learned of the program was in favor of the proposed changes; as a matter of fact, several...

   Here the author provides that not everyone was happy about the changes; after the semicolon you will likely learn more about some of those who were *unhappy* about the suggested changes.

---

3. The crossing of the mountain range in the dead of winter was considered an incredible feat. When one considers the significant portion of the army that was lost to freezing and drowning, though,...

   The word "though" provides some indication of direction that the author is about to take—a shift in focus to the terrible costs associated with that incredible feat.

---

4. While almost everyone present had been trained extensively in the building's emergency response procedures,...

   If this sentence had not started with the word "while," it would be more difficult to predict the next turn. As it is, however, we can predict contrast—perhaps that some in the building did not act in accordance with emergency procedures, or perhaps that the training did not preclude some type of detriment.

---

5. Following its initial publication, the physicist's controversial work was met with many different reactions. Some were quick to adopt his new theories, but many critics were immediately dismissive. Still others...

   Here the author begins by saying that there were widely varied reactions to the physicist's work. Some adopted his theories right away, others were completely dismissive. "Still others..." should lead to a discussion of yet another group, neither the early adopters nor the immediately dismissive critics.

Active Reading Drill I Answer Key

6. Jackson found these challenges nearly insurmountable. In fact…

   "In fact" will lead into a continuation of the previous thought. From here, the author will likely discuss the difficulty or nature of the aforementioned challenges.

7. Despite strong objections to the proposed legislation…

   Since this sentence begins with the term "despite," a directional change should follow—perhaps a discussion of those who supported the legislation (in spite of others' objections) or of the subsequent success of the legislation (in spite of previous objections).

8. Although the movement had encountered resistance at first, eventually…

   The word "although" in this example indicates that there is contrast—in this case, between the resistance initially encountered, and eventually, (most likely) some degree of acceptance.

9. It was indeed true that many of the men had volunteered for the difficult mission, but…

   In this case, the word "but" tells us that a turn is coming: Next, the author might discuss some of those others who *didn't* volunteer ("...but many chose not to go"), qualify the willingness of those who did volunteer ("...but they weren't very happy about it"), or perhaps discuss a level of difficulty that was surprising despite expectations.

10. Unlike the complex language that pervaded the writer's first three novellas...

    The straightforward language in this example indicates that the author will likely now discuss the writer's change, to more straightforward language.

11. The general mood at the conference was lighthearted. However...

    As alluded to in this drill's directions, the word "however" provides a clear indication that the author's discussion is about to shift to a less lighthearted subject.

12. On one side of the debate were those who had been
    directly affected by the storm...

    Since this sentence begins with the perspective from one side of the debate, the author will likely
    go on to provide information about those on the other side of the debate.

13. As the journey progressed, unfortunately for all those
    involved, conditions did not improve...

    At this point, the author will most likely continue to discuss the worsening conditions for the
    unfortunate journey.

14. Since the corporation rescinded its proposal to build
    a distribution center on the edge of town, the zoning
    commission's sole reason for approving the variance
    required by the proposal was gone. With this in
    mind,...

    The phrase "with this in mind" indicates that the author may proceed to tell us that the zoning
    commission will reject the proposed variance, an action consistent with the removal of the
    commission's only reason for approving it.

15. The cold case detective assigned to review
    the investigation file began to notice several
    inconsistencies between the crime scene photographs
    and the original investigator's notes
    describing the scene. For instance,...

    Here, the author begins by alluding to a relatively broad category of information, the several
    inconsistencies between the crime scene photographs and the investigator's notes. By beginning
    the next sentence with "for instance," the author signals the appearance of a description of at
    least one of those inconsistencies.

16. On one hand, the non-profit's treasurer was relieved to
    discover that it was not the organization's charismatic
    president who had embezzled the $125,000 missing
    from the organization's bank account. On the other
    hand,...

    In this case, it appears that the evidence satisfied the treasurer that the president had not
    embezzled the money. However, the money was taken by someone. It is most likely that the
    sentence beginning with "on the other hand" will conclude with an expression of the treasurer's
    concern that they still do not know who embezzled the money.

17. Last year, the school board wasted valuable tax
    dollars buying the football team new uniforms
    and equipment. Meanwhile,...

The author's word choice in the first sentence provides a hint as to what is likely to follow the word "meanwhile." By saying the school board "wasted" the "valuable" tax dollars, the author implies there was a better use for those funds. We can expect that the author will tell us about some other, more pressing, need that could have been addressed with the money spent on uniforms and equipment.

18. While it may be true that the government's newly
    announced passenger car fuel economy standards
    will enable vehicles meeting those standards to travel
    farther on a tank of gas,...

In this example, the author begins with a concession, that the new fuel economy standards achieve the desired effect of increasing fuel efficiency for compliant cars. However, we can predict that the author will continue by pointing out some trade-off or unintended consequence of the new standards that calls into question the wisdom of such regulation.

19. Early in the 20th century, astronomers discovered
    that the light emitted from nearly all observable stars
    was shifted into the red part of the color spectrum,
    meaning that the stars were moving away from Earth.
    In other words,...

Here, the author describes a scientific discovery that could be confusing to the reader, such that the reader may not fully comprehend the implication of the discovery that nearly all of the observable stars are moving away from Earth. The phrase "in other words" indicates that the author will restate the implication of the discovery to make it more accessible to the reader. Here, the author will tell us that the discovery indicates that the universe is expanding.

20. Historical data suggests that no one-term
    representative of the minority party will be able to
    successfully sponsor important legislation during the
    representative's first term in office. Even so,...

The author's presentation of historical data indicates that it is highly unlikely that a representative of such short tenure would be able to introduce important legislation and have it be approved by the legislative body. The term "even so" implies that the following information will discuss some positive impact that such a representative may have, whether it is a specific representative who may actually be successful in sponsoring important legislation, or a generalized statement of the positive contribution such a representative can make.

Active Reading Drill II Answer Key—page 11

Once again, do not be concerned if your predictions do not perfectly match those discussed below; the most important function of this exercise is to reinforce the habit of using context clues while reading the passage.

1. The small army suffered through a brutal winter; supplies had been extremely limited, and many of the men neared starvation. Their condition was not ideal for the battle that was to come...

    (A)   , and, predictably,...

    The beginning of this excerpt describes a worn-down army, not ideally prepared for the upcoming battle, so when the sentence continues with "and, predictably," we will probably soon be told of a battle that was not particularly successful for the group.

    (B)   , but even so...

    "But even so" tells us that the author is about to change direction—the army was worn down, but even so...things probably went somehow better than one might expect. This could mean a victory, but not necessarily—it could also lead to a conciliatory note, such as "But even so, the soldiers fought valiantly."

    (C)   To the enemy's amazement, however,

    "However" provides a clue that the direction of the passage is about to turn, and "To the enemy's amazement" foreshadows an outcome that was entirely unexpected by the enemy.

Active Reading Drill II Answer Key

2. It was to be one of the tallest buildings in the world,
    and the size and scope of the project would present
    many unique challenges. As the building continued,
    issues with the construction of the massive structure
    were numerous...

    (A)   Incredibly, though...

    > This example opens with a discussion of a difficult construction project with numerous
    > issues. "Incredibly, though" tells us that the next statement will be surprising in light of
    > the project's many difficulties.

    (B)   Challenges included...

    > "Challenges included" is a very straightforward context clue that says, "what follows is a
    > list of challenges." Lists, of course, are always worth noting when working through any
    > Reading Comprehension passage, and if you were to see this excerpt in an actual passage,
    > you could probably count on at least one question that deals with this list.

    (C)   As a result...

    > "As a result" is a phrase that generally precedes the discussion of an effect, so what
    > follows these words will be a reference to some outcome caused by the numerous
    > construction issues.

3. Having planned extensively for a variety of different
    emergency situations, including both hurricanes and
    flash floods, city officials had considered themselves
    well-prepared for just such an emergency.

    (A)   Thankfully...

    > This one begins with the fact that city officials felt prepared for a particular emergency—
    > this could potentially go in several directions. "Thankfully" leads into a positive outcome
    > of some sort, maybe that they were indeed prepared, or perhaps that their preparations
    > were not put to the test.

    (B)   Unfortunately...

    > "Unfortunately" does not suggest a positive direction—maybe the officials were not as
    > prepared as they thought, or perhaps they were presented with a different type of emergency.

    (C)   Some, however, were not quite so confident;

    > This example takes a slightly different direction. Since the sentiment begins with, "some
    > were not quite so confident," followed by a semicolon, the author is probably about to
    > begin a discussion about those who were less confident, or state reasons for their lack of
    > confidence.

Active Reading Drill II Answer Key

4. At the time of its publication, McMillan's first novel
    was lauded by many as one of the most important
    literary works of the era,

    (A)   but in retrospect...

    > The author begins by presenting the fact that McMillan's novel was released to
    > widespread acclaim. This introduction deals specifically with the time of the novel's
    > publication, so when it is followed by "but in retrospect," this is a clear indication that
    > the author is about to turn away from the positive initial reaction, perhaps to more critical
    > perspectives.

    (B)   and critics continue to praise the work's insights;

    > Rather than taking a new direction, this example would lead to a continuation of the
    > discussion of critical praise.

    (C)   although several of McMillan's contemporaries took issue with this
            characterization...

    > This is a clear indication that a shift in direction has come—the author will now most
    > likely turn the discussion to those contemporaries, or else to their specific criticisms.

---

5. The proposal was intended to provide a compromise
    that would be considered equitable by all concerned
    parties, but some who learned of the changes opposed
    the new plan.

    (A)   Regardless,...

    > In this example we see an early directional shift: the proposal was intended to be fair, but
    > some opposed the new plan. The word "regardless" probably indicates a shift back, away
    > from those opponents (i.e. "without regard for those opponents...") possibly leading to
    > the fact that the proposal would remain in place, despite the opponents.

    (B)   Indeed,...

    > "Indeed" generally continues a sentiment, so in this example the author will probably
    > further discuss those who opposed the plan.

    (C)   These opponents claimed...

    > This example will clearly lead to a discussion of the specific claims of opponents against
    > the referenced proposal.

6. The strike went on for months, and some wondered whether it would go on indefinitely. Management seemed completely intractable, and the union had no intention of giving up on what the group considered to be very reasonable demands...

(A)   Making matters worse,...

Here the author discusses a long-standing strike in which both sides are apparently committed to their agendas. "Making matters worse" tells us that the author is about to discuss further factors detrimental to the situation.

(B)   Eventually, though...

The word "though" implies a turnaround, and in this context we can probably expect to read about how they were able to overcome the strike.

(C)   , such as...

"Such as" follows the reference to reasonable demands, so the author is about to list examples of those demands.

Again, the main focus for this drill, and as you review these answers, should be on developing the habit of drawing what you can from the language chosen by the author.

1. For years, health officials have argued that a diet high in saturated fat contributes to an elevated risk of heart disease...

    The author introduces a view that will likely be rejected. She will probably argue that a diet high in saturated fat does not necessarily increase one's risk of heart disease.

2. Stevens rejected the student's application for a seat on the school's steering committee, based in part on the debatable assertion that no student who has been enrolled in school for less than two years can have sufficient knowledge of the school and its issues to make a real contribution to the committee's work...

    The author presents Stevens' reasoning for rejecting the student's application. The use of the term "debatable" allows us to predict that the author will probably disagree with Stevens' reasoning. This does not necessarily mean, however, that Stevens should have accepted the application. The author could agree with the Stevens conclusion, yet disagree with the reasoning behind this conclusion.

3. While the journalist maintains that she should be entitled to withhold the identity of her confidential source, citing the need to protect her reputation for integrity as an investigative reporter...

    We can infer from this opening that the author is going to disagree with the journalist's view. As we saw in the second example, however, the author will not necessarily conclude that the journalist should be forced to reveal her source. The author could disagree with the journalist's justification for refusing to identify her source, but still believe that she should be permitted to keep her source confidential.

4. A recent proposal by the federal government to establish a ratings system for colleges and universities has garnered the approval of several public universities, which urge the government to tie federal grants and subsidies to the proposed ratings. Private universities argue that the proposed ratings system is unnecessary, since market forces already in place set the value of these institutions of higher learning...

The author of this passage presents two competing viewpoints, those of the public universities and the private universities.

Occasionally, when two competing viewpoints are presented together, the author could insert a contrasting transition word, such as "however" or "yet," after the *second* viewpoint, and then conclude that the second view is incorrect. If she rejects both competing viewpoints, it is likely that a third viewpoint will be introduced later in the passage.

5. At a conference held last year, representatives from several traditional brokerage institutions expressed lingering doubts that the surprising growth of "in-app" purchases, in which consumers using applications on mobile communication devices can purchase ancillary products and services, will generate significant revenue streams in the near term...

Here, the author opens with the view shared by "traditional brokerage houses": in-app purchases will not provide significant sources of revenue in the short term. As we saw in the previous example, the author does not lead off with the viewpoint, making it more difficult to predict the author's perspective with any certainty.

6. Debate concerning the proposed 2021 manned Mars flyby mission has focused both on cost and astronaut safety. Some lawmakers publicly signaling support for the mission have indicated to administration officials during closed-door sessions that their support is limited to a privately funded mission...

The difficult sentence structure and word choice of this passage make it harder to track the argumentation. However, the second sentence explicitly uses the conventional "some people say..." language, suggesting that the author may ultimately disagree with the lawmakers' position. The author will probably argue that lawmaker support should not be limited to privately held missions.

Active Reading Drill III: Viewpoint Prediction Answer Key

7. A recent survey of tenured university faculty indicates that most rate as poor their students' ability to write a well-researched and cogent paper on an assigned topic within each individual student's primary field of study. Despite the data referenced by the respondents,...

In this case, the author has offered the view of tenured university faculty regarding their students' performance. We can predict that the author will go on to disagree with these faculty members, and state that students' ability to write papers would not necessarily rate as poor. Notice that the author used the word "respondents" in the second sentence to refer to the faculty. Such a shift in terms can make it somewhat difficult to track the viewpoint in question.

8. Many automobile safety experts have lobbied intently for the passage of legislation that would criminalize the use of any electronic device while driving. The theory is that a broadly stated usage ban of this nature will reduce accidents caused by distracted drivers. However,...

This example has two sentences presenting a viewpoint prior to the transition word, "however." Here, the two introductory sentences express the same position. The first sentence summarizes the position, while the second sentence provides support for this position. The adverb "however" suggests that the author will likely disagree with the assertion that the usage ban would have the desired effect.

Language Simplification Drill I Answer Key—page 20

As you continue to practice breaking down passages, you will likely note that in most cases, the information presented could be relayed in a much more straightforward manner.

1. The jurors will probably not be inclined to acquiesce
    to the defendant's plea for mercy.

    Basic Translation: Jurors will probably not be merciful to the defendant.

2. Expensive machinery is rarely, if ever, a necessary
    precondition for facilitation and enhancement of the
    manufacturing process.

    Basic Translation: Manufacturing does not require expensive machinery.

3. While there is some wisdom behind prohibiting the
    use of non-renewable resources, such an injunction
    does not preclude the use of renewable resources.

    Basic Translation: The ban against using non-renewable resources allows for the use of renewable resources.

4. The Prime Minister's recent announcement reaffirms
    his party's long-standing belief that a policy of
    nuclear deterrence is generally incompatible with
    long-lasting peace.

    Basic Translation: The Prime Minister restated his party's belief that the strategy of nuclear deterrence is not compatible with long term peace.

5. The requirement to document all tax-deductible
    expenses imposes a heavy burden on some taxpayers,
    though it does not obviate the need for compliance
    with all other provisions of the tax code as well.

    Basic Translation: One must comply with all provisions of the tax code; documenting one's tax-deductible expenses is not enough.

6. We strongly oppose the allocation of healthcare
    spending from the public to the private sector,
    which not only contradicts the government's alleged
    reluctance to increased private sector spending, but
    also threatens to disrupt continuity of care and deprive
    the public of medical services.

    Basic Translation: The author is unhappy with the current government. The government claims
    not to want increased private sector spending, but now healthcare spending has been shifted from
    the public to the private sector. According to the author, this has deprived some people of medical
    services.

7. Unless the candidate clarifies his recent statements,
    his position on several integral issues will likely be
    the subject of widespread misinterpretation.

    Basic Translation: If the candidate doesn't clarify what he intended to say, many people will
    probably misinterpret his recent statements.

8. The use of complicated wording as an overall literary
    technique does not always detract from the intended
    meaning of the text, though the ironic prevalence
    of this approach in some lowbrow literary journals
    raises important questions about the degree to which
    complexity of language may correlate with simplicity
    of thought.

    Basic Translation: Complicated wording might convey the intended meaning of the text, though
    complex language may often reflect much simpler concepts.

Language Simplification Drill II Answer Key—page 22

The summaries below are very condensed for illustrative purposes, drawing on only the big picture from each excerpt. Do not be concerned if your simplifications are a bit more detailed, as the goal here is to continue to practice taking long, seemingly complex passages and breaking them down into shorter, more easily comprehensible ideas.

1. Recent scholarship on the role of Eskimo women in ritual practice often relies on the dubious assumption that female participation in this activity simply supported the male role. Such interpretations of mere complementarity not only undervalue the distinctly unique and indispensable role of women in ritual practice, but also impose a decidedly patriarchal viewpoint upon its subject.

   Basic Translation: The study of Eskimo women often underestimates their role in ritual practice.

2. Comprehensive plans are statements of local governments' objectives and standards for future land development, including distribution of population, density, and infrastructure. Because such plans are usually prepared by experts, the standards they set are often overly technocratic for the complex and ever-changing area of urban planning. As a result, the practical enforceability of these standards remains somewhat dubious in some of the fastest-growing municipalities.

   Basic Translation: Comprehensive plans may be too rigid to apply to some types of urban land development.

3. Professor Lavin's simplistic interpretation of Hieronymus Bosch's disquieting religious paintings is more revealing of the professor's own inadequacies than of those that allegedly plagued the subject of his critique. Indeed, Lavin's attempts to explain Bosch's style as the result of a mental illness are as hackneyed as they are predictable, symptomatic of the cultural conventions to which many contemporary historians inadvertently cling.

   Basic Translation: The professor's interpretation of Bosch's paintings is too simplistic, revealing the professor's own shortcomings, not those of the painter.

4. The recently introduced city tax on cigarettes seeks to curb smoking by imposing a significant financial disincentive on people who choose to continue smoking. Some critics have contended that the tax can inadvertently lead to a counterproductive effect, because many residents resort to buying cigarettes in bulk from vendors outside the city. Studies show, however, that smoking trends correlate rather poorly with smokers' perception of the quantity of cigarettes available to them at any given time. These critics' fears are therefore unwarranted.

Basic Translation: Critics fear that the city tax on cigarettes might encourage people to smoke more, not less, because smokers would start buying cigarettes in bulk. These fears are thus unjustified.

5. One of Bertolt Brecht's major critiques of Western theater targets its dialogue as a text-bound performance whose compulsory repetition is devoid of spontaneity and therefore lacking in true meaning. The compulsion to repeat the text, however, can yield different interpretations, as the dialogue through which characters convey their versions of the written text can itself be a source of spontaneity in the performance of that text.

Basic Translation: Brecht's critique of Western theater is too harsh, because the same text can be performed and interpreted differently.

6. Under some common law jurisdictions, for an offer and acceptance to constitute a valid contract, the acceptance of the offer must meet and correspond with the offer in every respect, including the manner in which each is made. Not every variance between offer and acceptance, however, should render the intended acceptance ineffective or preclude formation of a contract, because acceptance can assume a variety of forms.

Basic Translation: In some jurisdictions, common law requires an offer to be in the same form as an acceptance, but not every variation weakens the validity of the contract.

7. One of the main goals of a criminal justice system is to optimize the control of crime by devising a set of punishments whose magnitude is sufficient to deter a reasonable person from committing any given crime. Although deterrence is an intuitively compelling strategic goal, there is a growing skepticism about the deterrent effect of criminal law itself. For instance, rather than imposing draconian sentencing guidelines for illegal drug users, there is a strong deterrence argument in favor of a public health doctrine that depicts the consequences of using such substances in order to discourage their use.

Basic Translation: Stricter punishments do not deter criminals as much as we think. It may be better to discourage illegal drug use by showing its effects on one's health.

8. Lawmakers argue that governance results from a fundamentally normative project of deliberation and consent. However, the modalities of deliberation and contractual obligation depend not upon the stability of civil government but rather on its occasional failure to deliver upon the promise it creates. Granted, such failures can be rightfully viewed as temporary setbacks, but they eventually occasion the discourse that is a hallmark of a well-functioning democracy.

Basic Translation: Deliberation and consent are both the cause, and the effect, of effective civil governance. Even stable governments occasionally fail to deliver on their promises, which generates public discourse. Such a discourse eventually leads to deliberation and consent— hallmarks of a well-functioning democracy.

9. In the absence of a statute providing otherwise, the admitting physician at McLean Hospital was under no legal obligation to render professional services to Jack Johnson, who was not a patient of the hospital at the time he arrived there. Regardless of whether one finds doctrinal or moral grounds for establishing a duty to treat, neither the existence of a license law nor the possession of a license to practice medicine can be construed as instruments that enlarge a physician's duty in regard to accepting an offered patient, because such laws are essentially a preventive, rather than compulsory, measure.

Basic Translation: The doctor was under no obligation to treat Jack, because the law does not compel doctors to treat every patient who shows up at their door. The law is meant to prevent unlicensed doctors to practice medicine, rather than compel licensed doctors to do the same.

Language Simplification Drill II Answer Key

10. There is little credibility to the claim that even a politically polarized nation can distinguish between legitimate calls to action and the voices of messianic demagoguery. To speak without listening is an exercise in futility, for no matter how informed or erudite the views, they are bound to fall on deaf ears. Unfortunately, the same cannot be said about shouting.

Basic Translation: A polarized nation cannot distinguish legitimate calls to action from messianic demagoguery. Unfortunately, the voices of demagoguery are much louder than the voices of reason.

---

11. Scholars of Antonin Artaud often argue that the dramatic effects of the satirical genre were not entirely consistent with his philosophy of truth and illusion. Whereas satire uses humor to ridicule the topical issues of the day, for Artaud the only "truths" worth deriding are supposedly those that cannot be proven as such, and may, in fact, be false. It would be too facile to assume, however, that by imbuing his plays with futuristic elements and absurd plot lines, Artaud drew a line between illusion and reality, or—worse—protected the sanctity of politics from satire's corrosive effects. A play need not be credible to be topical. As a skilled dramaturge, Artaud blurred the distinction between the boundaries we take for granted, often staging them as conditions for their mutually assured destruction.

Basic Translation: Scholars think that Artaud's plays focus on the absurd, and as such cannot be taken seriously as political satire. However, the author believes that the two are not mutually exclusive, because a play can be politically relevant even if it's not entirely credible.

12. Socrates defines timocracy as the regime closest to, but decidedly inferior to, aristocracy. However, the language used to differentiate them makes such proximity both essential and unsettling. The surprise emerging from the passage on timocracy lies precisely in a dialectic whose attainment of regime derivation and differentiation depends on a certain failure to obliterate difference and faction as constitutive elements of either regime. In seeing both regimes as mutually constitutive and co-extensive, rather than oppositional or mutually exclusive, Socrates inadvertently questions the valorized difference between the two.

Basic Translation: Socrates believes that timocracy is inferior to aristocracy. However, the two regimes are similar enough. Socrates' rhetoric reveals that neither regime is perfect or whole (i.e. he fails "to obliterate difference and faction as constitutive elements of either regime"), even as he attempts to differentiate between the two.

13. Scientists who reject the notion that excessive exposure to sunlight in tropical areas increases the risk of melanoma cannot reliably conclude that their theories cannot be disproved. Granted, none of the studies showing a correlation between ultraviolet radiation and skin cancer were conducted in tropical areas, and many of them failed to control for exposure to other potential carcinogens such as diet and smoking. Nevertheless, lack of evidence for a particular claim should not be interpreted as evidence undermining that claim.

Basic Translation: Some scientists believe that excessive exposure to sunlight does not cause melanoma, because the evidence supporting such causal relationship is murky. However, just because the evidence supporting a causal connection is weak does not mean that ultraviolet radiation does not cause melanoma.

Language Simplification Drill II Answer Key

14. More than a theory of governance proscribing
     the framework of a rather fragile social contract,
     Kobe's ideology describes the quintessence of a
     social contract that rescues us from the vicissitudes
     of anarchy. By relying upon the modality of
     retrospection, Kobe achieves his goal from the very
     vantage point it seeks to address—the vantage point
     of the modern constitutional state. Admittedly, such
     an ideology is a work of contradictions that resists
     a simple explanation, revealing in form as well as
     content a profound struggle with the contingency of
     its time. But this is true of most, if not all, doctrinal
     texts.

Basic Translation: Kobe wrote a theory of governance that recommends a certain social
contract, namely, the modern constitutional state. He writes from the "vantage point [he] seeks to
address," suggesting that Kobe resides in a state in which that contract is already established. The
author concedes that there are some contradictions in Kobe's work, but dismisses such criticism
because such contradictions are not unique to Kobe.

Do not be concerned if your diagram and summary do not match ours exactly. The point of this drill is to get you thinking about how to diagram, and about the types of notations that can be made. Again, the proper approach to notating passages varies from person to person. **There is no definitively correct or incorrect way to diagram.**

Passage #1:

Modern conceptions of the origin of large-scale architecture in the Americas often tend toward the belief that there was no significant construction until after 1700, when a mass immigration of
(5) European settlers began. However, this view ignores the significant contributions of the native peoples who inhabited the continent prior to the arrival of the Europeans. For example, the pyramidal structures built by the Mayans in El
(10) Mirador date back to the pre-Classic era, and represent some of the largest structures in the world to this day. In a more recent example, the pueblo peoples of the American Southwest constructed sprawling cliff dwellings that included unique
(15) apartment-like designs and immense public worship buildings capable of holding over 1000 people. These structures, still standing today, date as far back as 1500 years ago.
    While architectural historians do recognize the
(20) existence of these structures, appreciation for their importance in a historical context has largely been withheld. Historiographers have only recently started to recognize this error, suggesting that a more complete and accurate understanding of the
(25) true history of architecture in the Americas will soon be forthcoming.

V_{MC}

V_A

V_H
V_A

MP

Summary:

The passage begins by outlining the dominant views regarding large-scale architecture in the Americas. These views are quickly rejected in favor of a more inclusive perspective on the architectural contributions made by native cultures. Two examples are cited in support of the author's position.

In the second paragraph, the author criticizes architectural historians for not fully appreciating the architectural contributions outlined earlier. The passage closes on a hopeful note, suggesting that the omission has been recognized and may soon be rectified.

Passage Analysis and Diagramming Drill Answer Key

PRACTICE DRILL
EXPLANATIONS

<u>**Passage #2:**</u>

The legal concept of "freedom of the seas" can
be traced back to the 17th century Dutch jurist
Grotius. Relying on precepts from Roman law,
as well as on legal cases from other maritime
(5)   countries, Grotius asserted that no one country
could rightly claim ownership of the oceans, and
that therefore <u>all nations had an inherent right of
free passage on the high seas</u>. Although Welwood
and Selden would later argue against the notion of
(10) freedom of the seas, the concept slowly became
embedded in international law doctrine.

V_G

V_{WS}

Grotius' initial formulation of the principle
stipulated that <u>freedom of passage extended up to
the shoreline</u>. However, practical considerations,
(15) such as piracy and military aggression, soon
necessitated a policy of local governmental control
over shore waters. Although the extent of that
control was initially seen as controversial, in the
18th century it was agreed that <u>local governmental
(20) control would extend the distance of direct military
control from the shoreline</u>. As cannons had a
maximum impact distance of approximately (three)
miles, that became the standard of the time.

V_G

3 mi

While this standard is still in existence today,
(25) other significant demarcations are also in use. A
nation's <u>contiguous zone</u> extends out (24) miles from
shore, and allows control over all vessels in that
zone. Extending outward (200) miles from shore is a
nation's <u>exclusive economic zone</u>, largely granting
(30) ownership and control over resources in these
waters. Beyond (200) miles, general <u>international
maritime laws</u> apply, which can limit, but not
necessarily override, national law.

24 mi

200 mi

200+

Summary:

This passage opens by discussing the legal concept of "freedom of the seas," a concept that
originated with Grotius. Grotius believed in free passage of the seas, and although some others
disagreed (Welwood and Selden), the concept became part of international law. In the second
paragraph, we learn that Grotius' ideas about freedom of passage up to the shoreline were not
accepted for security reasons, and local governmental control was established to extend roughly 3
miles out from shore.

The last paragraph discusses other lines of demarcation, and along with the attendant rights in the
areas they demarcate.

Passage Analysis and Diagramming Drill Answer Key

__Passage #3:__

"Punishment" is the imposition of negative consequences upon perpetrators of intolerable activities, by entities with some type of authority over those who committed these activities. **Def**

(5)   There are several common justifications for punishment, including deterrence, retribution, and rehabilitation.

First, the threat of punishment is intended to deter future wrongdoers from breaking the law, and

(10)   to dissuade those who have been punished from committing further transgressions. Punishment for the sake of retribution seeks to address imbalances of justice by making sure that offenders pay a price for whatever wrongdoing has been committed.

(15)   When punishment is imposed in a rehabilitative effort, the purported goal is to improve the character of those who have acted unacceptably.

Summary:

This passage begins with a definition of the central concept of the passage, and closes with a list of three common justifications for the imposition of punishment: deterrence, retribution, and rehabilitation.

In the second paragraph, the author reiterates the list, this time providing a brief definition of each justification: punishment is imposed to deter crime, retribution—to address imbalances of justice, and rehabilitation—to improve the character of those who have committed a crime.

The author's main point in this passage is to discuss the concept of punishment, and briefly expand upon three common justifications for its imposition.

Passage Analysis and Diagramming Drill Answer Key

<u>Passage #4:</u>

The "domino effect" and the "butterfly effect" both describe causal chains of events, in which an initial cause leads to an effect, which in turn leads to another effect. Where one notion is
(5)   finite, however, the other is significantly more open-ended. The domino effect, as its namesake suggests, refers to a clear and exhaustive sequence of reactions that take place as a result of an initial occurrence; typically, these chains of events have
(10)   no relative scale of significance (that is, a small event can be followed by an event of smaller, greater, or similar magnitude).

     In contrast to the domino effect, the butterfly effect posits more expansive and complex causal
(15)   chains, allowing for even a very small change in initial conditions to have vast and varied "ripple" effects that often leave the line of causality unclear. Newton's third law of motion holds that for every action there is an equal and opposite reaction,
(20)   suggesting a potential for infinite butterfly effects in response to any given occurrence.

Compare/ Contrast

Def-domino

Def-butterfly

Summary:

The author begins this passage with a presentation of its two central concepts: the domino effect and the butterfly effect, and immediately begins to compare and contrast the two ideas. They are similar in that they both deal with causal chains, but the two concepts are readily distinguishable as well. The first paragraph closes by defining the domino effect as having a clear beginning and ending.

In the second paragraph, the author provides a second definition—that of the butterfly effect. This notion, in contrast with the domino effect, includes ripple effects which, the author points out, could be infinite according to Newton.

Students typically miss a few questions in this drill. Do not worry about how many you miss; the point of this drill is to acquaint you with the idea of Location as it is presented in different question stems. As you see more examples of each type of question, your ability to quickly and accurately identify the Location element will improve.

1. The author would be most likely to agree with which one of the following statements?

Location Designation: Global Reference

Because this stem makes no reference to any particular line, paragraph, or concept, it is best described as a Global Reference question.

2. Which one of the following does the author present as an example of 18th century justice?

Location Designation: Concept Reference

This question stem does not refer to a specific line or paragraph, so it cannot be a Specific Reference question. The reference to a particular notion of justice is enough to suggest that this is more specific than a Global Reference question, so this example can be classified as a Concept Reference question.

3. Which one of the following statements is affirmed by the second paragraph of the passage?

Location Designation: Specific Reference

This question refers to a particular paragraph, so it is a Specific Reference question.

4. In discussing 'the early efforts of the organization'
    (line 35), the author seeks primarily to:

Location Designation: Specific Reference

The specific reference to line 35 in this question makes it a Specific Reference question.

---

5. Which one of the following most accurately describes
    the organization of the passage?

Location Designation: Global Reference

This question stem does not refer to a specific line paragraph, or concept, so it should be categorized as a Global Reference question.

---

6. Which one of the following would the author be
    most likely to characterize as one of the 'institutional
    challenges' discussed in lines 13-14 of the passage?

Location Designation: Specific Reference

The specific reference to lines 13-14 in this example makes it a Specific Reference question.

Question Classification II: Location, Type, and Sub-type Drill Answer Key—page 32

The point of this drill, like that of the previous one, is to consider the different question types that you will encounter and what is required to effectively attack each question.

1. The author of the passage would be most likely to agree with which one of the following statements?

GR, Must, AP

Location: This example provides no direction, conceptual or otherwise, as to location in the passage, so it is a Global Reference question.

Type: This common question requires the reader to understand the author's perspective. The correct answer choice must pass the Fact Test, so this is a Must Be True question, and it must reflect the author's viewpoint, so it is also an Author's Perspective question.

---

2. Which one of the following, if true, would most undermine the claims of Sutton's early critics?

CR, Weaken

Location: Here we are asked to find the answer choice that would undermine a particular view referenced from the passage, so this is a Concept Reference question.

Type: A question stem that begins with "Which of the following, if true" is nearly certain to be a Strengthen or Weaken question. In this case, the information in the correct answer will call the referenced assertion into question, so this should be classified as a Weaken question.

---

3. Which one of the following, if true, would most strengthen the claims of the critics mentioned in the second paragraph of the passage?

SR, Strengthen

Location: Although no line reference is provided in this example, the reader is directed to the second paragraph of the passage, so this is a Specific Reference question.

Type: In this case, since the correct answer will support the referenced view, this is clearly a Strengthen question.

Question Classification II: Location, Type, and Sub-type Drill Answer Key

4. Which one of the following statements would provide
    the most logical continuation of the discussion in the
    last paragraph of the passage?

SR, Must, E

Location: This example provides a particular location of the referenced quote (the end of the final paragraph), so this is a Specific Reference question.

Type: The correct answer must provide a reasonable continuation of the last paragraph of the passage, so it is a Must Be True Expansion question.

5. Which one of the following most accurately expresses
    the main point of the passage?

GR, Main Point

Location: This question refers to the passage as a whole so it is a Global Reference question.

Type: The question asks about the main point of the passage, a clear example of a Main Point question. The correct answer choice will be the one which most accurately and completely reflects the central focus of the passage.

6. According to the passage, Harding would most likely
    agree with which one of the following statements?

CR, Must, SP

Location: Without reading the passage, it might be difficult to assess the scope of this question's reference. Note that if the passage is largely focused on Harding, this is a Concept Reference question.

Type: The correct answer choice must be confirmed by the passage and reflect the subject's perspective, so this is a Must Be True, Subject Perspective question.

THE POWERSCORE LSAT READING COMPREHENSION BIBLE WORKBOOK

7. Which one of the following most accurately describes
the organization of the passage?

GR, Must, O

Location: This question refers to the passage as a whole, so it is a Global Reference question.

Type: This question requires that the reader understand the overall structure of the given passage, and the right answer must reflect that structure. This is a Must Be True, Organization question.

---

8. The author mentions each one of the following as an
example of early technological innovations, EXCEPT:

CR, MustX

Location: In this case, since the question refers to technological innovation, this would be a Concept Reference question.

Type: Since this is a MustX question, the four incorrect answer choices will be examples that are provided in the passage, and the correct answer choice will not be listed as an example of an early technological innovation.

---

9. Which one of the following principles most closely
conforms to the author's notion of justice, as it is
expressed in the passage?

CR, Must—PR

Location: This question refers to the notion of justice, so it is a Concept Reference question.

Type: As it requires identifying the underlying principle in the passage, this is a Must Be True, Principle question.

Question Classification II: Location, Type, and Sub-type Drill Answer Key

10. Which one of the following most accurately describes the organization of the material presented in the first paragraph of the passage?

SR, Must, O

Location: The reference to the first paragraph makes this a Specific Reference question.

Type: Since the question asks about the organization of the first paragraph of the passage, it is a Must Be True, Organization question.

---

11. The author's attitude regarding the early views of the skeptics can most accurately be described as:

CR, Must, AP

Location: This question deals with the author's attitude toward a particular viewpoint, so it is a Concept Reference question.

Type: Since the question requires the reader to understand the author's perspective, it is a Must Be True, Author's Perspective question.

---

12. With which one of the following would the author of the passage be LEAST likely to agree?

GR, Cannot, AP

Location: This example provides no direction, so it is a Global Reference question.

Type: This question requires you to find an answer choice with which the author would disagree. Because the correct answer choice will be inconsistent with the author's attitude, this question stem can be classified as a Cannot Be True, Author's Perspective question.

13. Which one of the following views can most reasonably be attributed to the experts cited in line 14?

SR, Must, SP

Location: The line reference at the end of this question stem makes it a Specific Reference question.

Type: Since the question requires an understanding of the referenced "experts," this is a Must Be True, Subject Perspective question.

14. Which one of the following relationships would be most closely analogous to the symbiotic business relationship discussed in the passage?

CR, Parallel

Location: Since this question refers to a relationship discussed in the passage, this is a Concept Reference question.

Type: Here the reader is asked to find an answer choice which is most closely analogous to a particular relationship, which makes it a Parallel Reasoning question.

15. Which one of the following most closely expresses the author's intended meaning of the word "compromised," as it is used in line 32 of the passage?

SR, Must, P

Location: The line reference identifies this question as a Specific Reference question.

Type: The answer to this question must accurately reflect the author's purpose in using a particular term, so it is properly characterized as a Must Be True, Purpose question.

16. Which one of the following, if true, would cast the most doubt on Ellison's argument concerning the role of the American middle-class in the first half of the 20th Century?

CR, Weaken

Location: This question stem refers to a concept (Ellison's argument concerning the role of the American middle-class during the first half of the 20th Century), so it is a Concept Reference question.

Type: Since the question asks for the answer choice that would cast doubt on the referenced argument, this is a Weaken question.

---

17. The researcher mentioned in lines 15-16 would be most likely to agree with which one of the following statements?

SR, Must, SP

Location: Since this question refers specifically to lines 15-16, it is a Specific Reference question.

Type: This question deals with the perspective of a researcher discussed in the passage so this is a Must Be True, Subject Perspective question.

---

18. Which one of the following is most closely analogous to the process of automation discussed in lines 23 - 31?

SR, Parallel

Location: This question points to a very specific location in the passage, so it is a Specific Reference question.

Type: Since it asks for the choice that is most closely analogous to a process discussed in the passage, this is a Parallel Reasoning question.

19. Which one of the following studies would provide the most support for the claim mentioned in the last paragraph of the passage?

SR, Strengthen

Location: This question refers to the last paragraph of the passage, so it is a Specific Reference question.

Type: Since the question requires identifying an answer choice that would provide support for the given claim, this is a Strengthen question.

---

20. The author of the passage would be LEAST likely to agree with which one of the following statements about interstate commerce?

CR, Cannot, AP

Location: This question refers to interstate commerce, so this is a Concept Reference question.

Type: This question asks about a statement with which the author would be least likely to agree, making this a Cannot Be True, Author's Perspective question. The four incorrect choices in this case would provide statements with which the author would agree, and the correct answer choice would be one with which the author would disagree.

Once again, the point of this drill is for you to consider the different question types that you will encounter and what is required of each question.

1. The author provides at least one example of each of the following EXCEPT:

Question Type: MustX

The four incorrect answer choices will each be exemplified in the passage; the correct answer choice will not be.

2. The information in the passage provides the LEAST support for which one of the following claims?

Question Type: MustX

The four incorrect answer choices will present a claim that is supported by the information in the passage; the correct answer choice will feature a claim that is not supported by the passage.

3. It can be inferred from the passage that each of the following was achievable before the rise of modern computing EXCEPT:

Question Type: Cannot Be True

The four incorrect answer choices will present achievements that were possible before the rise of modern computing; the correct answer choice will feature an achievement that would not have been possible prior to the advent of modern computing.

4. The author mentions each of the following as a potential detriment associated with fracking EXCEPT:

Question Type: MustX

The four incorrect answer choices can be explained by the information in the passage; the correct answer choice cannot be.

5. Which one of the following, if true, is LEAST consistent with the theory mentioned in the first paragraph of the passage?

Question Type: Cannot Be True

The four incorrect answer choices will be consistent with the referenced theory; the correct answer choice will be inconsistent with that theory.

6. The author mentions each of the following as a potential detriment associated with fracking EXCEPT:

Question Type: MustX

The four incorrect answer choices are mentioned as potential detriments associated with fracking; the correct answer choice is not mentioned as such.

Please keep in mind that this drill is designed to help you develop the habit of identifying viewpoints and understanding the relationship between various perspectives. In some instances, the "No Specific Viewpoint" designation used below could be included in an "Author's Viewpoint" categorization; however, the point isn't to worry about finding a "perfect" answer, but to understand how viewpoints can be presented.

Passage #1:

Psychogeography is the study of how the physical geography of an environment affects human emotion and perception. First articulated in 1953 by French theorist Ivan Chtcheglov, and
(5)   later expanded by fellow Frenchman Guy Debord, psychogeography sought to alter contemporary architecture and to re-imagine the interaction of man and environment. But, the field struggled to find a defining ethic, and the intensely personal
(10)   nature of psychogeography made the creation of a unifying interpretation difficult, if not impossible. In recent years, psychogeography has been repopularized, primarily through performance art and literature.

Number of Viewpoints: 1

<u>Lines 1-14: Author</u>. This excerpt does not provide multiple viewpoints; it is simply the author's presentation of information about psychogeography. Note that lines 1-8 provide contextual information that serves to clarify the author's position in lines 8-11. The views of Chtcheglov and Debord are not presented as separate viewpoints.

1. The author would be most likely to agree with which one of the following statements?

    (A) Recently, psychogeography has repopularized performance art and literature.
    (B) The intensely personal nature of psychogeography allowed for the creation of a complex unifying interpretation.
    (C) Psychogeography should be repopularized despite the field's ongoing struggles to find a defining ethic.
    (D) The creation of a unifying interpretation of psychogeography may have been an impossibility.
    (E) The repopularization of psychogeography has been a long but well-planned process.

VIEWSTAMP Analysis: Viewpoint Identification Drill Answer Key

Question #1: GR, Must, AP. The correct answer choice is (D)

In approaching this broad Must Be True, Author's Perspective question, the formation of a precise prephrase might be nearly impossible, but the correct answer choice will be the one that passes the Fact Test and can be confirmed by the information provided in the passage.

Answer choice (A): In the last sentence of the passage, the author provides that psychogeography has been repopularized by performance art and literature, not the other way around, so this choice fails the Fact Test and cannot be correct

Answer choice (B): This is an Opposite Answer, since the passage provides that the intensely personal nature of the field made the creation of a unifying interpretation difficult, if not impossible.

Answer choice (C): In lines 12-13, the author observes that the field of psychogeography has been repopularized. However, her views as to whether this is a good idea or whether it *should* be done remain unknown. Note that the author's tone is descriptive, not prescriptive, and that the content is factual, not normative.

Answer choice (D): This is the correct answer choice. In lines 9-11, the author provides that "the intensely personal nature of psychogeography made the creation of a unifying interpretation difficult, if not impossible."

Answer choice (E): In the last sentence of the passage the author provides that psychogeography has been repopularized in recent years, not that repopularization has been a long, well-planned process, so this cannot be the right answer choice.

VIEWSTAMP Analysis: Viewpoint Identification Drill Answer Key

Passage #2:

Research into the physiology of lying has yielded mixed results. Initial research seemed to indicate that individuals engaged in the act of lying have certain immediate and consistent physical
(5) responses, including elevated blood pressure and pupil dilation. Researchers have recently shown that physiological reactions are an unreliable indicator of lying, because some individuals either do not experience such reactions, or else are able
(10) to actively suppress them. Newer studies using magnetic resonance imaging have shown that compulsive liars have more "white matter"—the brain's version of wiring—than individuals who do not lie compulsively. However, the validity of
(15) such studies is clearly questionable because the individuals classified as "liars" were largely self-reported, potentially biasing the study.

Number of Viewpoints: 4

Lines 1-2 and Lines 16-19: Author. The author first notes that research into the physiology of lying has yielded mixed results (an opinion of sorts), and then later notes that the results of the "newer studies" are in question due to possible validity issues.

Lines 2-6: Initial Researchers. Initial research (and thus initial researchers) suggest that liars had certain physical responses when lying.

Lines 6-12: Recent Researchers. These researchers disagree with the initial researchers, because some individuals do not display the expected physical reactions.

Lines 12-16: Newer Studies. The newer studies claim that liars have more "white matter" than non-liars.

2. The author would most likely agree with each of the following statements EXCEPT:

   (A) Initial research into the field of lying suggested that certain immediate and consistent physical responses were associated with the act of lying.

   (B) The results yielded by research into the psychology of lying have been inconsistent.

   (C) Compulsive liars have more "white matter" than individuals who do not lie compulsively.

   (D) Some researchers in the field believed physical reactions to be unreliable indicators of the act of lying.

   (E) The validity of certain studies in the field of lying is somewhat questionable.

Question #2: GR, MustX, AP. The correct answer choice is (C)

In responding to this MustX, Author's Perspective question, remember that the author must agree with four of the five answer choices. The correct answer choice will be a statement with which the author will *not necessarily agree*. Note that lack of evidence for an agreement is not the same as having evidence for a disagreement (this is one of the classic Errors in the Use of Evidence). In other words, the author need not overtly disagree with the correct answer choice; all we need to do is prove that she would not necessarily agree with it.

Answer choice (A): This fact is stated in the passage (lines 2-5).

Answer choice (B): This view is stated in the passage (lines 1-2).

Answer choice (C): This is the correct answer choice, since it is the only choice that is *not* confirmed by the information in the passage. Although some suggest that compulsive liars have more white matter than individuals who do not lie compulsively, the author makes a point of questioning the validity of this claim.

Answer choice (D): This view is stated in the passage (lines 6-8).

Answer choice (E): This view is stated in the passage (lines 14-15).

VIEWSTAMP Analysis: Viewpoint Identification Drill Answer Key

Passage #3:

Patent laws are thought to have originated in Italy, but legal history professors have convincingly shown that the concept of patents existed as far back as the third century in ancient Greece.
(5) Despite the long legal history of patents, recent commentators have suggested that their use should be either abolished or curtailed significantly. They argue that social and technological changes have surpassed the capacities of the patent system,
(10) and instead of being an engine of expansion, patent laws are now more commonly used as a means of suppression.

Number of Viewpoints: 3

Lines 1-2: Author. By using the word "convincingly" to describe the views of legal history professors, the author indicates that he or she agrees with the idea that the concept of patents has existed as far back as the third century. Line 1 presents a belief that is immediately discredited by the legal history professors with whom the author agrees.

Lines 2-4: Legal History Professors. This group holds that the concept of patents has existed as far back as the third century in ancient Greece.

Lines 5-12: Recent Commentators. The commentators believe that the use of patents should be restricted or eliminated.

3. It can be inferred from the passage that the commentators mentioned in line 6 would be most likely to agree with which one of the following statements regarding patents?

(A)   The patent system is now commonly used as an engine of expression.
(B)   Changes within the patent system have outpaced technological and social changes.
(C)   The use of patents should be abolished or significantly reduced.
(D)   Social and technological changes slowed the creation of the patent system that is currently in use.
(E)   The concept of patents has traditionally been thought to have originated in ancient Greece.

Question #3: CR, Must, SP. The correct answer choice is (C)

Since this is a Must Be True, Subject Perspective question, it is important to note the perspective of the commentators, who are in favor of either reducing or completely eliminating the use of patents.

Answer choice (A): At the end of the passage, the author provides that the patent system has come to be used more commonly as a means of suppression than as an engine of expression, so this choice cannot be confirmed by the passage, and should be eliminated from contention.

Answer choice (B): This is the Opposite answer. In lines 8-9, the commentators clearly state that technological and social changes have actually surpassed the capacity of the patent system.

Answer choice (C): This is the correct answer choice. In lines 6-8, the author mentions that some commentators have argued for abolishing or significantly curtailing the use of patents, thus confirming this as the correct answer choice.

Answer choice (D): The passage does not suggest that the creation of the patent system currently in use may have been slowed by social and technological changes, so this cannot be the right answer choice.

Answer choice (E): At the beginning of the passage, the author provides that patent laws were thought to have originated in Italy, though legal history professors have convincingly claimed that the concept may date back to third-century Greece. However, the passage provides no information about what the *recent commentators* believe about the origins of patents. Make sure to differentiate between various viewpoints in the passage, especially when they are not explicitly contrasted. The incorrect answers to Subject Perspective questions often state positions with which *other* subjects (or the author) would agree.

VIEWSTAMP Analysis: Viewpoint Identification Drill Answer Key

Passage #4:

Peruvian poet César Vallejo left behind a relatively small body of work, but his poetry has been lauded as uniquely insightful by many commentators. The monk-poet Thomas Merton called him the greatest
(5) poet since Dante, and others praised him as "a sublime wordsmith with no contemporary peer." His notably low level of output excludes him from the group of poets that would later be considered as the best of the 20th century, although he certainly
(10) would have warranted inclusion in that group had he produced a larger body of work.

Number of Viewpoints: 4

<u>Lines 1-2 and 7-12: Author</u>. The author believes that Vallejo is an excellent poet, but that his low output excludes him from consideration as the best of the century. Note that lines 1-2 provide an opinion of Vallejo's output—"relatively small body of work" and "justifiably"— that the author re-affirms later in the passage, and lines 1-2 are thus included in the author's viewpoint.

<u>Lines 2-4: Many Commentators</u>. This group believes Vallejo is uniquely insightful.

<u>Lines 4-5: Thomas Merton</u>. Merton lauds Vallejo as the "greatest poet since Dante."

<u>Lines 6-8: Others</u>. These commentators also believe Vallejo is a phenomenal poet.

4. Based on the information provided in the passage, Thomas Merton would be most likely to agree with which one of the following statements?

    (A) César Vallejo left behind a large and impressive body of work.
    (B) Vallejo's low level of output is one of the reasons why his poetry was so impressive.
    (C) Vallejo's work has been lauded by many uniquely brilliant commentators.
    (D) Vallejo's level of output was roughly equivalent to that of many of the 20th century's greatest poets.
    (E) Dante was a great poet.

Question #4: CR, Must, SP. The correct answer choice is (E)

In response to this Must Be True, Subject Perspective question, note the fact that all we know of Merton is that he referred to Vallejo as "the best poet since Dante."

Answer choice (A): The passage specifically provides that Vallejo left behind a relatively small body of work, so Merton would not agree with the statement in this answer choice.

Answer choice (B): The passage mentions that Vallejo had a relatively low level of output, and that Vallejo was a great poet, but there is no suggestion that Merton drew this causal connection, so this choice should be eliminated from contention.

Answer choice (C): While the *author* indicates that many commentators have lauded Vallejo as uniquely brilliant, there is no information supporting the notion that *Merton* saw those commentators as such. Therefore, this cannot be the correct answer to this Must Be True, Subject Perspective question.

Answer choice (D): The passage provides that Vallejo produced a relatively small body of work, so there is no basis for the assertion that Merton would agree with this statement. As such, it should be eliminated from contention.

Answer choice (E): This is the correct answer choice. By referring to Vallejo as the "greatest poet since Dante" (lines 4-5), Merton expresses a clear belief that both Vallejo and Dante are great poets.

Passage #5:

While often maligned by political commentators of the 1970s, the early success of the Five Year Plans for the Soviet economy is indisputable. After languishing for decades economically, in
(5)   just 13 years under Plan stewardship the Russian economy produced double-digit growth.

Number of Viewpoints: 2

Line 1: Political Commentators. The commentators are clearly critical of the Five Year Plans.

Lines 2-7: Author. The author defends the Plans and lauds their early success as "indisputable."

5. The author would most likely agree with which one of the following statements regarding the Five Year Plans?

    (A) The Plans were justifiably maligned by political commentators.
    (B) The Plans brought the Russian economy double-digit growth for 13 years.
    (C) The Plans were intended to stimulate double-digit growth within 13 years.
    (D) The Plans, which were criticized by some, were initially successful.
    (E) The Russian economy languished for decades under Plan stewardship.

Question #5: CR, Must, AP. The correct answer choice is (D)

In response to this Must Be True, Author's Perspective question, we should note that the author has a very high opinion of the Five Year Plans, referring to their early success as "indisputable."

Answer choice (A): The author does not suggest that the commentators' critiques were justified, so this answer choice cannot be correct.

Answer choice (B): The author provides that within just 13 years under Plan stewardship, the Russian economy produced double-digit growth. This does not mean, however, that growth continued for 13 years.

Answer choice (C): Although the author does provide that the Russian economy achieved double-digit growth within 13 years of Plan stewardship, there is no reason to believe that this achievement was specifically intended.

Answer choice (D): This is the correct answer choice. In line 3, the author describes the early success of the Five Year Plans as "indisputable." Clearly she would agree that the plans were, at least initially, successful.

Answer choice (E): This answer choice is directly disproven by the passage. Just because you know something to be true in the real world does not make it correct on the LSAT.

You should not be concerned if your shorthand summations look a bit different from the very condensed summaries presented below, as long as you sought to draw information that was brief enough to remember, but detailed enough to have some practical value in responding to the questions that would accompany an actual Reading Comprehension passage.

Passage #1:

When considering the rate of expansion of the Universe, astrophysical theorists have long held that the universe's growth must be slowing due to gravity. However, recent observations from
(5)   the Hubble Telescope suggest that the Universe is actually expanding more rapidly today than it has in the past. What, then, would account for this surprising observation? One explanatory model involves vacuum energy, a form of dark energy that
(10)   exists in space throughout the Universe. The precise nature of this energy, however, remains unknown. Another explanation allows for the possibility of a cosmological model containing phantom energy that could cause the expansion of the universe to
(15)   accelerate beyond the speed of light, and eventually rip it apart. A third hypothesis argues that the accelerating universe could be due to a repulsive gravitational interaction of anti-matter. Of course, it is entirely possible that the rate of expansion is not
(20)   homogeneous, and that we are, coincidentally, in a temporary period where expansion is faster than the background. The benefit of this model is that it does not require any new physics such as dark energy, whose fundamental properties are yet to be fully
(25)   understood.

The author begins by rejecting a commonly held view, and then proposes several explanations for a new view. At the end of the passage, the author defends an entirely different hypothesis.

VIEWSTAMP Analysis: Structure Identification Drill Answer Key

1. Which one of the following best describes the organization of the passage?

   (A) A scientific conundrum is described, discrepancies among proposed solutions to it are evaluated, and a course of action is recommended.

   (B) A phenomenon is described, three different theories regarding its effects are presented, and an argument that the phenomenon may be short-lived is defended.

   (C) A commonly held scientific belief is rejected, three explanations for the new belief are evaluated, and a fourth hypothesis is presented as more plausible than the other three.

   (D) Three solutions to a scientific puzzle are advanced, the implications of a fourth solution are evaluated, and an assumption underlying these solutions is rejected as not yet fully understood.

   (E) A scientific dispute is discussed, the case for one side is made and supported by examples, and a new hypothesis is advocated.

Question #1: GR, Must, Organization. The correct answer choice is (C)

Organization questions exemplify the value of understanding passage structure. In some ways, they resemble Method of Reasoning questions from the Logical Reasoning section of the test. Due to the highly abstract nature of the terms used in each answer choice, you must think about argument structure, not content. While prephrasing an answer will help you understand how the argument is organized, there are many ways to describe the same argument. So, do not expect to see your exact prephrase as the answer.

Answer choice (A) is incorrect, because no course of action is recommended.

Answer choice (B) is attractive, but incorrect. Although the author certainly describes a phenomenon (accelerating expansion of the universe) and later argues that the phenomenon may be short-lived, the effects of this phenomenon are never discussed. The theories discussed seek to explain the phenomenon in question, i.e. to present a plausible cause for it: the debate is over *why* the universe is expanding. Accordingly, it would be imprecise to say that "three different theories of its *effects* are presented."

Answer choice (C) is the correct answer choice. The author begins by rejecting the commonly held view that the universe's growth must be slowing, and then proposes several explanations for the new view, which is that the expansion of the universe is accelerating. At the end of the passage, the author defends an entirely different postulate, namely, that the expansion is temporary. This hypothesis is advocated as more understandable because it does not require any new physics, such as dark energy, which is not yet fully understood.

VIEWSTAMP Analysis: Structure Identification Drill Answer Key

Answer choice (D) is incorrect, because only three of the four proposed explanations require making an assumption about energy or matter that are not yet fully understood. The fourth explanation is advocated precisely because it does not require making such assumptions.

Answer choice (E) is incorrect, because the author does not *discuss* a scientific dispute as much as mention—and quickly reject—the commonly held belief that the universe's growth is slowing. The claim that "a scientific dispute is discussed" overstates the importance of that element in the passage. More importantly, the theories mentioned to not exemplify the hypothesis that expansion is accelerating; rather, they seek to explain the cause for such acceleration.

Passage #2:

On War, the posthumously published seminal work of military theorist Carl von Clausewitz (1780-1831), is regarded as an effort, unique in its time, to marry the concepts of political and military
(5)   strategy. Guided by the principle that war is "simply the expression of politics by other means," Clausewitz rejected a succession of preceding works of military theory for being focused too heavily on practical, geometrical, and unilateral
(10) considerations. In short, Clausewitz sought a unified theory of war that encompassed both the practical considerations of conducting war and the constant, reciprocal application of intelligent forces that permit military genius to rise above the fixed
(15) rules of traditional military doctrine.

The author mentions two strategies for conflict resolution (political and military), and describes the work of a military theorist who believed that these strategies can be combined into a unified theory of war.

2.   Which one of the following most accurately describes the organization of the passage?

   (A)   Two strategies are described and a general principle is used to resolve the conflict between them.

   (B)   A general principle is described and instantiated by two different ways of resolving a conflict.

   (C)   Two ways of resolving a conflict are introduced, and a principle is used to show that they are not incompatible with each other.

   (D)   A general principle is described and used to discredit a commonly held belief.

   (E)   Two theories are outlined and a general principle is applied to decide between them.

Question #2: GR, Must, Organization. The correct answer choice is (C)

To answer this Organization question, you first need to summarize the passage: Clausewitz was a military theorist who, unlike prior theorists, combined military and political theory. Guided by the principle that war is an expression of politics, Clausewitz was able to account for both the practical considerations of war and the potential impact of military genius. It is not uncommon to find that your prephrase to Organization questions does not have an exact match, because of the variety of ways in which test makers can characterize a given argument or passage. This is not a problem: as long as you know how the passage is organized *in general*, you should have no problem answering the question.

Answer choice (A) is incorrect, because there is no evidence that there is a presumed *conflict* between the concepts of political and military strategy that the principle needs to resolve.

Answer choice (B) is incorrect, because neither strategy exemplifies, or instantiates, the principle that war is an expression of politics. The principle in question is not represented by an actual example.

Answer choice (C) is the correct answer choice. The political and military strategies are introduced as two ways of resolving a conflict (war). The principle in the second sentence is then used to show that these two strategies are not incompatible with each other, i.e. that they can be combined in a unified theory of war.

Answer choice (D) is incorrect, because there is no reason to suspect that the succession of preceding works amounts to a "commonly held belief."

Answer choice (E) is incorrect, because the principle in question is not used to *decide*, or arbitrate, between the concepts of political and military strategy. Instead, the principle shows that the two are inextricably linked.

Passage #3:

Harriet Tubman was born a slave in Maryland in 1819 or 1820. Having suffered vicious beatings as a child, she escaped north to Philadelphia when she was approximately thirty years old. Over the
(5)   next several years, Tubman learned the duties of a conductor on the Underground Railroad, a network of people and secret places used to help slaves escape to non-slave-holding territories, and to freedom. During this time she worked tirelessly,
(10)   devoid of fear for her personal safety, to help others escape as she had done. Through her work, Tubman became acquainted with other figures whose words and actions would echo down through history, telling both her story and their own.

Tubman, born a slave, escaped from slavery to become a conductor on the Underground Railroad. The remainder of the passage praises Tubman for helping others do the same.

3. The author's discussion proceeds in which one of the following ways?

    (A)   from a common claim about slavery to an inference regarding a particular individual to whom that claim applies
    (B)   from an account of an individual's overcoming an obstacle to a recognition of that individual's ability to help others overcome a similar obstacle
    (C)   from a specific observation about an individual to a more general claim about the applicability of that observation to other, similar individuals
    (D)   from a depiction of a predicament faced by a particular individual to a more general observation about the extent to which this predicament was shared by other individuals
    (E)   from general comments about a historical fact to a counterexample to these comments as applied to a particular individual

VIEWSTAMP Analysis: Structure Identification Drill Answer Key

Question #3: GR, Must, Organization. The correct answer choice is (B)

To understand the structure of the passage, it is essential to synthesize the information in it. The first half of the passage describes Tubman's escape from slavery and work on the Underground Railroad, whereas the second half praises Tubman for helping others do the same.

Answer choice (A) is incorrect, because the author makes no common claims about slavery.

Answer choice (B) is the correct answer choice. See prephrase above.

Answer choice (C) is incorrect, because the author does not evaluate the extent to which his observations about Tubman also apply to others who escaped.

Answer choice (D) is incorrect, because the extent to which slavery (a predicament) was shared by other individuals is never explicitly addressed.

Answer choice (E) is incorrect, because Tubman is not used as a counterexample to a general comment about slavery.

Passage #4:

Forensic handwriting analysis, a pattern matching discipline in which an examiner compares a "known" handwriting sample to the handwriting on a "questioned" document to determine whether
(5)   the person who created the known sample also wrote the questioned document, has been the subject of ongoing and vigorous debate within the legal community. Granted the status of "expert testimony," such forensic analysis is an infrequently
(10)   used but often powerful evidentiary tool employed by prosecutors to convince juries of a defendant's guilt. But, should such evidence even be admissible at trial? The answer to this question begins with another question: Is forensic handwriting analysis
(15)   a science? Recent federal appeals court decisions are split on this issue, which is critical to the determination of the proper legal standard to be used by trial courts in ruling on the admissibility of forensic handwriting evidence.

The author introduces forensic handwriting analysis as controversial, mentions its use in courtroom proceedings, and then asks if such an analysis is scientific enough to be admissible as evidence at trial.

4. Which one of the following best describes the organization of the passage as a whole?

   (A) A type of forensic analysis is described as controversial, its value in courtroom proceedings is presented, and questions regarding its admissibility at trial are raised.

   (B) The benefits of using an evidentiary tool are debated, its adoption is criticized as unreliable, and the implications of that adoption are evaluated.

   (C) The value of a particular type evidence is viewed as theoretically plausible, the practical difficulties of using such evidence at trial are enumerated, and the validity of that evidence is called into question.

   (D) A type of forensic evidence is discussed, two viewpoints regarding its admissibility are outlined, and one of those viewpoints is endorsed at the expense of the other.

   (E) The advantages of using a type of forensic analysis are discussed, its fairness is questioned, and a more fundamental question is introduced as controversial.

Question #4: GR, Must, Organization. The correct answer choice is (A)

There is a debate within the legal community over whether forensic handwriting analysis is science, and—if so—whether it should be admissible at trial.

Answer choice (A) is the correct answer choice. The author introduces forensic handwriting analysis as controversial (first sentence), presents its value in courtroom proceedings (second sentence), and then raises several questions regarding its admissibility at trial (rest of the passage).

Answer choice (B) is incorrect, because the author never evaluates the implications of actually adopting forensic handwriting evidence in the courtroom. Its admissibility is questioned, but its implications are never evaluated.

Answer choice (C) is incorrect, because the author does not enumerate the practical difficulties of using handwriting evidence in legal proceedings.

Answer choice (D) is incorrect, because the author does not outline *two* viewpoints regarding its admissibility of handwriting forensic evidence. There is only one viewpoint, i.e. that such admissibility is questionable. The precise arguments for and against accepting such evidence are not laid out as such.

Answer choice (E) is incorrect, because the fairness of using forensic handwriting evidence is never debated.

Passage #5:

In the early 1950s, a diagnosis of autism—a broad
term used to describe developmental brain disorders
resulting in difficulties in social interaction and
communication, both verbal and non-verbal, and
(5)   also resulting in repetitive behaviors—almost
always meant a life of institutionalization for the
person diagnosed, beginning in childhood and
lasting throughout the rest of the person's life.
Temple Grandin, born in the late 1940s, was
(10)   herself diagnosed with autism in 1950. As a child,
Grandin did not speak until she was more than three
years old, communicating only through screams
and other non-verbal vocalizations. Despite these
disadvantages, Grandin went on to earn a doctorate
(15)   in animal science and to invent a livestock restraint
system used for the humane handling of nearly
half of the cattle in North America. One key to Dr.
Grandin's success was a symptom of her autism:
she was a photo-realistic visual thinker able to
(20)   construct and examine complex designs in her mind
before they are constructed, just as someone might
examine a photograph of the built object, down to
the last detail.

The passage describes the life of Dr. Grandin, who became an accomplished inventor in part by
turning a symptom of her condition—photo-realistic visual thought—into an advantage.

5.   The primary purpose of the passage is to

(A)   provide a biographical account of an
         accomplished scientist
(B)   examine the hidden consequences of a
         developmental disorder
(C)   outline the historical understanding and
         treatment of a medical condition
(D)   show that a specific disorder may confer
         unique benefits that would otherwise be
         unobtainable
(E)   praise an accomplished inventor for turning an
         apparent disadvantage into an advantage

Question #5: GR, Must, P. The correct answer choice is (E)

Sometimes, your understanding of Passage Structure will be tested with a Global Reference, Purpose question. These questions are quite similar to Organization questions, both of which highlight the importance of understanding the information presented at an abstract level. Purpose questions often produce answers that are even more abstract than Organization questions: they ask about what the author *did*, not what she *said*.

Answer choice (A) is incorrect, because the purpose of the passage is not merely to provide a biographical account of Dr. Grandin's achievements, but rather to situate these achievements in the context of her developmental disorder.

Answer choice (B) is incorrect. Even if Dr. Grandin's photo-realistic visual skills can be regarded as a "hidden consequence" of her condition, the author does not seek to examine the hidden consequences of autism.

Answer choice (C) is incorrect, as it only captures the content of the first sentence of the passage, not of the passage as a whole.

Answer choice (D) is attractive, but incorrect. Just because Dr. Grandin's autism conferred a certain advantage does not mean that this advantage is unique to autism, and unobtainable for anyone not suffering from autism. It is entirely possible that some photo-realistic visual thinkers are not autistic.

Answer choice (E) is the correct answer choice. The passage provides a biographical account of Dr. Grandin, who became an accomplished inventor in part by turning a symptom of her condition—photo-realistic visual thought—into an asset.

This drill is designed to help you identify the author's attitude and tone. For each passage, we have selected a handful of words to concisely describe that tone. Rest assured that you need not write down tone descriptor words while taking the LSAT!

Also, the descriptors provided in the answer key are general; if you provided a different term, that is acceptable as long as your answer is in the general vicinity of the answer provided. For example, if the answer key uses "congratulatory" as the tone, and you answered "complimentary," then that would still be correct.

<u>Passage #1</u>:

Hydraulic fracturing, or "fracking," is the practice of introducing pressurized fluids into rock layers—such as those in shale—in order to assist in the removal of petroleum and natural gas from
(5)   the rock strata. While fracking has increased the recovery of oil and gas from U.S. reserves and has provided economic growth in areas of the country that had been depressed, the environmental risks are unquestionably cause for concern. Groundwater
(10)   contamination is the primary threat, because fracking fluids can migrate into water supplies. Other threats exist as well, including air pollution and toxic waste. These concerns need to be addressed if fracking is allowed to continue.

Cautious; Concerned.

The author admits that fracking has provided some benefits, including economic growth and increased energy production. However, the author also notes that there are concerns, and that these concerns need to be addressed if fracking is to continue.

1.   The author's attitude toward fracking can best be described as one of

     (A)   admiration
     (B)   fascination
     (C)   disbelief
     (D)   caution
     (E)   confusion

Question #1: CR, Must, AP. The correct answer choice is (D)

The author recognizes that fracking is beneficial to the oil and gas industries, but is concerned about possible threats to residents and the environment.

Answer choice (A): Although the author concedes that fracking has increased oil and gas recovery in the United States, this does not amount to "admiration," and the point is immediately followed by a reference to the associated environmental risks.

Answer choice (B): The author does not appear to be "fascinated" with fracking.

Answer choice (C): The author is not "incredulous" at the environmental risks posed by fracking: on the contrary, she is convinced that such risks do exist (lines 8-9).

Answer choice (D): This is the correct answer choice. The author states that "the environmental risks are unquestionably a cause for concern" (lines 8-9), clearly expressing caution and worry about the environmental impact of fracking.

Answer choice (E): The author refers to the environmental risks of fracking and states that such concerns must be addressed if fracking is to continue. The author does not seem "confused," so this is not the right answer choice.

<u>Passage #2</u>:

The works of Maya Angelou reflect a passion for living and a breathtaking range of life experience. Her dazzling 1969 autobiographical work, *I Know Why the Caged Bird Sings*, rightly brought her
(5)   worldwide recognition and fame, but "author" was just one of many artistic endeavors at which she excelled. Angelou was also an acclaimed poet, playwright, screenwriter, editor, dancer, narrator, journalist, broadcaster, composer, actor, producer,
(10)   and director.

Enthusiastic; Appreciative; Adulatory.

The author's attitude towards Angelou's work is extremely complimentary. Phrases such as "breathtaking range," "dazzling 1969 autobiographical work," "rightly brought her worldwide recognition," and "just one of many artistic endeavors at which she excelled" indicate not just respect, but an attitude closer to adoration or adulation.

2. The author would be most likely to agree with which one of the following statements regarding Maya Angelou?

    (A) After Angelou wrote *I Know Why the Caged Bird Sings*, she was able to attain her justifiable goal of achieving worldwide recognition and fame.

    (B) Angelou's worldwide recognition and fame was probably attributable to her many artistic endeavors.

    (C) Angelou would not have been famous had it not been for the success of *I Know Why the Caged Bird Sings*.

    (D) The fame that *I Know Why the Caged Bird Sings* brought to Maya Angelou was justified.

    (E) Angelou had many talents, but her poetry deserves the most acclaim.

Question #2: CR, Must, AP. The correct answer choice is (D)

The author is impressed with Maya Angelou, so the correct answer choice to this Must Be True, Author's Perspective question is likely to reflect that positive attitude.

Answer choice (A): Although the passage does provide that Angelou became internationally famous after the publication of her autobiography, there is no suggestion that this was Angelou's *intended* goal.

Answer choice (B): The author clearly admires Angelou for her many artistic endeavors, but it was Angelou's autobiography that was specified as having brought the artist worldwide fame.

Answer choice (C): The passage does provide that *I Know Why the Caged Bird Sings* brought Angelou worldwide recognition, but there is no suggestion that Angelou would not have become famous in some other way in the absence of her autobiography.

Answer choice (D): This is the correct answer choice. In lines 3-5, the author refers to Angelou's autobiographical work as "dazzling," and makes a point of saying that the book "rightly brought her recognition and fame."

Answer choice (E): The passage provides that Angelou was an "acclaimed poet" but then goes on to list several other areas of the artist's expertise. Since the author makes no suggestion that Angelou's poetry necessarily deserves more acclaim than her other talents, this choice fails the Fact Test and should be ruled out of contention.

VIEWSTAMP Analysis: Tone Identification Drill Answer Key

Passage #3:

In the aftermath of the Great Depression, the
Glass-Steagall Act of 1933 reformed the American
banking system. Later congressional actions
weakened Glass-Steagall until, ultimately,
(5)   significant sections were repealed in 1999.
These developments directly led to the financial
meltdown of the late 2000s, an event that affected
millions of citizens. However, with the recent shift
in voter attitudes, I am certain that changes will
(10)   be made to the current banking statutes that will
result in greater stability and sustained economic
growth.

PRACTICE DRILL
EXPLANATIONS

Optimistic; Confident.

The first eight lines of the passage suggest that the author may take a rather negative view of
the subject, but this is only because the events under discussion are, by definition, negative. In
lines 8-12, however, the author displays a confident and optimistic attitude that changes will be
made.

3.   Which one of the following most accurately identifies
the attitude shown by the author toward future bank
regulations?

    (A)   incensed
    (B)   ambivalent
    (C)   cynical
    (D)   acquiescent
    (E)   optimistic

Question #3: CR, Must, AP. The correct answer choice is (E)

The author is quite confident about prospects for the future, claiming to be "certain that changes will
be made...that will result in greater stability and sustained economic growth." (Lines 8-12).

Answer choice (A): The author is not "incensed," or angry, about the current banking statutes.
Extreme tone is rarely observed on the LSAT.

Answer choice (B): The author does not reflect mixed emotions about the statutes, but is rather quite
optimistic about the prospects going forward.

Answer choice (C): This is an Opposite answer, because the author is hopeful and confident, not
cynical, regarding the future impact of any changes to the current bank regulations.

VIEWSTAMP Analysis: Tone Identification Drill Answer Key

Answer choice (D): The author is not acquiescing to the new regulations as much as openly embracing them. "Acquiescent" implies a tacit consent without protest, which is quite different from the confidence and hope displayed in the last sentence of the passage.

Answer choice (E): This is the correct answer choice, as implied by the views expressed in lines 8-12.

PRACTICE DRILL
EXPLANATIONS

Passage #4:

The legal system of Yemen has traditionally been weak and disorganized. Although Sharia (the religious law of Islam) is the constitutionally mandated source of Yemeni law, in practice the
(5)   system is administered by the Supreme Judicial Council (SJC). The SJC appoints judges (and can remove them at will), leading to an uncertain system prone to corruption, harassment, and manipulation. While many attempts to reform the
(10)   judiciary have been made in recent years, real reform remains unlikely, and Yemen is liable to continue to suffer without genuine rule of law.

Negative; Pessimistic; Doubtful.

The description of the Yemeni legal system is unquestionably negative ("uncertain system prone to corruption, harassment, and manipulation"). Note, also, that the author closes with a series of pessimistic statements: "real reform remains unlikely" and "liable to continue to suffer."

4.   The author's attitude toward the prospect of reforming the Yemeni legal system is best revealed by which of the following phrases?

   (A)   "genuine rule of law" (line 12)
   (B)   "traditionally … weak" (lines 1-2)
   (C)   "attempts…have been made" (lines 9-10)
   (D)   "remove them at will" (line 7)
   (E)   "reform remains unlikely" (line 11)

Question #4: CR, Must, AP. The correct answer choice is (E)

To attack this Author's Perspective question, note the dubious tone used throughout the passage. The correct answer choice will clearly reflect a pessimistic outlook.

Answer choice (A): At the end of the passage, the author provides that without genuine rule of law, the country is liable to continue to suffer. However, "genuine rule of law" does not reflect the author's attitude toward the prospect of reforming the Yemeni legal system.

Answer choice (B): This answer choice alludes to the state of the Yemeni legal system, but it does not specifically reveal the author's attitude toward the system's *future* prospects.

Answer choice (C): While attempts at reform have been made in the past, this phrase does not reveal the author's attitude regarding prospects for improving Yemen's legal system.

Answer choice (D): The author uses these words to describe the broad powers of the Supreme Judiciary Committee to appoint and remove judges, but this phrase does not reveal her attitude toward the prospect of reforming the Yemeni legal system.

Answer choice (E): This is the correct answer choice. As prephrased above, this choice reflects the pessimistic perspective manifest throughout the passage. "Reform remains unlikely" so accurately reflects the author's perspective in this case that it could have been the title of the passage.

Passage #5:

West Indian manatees are aquatic mammals that inhabit the Caribbean and U.S. Southeastern coastal area. The large, slow-moving manatee has an inquisitive nature and amiable temperament, and
(5)   presents no threat to humans. For a number of years, manatee populations have been decreasing, and encounters with humans or man-made refuse is often the cause. For example, fast-moving watercraft regularly strike these gentle mammals,
(10)   sometimes killing them and often inflicting serious injury. In other instances, discarded fishing gear such as hooks, sinkers, and monofilament line, is ingested by the curious manatee, causing distress and sometimes agonizing death. We should do
(15)   more to save the manatee from this inhumane treatment.

Sympathetic; Compassionate; Prescriptive; Descriptive.

The author refers to the manatees in positive terms ("inquisitive," "amiable," "gentle," "curious," "agreeable"). Meanwhile, the language used to describe their suffering displays feelings of compassion and outrage ("serious injury," "distress and agonizing death," "inhumane"). This fact, coupled with the closing statement that "we should do more", suggests that the author's attitude is one of sympathy and compassion. Since the passage contains both observations and recommendations regarding the treatment of manatees, the tone can be classified both descriptive and prescriptive.

5. The author's attitude toward the manatee can best be described as

    (A) angry
    (B) hopeless
    (C) concerned
    (D) jocular
    (E) inquisitive

Question #5: CR, Must, AP. The correct answer choice is (C)

Based on the wording chosen by the author of the passage, the author's attitude would properly be described as both sympathetic and concerned.

Answer choice (A): The author is alarmed by the inhumane treatment of manatees, but his concern does not amount to outright anger. This answer choice is too extreme to be correct.

Answer choice (B): The author is worried about the plight of the manatee but does not seem "hopeless," so this choice should be eliminated from contention.

Answer choice (C): This is the correct answer choice. The author discusses some of the issues causing the manatee to suffer or die, closing the passage with the sentiment that "we should do more to save the manatees" (lines 14-15). Clearly, the author is concerned about their well-being.

Answer choice (D): There is no jest in the tone of this passage, so this cannot be the right answer choice.

Answer choice (E): While concern is clearly present, there is no particular sign of "inquisitiveness."

Awareness of the shifts in perspective and various arguments that you encounter within the passages will be vital as you attack the questions on the Reading Comprehension section.

Passage #1:

Incentivization has recently become a hotly debated topic. On one side of the debate are theorists who believe that the use of incentives is fraught with dangers, including unintended

(5)   side effects that could lead to the distortion of our social values and goals. On the other side of the debate are pragmatists who insist that, while such dangers exist and are legitimate causes for concern, there is no other feasible

(10)   way to induce needed social changes.

Lines 2-6: Theorists. The theorists believe that the use of incentives is troubling and dangerous.

Lines 6-10: Pragmatists. This group agrees with the theorists that dangers exist, but argue that incentivization is necessary to bring about required social changes.

1. With which one of the following statements regarding incentivization would the theorists and the pragmatists discussed in the passage be most likely to agree?

   (A)   The use of incentives is not advisable.
   (B)   Incentivization is not likely to distort social values and goals.
   (C)   Incentivization is the only feasible way to induce needed social changes.
   (D)   There are risks associated with the use of incentives.
   (E)   The use of incentives will likely distort social values and goals.

VIEWSTAMP Analysis: Argument Identification Drill Answer Key

Question #1: CR, Must, SP, Point of Agreement. The correct answer choice is (D)

To attack this Point of Agreement question, find an answer choice containing a statement with which both groups would agree. Recall that the theorists are concerned about the dangers associated with the use of incentives, and that the pragmatists also concede that such risks do exist. Since this is the only point of agreement mentioned in the passage, it should make for a reliable prephrase.

Answer choice (A): This is the Opposite answer choice, as the theorists would probably agree with it, while the pragmatists would most likely disagree.

Answer choice (B): We have direct evidence that the theorists would disagree with this statement, because they are afraid that the unintended effects of incentivization could distort social values and goals (lines 3-6). The pragmatists concede that risks do exist, but their exact views regarding this statement are unknown.

Answer choice (C): This is an attractive answer choice, as we have clear evidence that the pragmatists would agree with it (lines 9-10). Unfortunately, we have no reason to suspect that the theorists would also agree. In fact, judging from the latter group's decidedly skeptical attitude toward incentives ("fraught with dangers" [lines 3-4]), they probably believe that there is a better way to induce social change.

Answer choice (D): This is the correct answer choice. The theorists believe that the use of incentives is fraught with danger (lines 3-4), and the pragmatists also agree that legitimate concerns exist (lines 8-9).

Answer choice (E): Although both groups consider the use of incentives to be potentially dangerous, neither group suggests how likely it is that incentivization will distort social values. This answer choice conflates possibility with probability, and represents a classic "decoy" answer to questions in the Prove family, such as Must Be True and Point of Agreement.

Passage #2:

The Universal Declaration of Human Rights, drawn up in 1946 after consultation with leading politicians and philosophers from around the world, was a much needed proclamation of fundamental
(5)   human rights. While the opinions of those who supported the Declaration were surprisingly consistent, the practical application of these rights proved much more controversial. An early criticism came from cultural relativists, who argued that
(10) the concept of human rights derived from Western individualism and was thus a form of Western cultural imperialism. These criticisms were ultimately dismissed, and rightly so. As the critics of the cultural relativists noted, no culture
(15) contains a wholly separate set of values, and many of the values that the cultural relativists attributed solely to Western thinking were also present in non-Western cultures. The cultural relativists also assumed, erroneously, that each country possesses a
(20) single uniform "culture," rather than a large number of sub-cultures blended together to create the whole.

Lines 4-7 and Line 13: Author. In line 4, the author refers to the Universal Declaration of Human Rights as "needed," and later remarks that the relativists' criticisms were "rightly" dismissed (line 13).

Lines 8-12: Cultural Relativists. This group argues that rights are a Western ideal, and thus that establishing a universal statement of rights is culturally imperialistic.

Lines 13-22: Critics. The critics of cultural relativists argue that no culture contains a wholly separate set of values, and also that no country has a single uniform "culture."

2. The observation that "no culture contains a wholly separate set of values" (lines 14-15) plays which one of the following roles in the passage?

(A) It is a claim that the rest of the passage is designed to establish.

(B) It is a statement serving merely to introduce the critics' objection to the cultural relativists, and plays no logical role.

(C) It is used to support the conclusion that many of the values that the cultural relativists attributed solely to Western thinking are also present in non-Western cultures.

(D) It is offered to call into question the claim that the concept of rights is a form of Western cultural imperialism.

(E) It is supported by the observation that the cultural relativists were wrong in their criticism of human rights.

Question #2: SR, Must, P. The correct answer choice is (D)

To answer this Purpose question, formulate a suitable prephrase first: the fact that no culture contains a wholly separate set of values is an observation used by the critics to object to the cultural relativists: it suggests that human rights are not an exclusively Western phenomenon.

Answer choice (A) is incorrect, because this claim is not the main point of the passage. The latter can be found in line 11.

Answer choice (B) is incorrect, because this statement supports the argument that the cultural relativists are wrong in their criticism. Thus, it plays a logical role in the critics' argument.

Answer choice (C) is incorrect, because the claim that many of the values attributed solely to Western thinking are also present in non-Western cultures is not a conclusion. Rather, it is a premise used to support the main conclusion that the cultural relativists were wrong in their criticism.

Answer choice (D) is the correct answer choice, as it agrees with our prephrase above.

Answer choice (E) is the Reverse answer, because this claim *supports* the conclusion that the cultural relativists were wrong in their criticism of rights.

Passage #3:

Before creating any of his seminal works, at the age of 13, Michelangelo was apprenticed to painter Domenico Ghirlandaio. Many historians believe that Ghirlandaio played a pivotal role in the
(5) artistic development of Michelangelo, while others argue that Michelangelo's inherent talent would have similarly developed at any of the academies at that time, and that Ghirlandaio was simply a stepping stone. According to the latter theory, the
(10) Medici played a far greater role in Michelangelo's artistic development than Ghirlandaio, in part because the Medici were Michelangelo's patrons and commissioned a number of his works. While acknowledging the significance of the Medici
(15) to Michelangelo's career, the opposition maintains that it was Ghirlandaio who introduced Michelangelo to the Medici: when asked to name his two best pupils, Ghirlandaio pointed at Michelangelo without hesitation, even though
(20) the young artist's apprenticeship had not yet been completed.

Lines 3-5 and 13-21: Many Historians. This group believes that Ghirlandaio played a critical role in the artistic development of Michelangelo. The reference to "the opposition" (line 15) can be linked back to this viewpoint.

Lines 5-13: Other Historians. This group believes that Ghirlandaio did not play a major role in Michelangelo's life, and that the Medici were more significant.

3. Which one of the following, if true, would most strengthen the contention that Ghirlandaio played a pivotal role in the artistic development of Michelangelo?

(A) The Medici would not have become Michelangelo's patrons without Ghirlandaio's initial endorsement.

(B) Ghirlandaio had many apprentices, none of whom were as successful as Michelangelo.

(C) Given that patronage by the Medici was invariably associated with superb artistic skill, it conferred instant status and prestige upon the artist.

(D) As patrons, the Medici allowed Michelangelo more artistic freedom than Ghirlandaio had.

(E) Some of the earliest works of Michelangelo, created under the guidance of Ghirlandaio, were not appreciated by the Medici.

VIEWSTAMP Analysis: Argument Identification Drill Answer Key

Question #3: CR, Strengthen. The correct answer choice is (A)

To strengthen the argument that Ghirlandaio played a pivotal role in the artistic development of Michelangelo, you either need to downplay the importance of the Medici to Michelangelo's life, or else emphasize the significance of Ghirlandaio's mentorship.

Answer choice (A) is the correct answer choice. If the Medici only hired Michelangelo thanks to Ghirlandaio's endorsement, this would strengthen the argument made at the end of the passage (lines 16-21) and reaffirm the belief that Ghirlandaio played a pivotal role in the young artist's development.

Answer choice (B) is incorrect, because it lends more credibility to the belief that Michelangelo was inherently talented, and that his success had little to do with Ghirlandaio himself.

Answer choice (C) is incorrect, because it suggests that Michelangelo because famous, at least in part, because of the Medici's patronage. This strengthens the opposite argument.

Answer choice (D) is incorrect. If Ghirlandaio allowed Michelangelo less artistic freedom than did the Medici, Ghirlandaio may have hindered Michelangelo's artistic development. Of course, it is also possible that lack of artistic freedom cultivated discipline and focus. There are several ways of interpreting this answer choice, with each interpretation carrying a different set of assumptions. Since the correct answer choice must unequivocally strengthen the argument that Ghirlandaio played a pivotal role in the artistic development of Michelangelo, this answer choice is incorrect.

Answer choice (E) is incorrect. Neither argument assumes that the Medici liked all of Michelangelo's works, and it is entirely possible that some of his earliest works were not anything special (he was, after all, only 13). This has no bearing on the issue at stake.

<u>**Passage #4:**</u>

Neutrinos are subatomic particles, similar to
electrons but lacking an electrical charge. In a
recent scientific controversy, experimental results
indicated that neutrinos were able to travel faster
(5)   than the speed of light, a violation of Einstein's
theory of special relativity. While some researchers
hailed the results as a breakthrough with profound
implications for the future, other researchers
immediately questioned the credibility of the
(10)   reported findings.

<u>Lines 5-6: Einstein.</u> This can be a tough viewpoint to identify, because it is inserted so briefly. Einstein asserted the theory of special relativity, and since that theory is violated by the experimental results, we can infer that, according to his theory, neutrinos cannot travel faster than the speed of light.

<u>Lines 6-8: Some Researchers.</u> These researchers see the experimental results as having a broad and important effect on society.

<u>Lines 8-10: Other Researchers.</u> These researchers believe the experimental results are possibly false.

4.   Based on the information presented in the passage,
it can be inferred that Einstein would probably agree
with which one of the following assertions?

(A)   Electrons lack an electrical charge.
(B)   Neutrinos are able to travel at speeds faster
       than the speed of light.
(C)   The findings reported from recent neutrino
       experiments lack credibility.
(D)   The results of recent experiments involving
       neutrinos represent a breakthrough with
       profound implications for the future.
(E)   Neutrinos cannot travel faster than the speed of
       light.

VIEWSTAMP Analysis: Argument Identification Drill Answer Key

Question #4: CR, Must, SP. The correct answer choice is (E)

To attack this Must Be True, Subject Perspective question, note that Einstein's perspective is only referenced indirectly, and that the correct answer will contain an inference that may not be directly stated in the passage, but that can still be proven by reference to the information contained in it.

Answer choice (A): Since neutrinos are "similar to electrons but lacking in electric charge" (lines 1-2), we can infer that electrons do have an electric charge. This answer choice is therefore false.

Answer choice (B): This is an Opposite answer. The proposition that neutrinos can travel faster than the speed of light is described as a *violation* of Einstein's theory of special relativity, so Einstein would probably disagree with this statement.

Answer choice (C): This statement does not express Einstein's views or beliefs, and is therefore incorrect.

Answer choice (D): Though some researchers hailed the recent results as a breakthrough, this is not an assertion made by Einstein, so this choice can be confidently eliminated from contention.

Answer choice (E): This is the correct answer choice. Experimental results indicate that neutrinos can travel faster than the speed of light, which the author describes as a violation of Einstein's theory of special relativity. So, Einstein would probably agree that neutrinos *cannot* travel faster than the speed of light.

VIEWSTAMP Analysis: Argument Identification Drill Answer Key

Passage #5:

Bitcoin, a peer-to-peer digital currency that permits electronic payments between strangers without third-party intervention, has left state, national, and international governmental organizations
(5) grasping to understand the technology and predict its potential impact on monetary policy. To some, bitcoin is simply a novelty that is entirely independent of the traditional banking system, and without effect on the process by which the
(10) monetary authority of a country controls the supply of money. Others, however, argue that bitcoin's independence and potential for nearly instantaneous geometric expansion could seriously threaten a nation's financial security.

Lines 6-11: Proponents. The proponents argue that bitcoin is a novelty that is independent of the traditional banking system.

Lines 11-14: Opponents. The opponents see bitcoin as a potential threat to a nation's financial security.

5. The two groups discussed in the passage would most likely disagree over which one of the following statements?

(A) Bitcoin can simplify large, international monetary transactions.
(B) Bitcoin is a form of peer-to-peer, digital currency.
(C) Bitcoin has the potential for nearly instantaneous geometric expansion.
(D) Bitcoin's potential impact might be difficult to predict.
(E) Bitcoin represents a serious threat to the nation's financial security.

Question #5: GR, Point at Issue. The correct answer choice is (E)

The correct answer to this Point at Issue question will contain a factual statement that passes the Agree/Disagree Test, i.e. it must produce responses where one group would say, "Yes, I agree with this statement" and the other group would say, "No, I disagree with it." Unless both responses are produced, the answer choice is incorrect.

Answer choice (A): Neither group makes any mention of how bitcoin would affect international monetary transactions.

Answer choice (B): The fact that bitcoin is a form of peer-to-peer currency is not disputed by either group.

Answer choice (C): This answer choice is incorrect, because it does not pass the Agree/Disagree Test. The opponents (lines 11-14) would clearly agree that bitcoin has the potential for nearly instantaneous geometric expansion; however, the proponents would not necessarily disagree with this statement.

Answer choice (D): Neither group discusses the difficulty of predicting bitcoin's impact.

Answer choice (E) This is the correct answer choice, because the proponents would disagree with this statement and the opponents would agree. To the proponents, bitcoin has no "effect on the process by which the monetary authority of a country controls the supply of money" (lines 9-11). By contrast, the opponents believe that bitcoin "could seriously threaten a nation's financial security" (lines 11-14). Since the two groups differ in their evaluation of risk, this answer choice is correct.

Each passage from this exercise is replicated below, with the main point highlighted in grey. You should not be concerned if your version of the main point is at variance with the answer key provided. Such differences are normal, as there are usually many ways to describe the main point of a given passage.

Passage #1:

Several members of the Appropriations Committee have taken the stance that public funds should only be given to projects that have proven successful in the past. Such a position does not actually serve
(5)   the public good, however. This criterion, though intended to help ensure that public funding is provided for projects with the greatest chances of success, unfortunately also precludes consideration of new and potentially beneficial uses of those
(10)   funds.

Main Point: The author takes issue with the policy of giving money only to groups with proven track records. Since new groups would never be eligible for consideration, the author concludes that such a position does not serve the public good.

1. Which one of the following best states the main idea of the passage?

    (A)   Public funds should be limited to projects that have proven successful in the past.

    (B)   The strategy of limiting public funding to projects that have proven successful is intended to ensure that funding is provided to projects with the greatest chance of success.

    (C)   The public good is not well-served by the stance that public funding should be limited to projects that have proven successful in the past.

    (D)   Several Appropriations Committee members have taken the stance that public funds should only be given to projects that have proven successful in the past.

    (E)   Funding only projects that have proven successful in the past would preclude consideration of new uses of those funds.

VIEWSTAMP Analysis: Main Point Identification Drill Answer Key

Question #1: GR, Main Point. The correct answer choice is (C)

The main point of the passage, as highlighted above, is that limiting public funds to proven projects "does not actually serve the public good" (lines 4-5).

Answer choice (A): This is a stance with which the author disagrees, so this choice can be confidently ruled out of contention.

Answer choice (B): This answer choice restates the main rationale for the position with which the author disagrees, so this cannot be the correct answer choice.

Answer choice (C): This is the correct answer choice, because the highlighted claim (lines 4-5) is supported by the rest of the passage, and therefore represents the main conclusion of the argument.

Answer choice (D): This choice restates the first sentence of the passage, but it does not reflect the author's main point.

Answer choice (E): Although this is a statement with which the author would clearly agree, it merely supports the main point of the passage by explaining *why* the strategy of limiting public funds to proven projects does not serve the public good.

Passage #2:

Although the eagle became the national emblem of the United States in 1782, according to Benjamin Franklin the turkey would have been a more suitable symbol. In a letter he wrote to his daughter,
(5)   he described the eagle as "a bird of bad moral character" and "a rank coward." He felt that the bald eagle lacked many positive attributes of the turkey, which he described in the letter as a "much more respectable bird, and withal a true original
(10)   native of America."

Main Point: The central focus of this passage is Ben Franklin's belief that the turkey would have been a more suitable national American symbol than the bald eagle. This belief is stated in the first sentence. The rest of the passage is intended to support and explain it.

2. Which one of the following most completely and accurately reflects the main point of the passage?

   (A) The eagle became the national emblem of the United States in 1782.
   (B) Benjamin Franklin believed that the turkey was less suitable as a national symbol than the eagle would have been.
   (C) Benjamin Franklin saw the eagle as "a bird of bad moral character."
   (D) Benjamin Franklin believed that the bald eagle lacked many of the positive attributes of the turkey.
   (E) Benjamin Franklin regarded the eagle as a less suitable emblem than the turkey.

Question #2: GR, Main Point. The correct answer choice is (E)

The author's main point is that, based on the respective attributes of the two birds being discussed, Franklin saw the turkey as a more suitable national emblem than the eagle.

Answer choice (A): This answer choice restates the first sentence of the passage, which is a factual claim that is not supported by other claims. Therefore, it is not the main point of the passage.

Answer choice (B): This is an Opposite Answer, since Franklin believed that the eagle was less suitable than the turkey would have been.

Answer choice (C): This is a premise in support of Franklin's conclusion; it is not the main point of the passage.

Answer choice (D): This claim supports Ben Franklin's conclusion that the bald eagle is not as suitable of a symbol as the turkey; however, it is not the main point of the passage.

Answer choice (E): This is the correct answer choice, as it agrees with our prephrase above.

Passage #3:

Since corporations are driven, in large part, by the motivation to increase profits, they cannot always be relied upon to make morally or ethically sound decisions. This is especially true if there are no
(5) legal disincentives for making unethical decisions. While the practices of some companies are beyond reproach, many corporations act in a manner that is clearly devoid of ethical or moral fortitude.

Main Point: Since corporations are driven by profits, the author concludes that they cannot be relied upon to make ethically sound decisions. The premise indicator "since" suggests that the first clause of this sentence is a premise for the second clause, which is thereby the conclusion. The rest of the passage serves to clarify this conclusion.

3.   Which one of the following statements best expresses the main idea of the passage?

(A)   Corporations are driven by their motivation to increase profits.

(B)   The actions of many corporations are driven exclusively by moral and ethical considerations.

(C)   The law allows corporations to make morally or ethically questionable decisions.

(D)   Corporations cannot always be relied upon to make morally or ethically sound decisions.

(E)   Some companies' practices are beyond reproach.

Question #3: GR, Main Point. The correct answer choice is (D)

The main idea of this passage, as expressed in the first sentence, is that corporations, which are largely profit-driven, cannot be relied upon to make morally or ethically sound decisions.

Answer choice (A): The fact that corporations are driven by their motivation to increase profits explains *why* corporations cannot be relied upon to make ethically sound decisions. Since this claim supports another claim in the argument, the former is not the conclusion of that argument.

Answer choice (B): Although the actions of many corporations are beyond reproach, there is no reason to believe that they are driven *exclusively* by moral and ethical considerations. Since this choice fails the Fact Test, it cannot be the right answer.

VIEWSTAMP Analysis: Main Point Identification Drill Answer Key

Answer choice (C): As with answer choice (A), this observation explains *why* corporations cannot be relied upon to make ethically sound decisions: there are no legal disincentives for making unethical ones. However, since this claim supports another claim in the argument, it is not the conclusion of that argument.

Answer choice (D): This is the correct answer choice, as prephrased above.

Answer choice (E): The author concedes that some companies' practices are beyond reproach, but still argues that many others cannot be trusted to make the right decisions. This claim therefore raises a side issue that has no logical relationship to the argument's main conclusion. Note that just because a claim is mentioned at the end of the passage does not necessarily make it the main point of that passage.

<u>Passage #4:</u>

People should not be surprised that the number of movie tickets sold annually nationwide has been decreasing precipitously for several years. Even as the prices of movie tickets—and the various
(5) concessions sold at those theaters—have continued to increase year after year, the public has been provided access to a vast and ever-increasing array of other entertainment options. While some theaters have continued to draw crowds on a regular basis,
(10) sales numbers have dropped steadily as a result of rising ticket prices, coupled with an increased competition for the public's attention.

Main Point: This excerpt presents evidence suggesting that rising ticket prices and increased access to other forms of entertainment have decreased the number of movie tickets sold every year. Accordingly, the problems experienced by movie theaters should not be seen as a surprise. Since the second and third sentences support the observation made in the first, the first sentence contains the main point of the passage.

4. Which one of the following best states the main idea of the passage?

    (A) The decreasing sales of movie tickets should have been expected.
    (B) Some theaters have continued to draw crowds on a regular basis.
    (C) Movie ticket sales have increased steadily as a result of falling ticket prices.
    (D) Prices of movie tickets and concessions have continued to rise year after year.
    (E) In recent years the public has been provided access to a vast and ever-increasing array of entertainment options.

VIEWSTAMP Analysis: Main Point Identification Drill Answer Key

Question #4: GR, Main Point. The correct answer choice is (A)

The main point is presented at the very beginning of the passage: It should come as no surprise that movie ticket sales have been falling for years. We know this is the main point, because the remainder of the passage outlines the factors contributing to this decrease.

Answer choice (A): This is the correct answer choice, as prephrased above.

Answer choice (B): Although this answer choice can be proven with the information contained in the passage (lines 8-9), it represents a concession and is not the main point of the argument.

Answer choice (C): This is the Opposite answer choice, as ticket sales have *decreased*, not *increased*, as a result of falling ticket prices.

Answer choice (D): As with answer choices (B) and (E), this answer choice contains a provable claim that is not, however, the main point of the passage. No additional support is given for this claim.

Answer choice (E): This statement can be proven by reference to lines 6-8; however, since it supports another claim in the passage, it is not the main point.

Passage #5:

Zoologist: Despite their size, honey badgers are well-equipped for survival, with large, strong claws and skin thick enough to ward off attacks by almost any predator. They have been known to challenge
(5)   animals much bigger than themselves, including lions, horses, cattle, and buffalo. In addition to their fighting prowess, honey badgers are also extremely intelligent, as members of one of the few species on earth with a documented capacity to
(10)   utilize basic tools.

Main Point: The zoologist presents several interesting facts in support of the general conclusion that honey badgers are well-equipped for survival.

5. Which one of the following most accurately states the author's main point?

(A) Honey badgers are extremely intelligent, as reflected in their ability to use basic tools.
(B) Honey badgers are skilled fighters and are also extremely intelligent.
(C) Honey badgers are well equipped for survival despite their size.
(D) Honey badgers are able to use basic tools to protect themselves from predators.
(E) Honey badgers have many natural predators, including lions, horses, cattle, and buffalo.

Question #5: GR, Main Point. The correct answer choice is (C)

The main idea in this passage is that honey badgers are well-equipped for survival despite their diminutive size. The first sentence contains the main point, and the rest of the passage serves to clarify it by remarking on the honey badgers' fighting prowess and intelligence.

Answer choice (A): Honey badgers' intelligence helps explain *why* they are so well-equipped for survival. Given the supporting role that this claim plays in the argument, it is a premise, not a conclusion.

Answer choice (B): As with answer choice (A), this choice is supported by the information in the passage, but it is not the main point.

Answer choice (C): This is the correct answer choice, as prephrased above.

Answer choice (D): The author never suggests that the badgers can use basic tools to protect themselves, so this answer choice fails the Fact Test and cannot be the right answer to this Main Point question.

Answer choice (E):These are mentioned as examples of animals much bigger than the honey badger, but that does not make them natural predators. (And even if they were, this would not be the main point of the passage.)

This drill seeks to assist you in identifying the elements and formations often found in Reading Comprehension passages. Writing down one or two descriptor words is intended to assist you in concisely identifying these elements. This is *not* a suggestion that you should write down the names of the elements while taking the LSAT. See *Chapter Three* of the *Reading Comprehension Bible* for more on passage elements and formations.

PRACTICE DRILL EXPLANATIONS

Passage #1:

Mozart composed his first musical piece in 1761, at age 5. The following year, he and his sister performed at the court of Maximilian III. Mozart spent much of his youth traveling throughout
(5)   Europe and performing. By 1773, he had gained a number of admirers in his hometown of Salzburg, and secured a position as court musician to Count Colloredo. However, financial concerns and artistic limitations caused Mozart to resign the Salzburg
(10)   court position in 1777.

Dates and Numbers

The passage provides three dates, as well as a Mozart's age, which together form a timeline within the passage. LSAT passages that feature dates and numbers often reference the timeline in the questions in order to see if you followed the narrative.

Passage #2:

Antiquities law addresses the ownership, sale, and protection of cultural items of value. While these laws are clear in their protective intent, they remain, to some extent, open to interpretation,
(5)   and consequently, in some cases the public good is not protected as intended. What priorities, then, should a jurist consider when overseeing a case that involves antiquities?

Text Question

The passage closes with a classic text question. Antiquities law is also explained, though this is not a definition in the classic sense.

Passage Elements and Formations Recognition Drill Answer Key

Passage #3:

About 5,000 years ago, the Harappan civilization
sprawled over nearly 400,000 square miles (1
million square kilometers) on the plains of the
Indus River in modern-day India and Pakistan.
(5)   At its peak, this civilization accounted for nearly
10 percent of the world population. Only recently
have scientists determined why this civilization
disappeared, and climate change was a key
ingredient in this collapse. As weather patterns
(10) shifted, the monsoons that fed the Indus River plain
began to move eastward, and many of the rivers
coursing through the region began to dry up. The
resulting population shift deprived the Harappans of
vital economic resources, which led to the
(15) civilization's eventual demise.

Dates and Numbers
Causality

The passage opens with references to dates, land occupation size, and population size.
However, the most notable feature is the series of causal statements that seek to explain why
the Harappan civilization disappeared. While many LSAT passages contain causal statements,
this section is notable because it details a series of causal relationships, creating a chain of
causation that explains what led to the civilization's disappearance.

Passage #4:

Polychlorinated biphenyls (PCBs), which were
once widely used in coolants and insulators, have
been banned by Congress because of the severe
danger they presented to the public.
(5)   Epidemiological studies of the effects of PCBs
on humans revealed potential carcinogenicity
and significant long-term persistence in the
environment. Non-carcinogenic effects include
damage to the immune system, reproductive
(10) system, nervous system, and endocrine system.

Difficult Topic and Terminology
Causality

The passage refers to a number of challenging words, including polychlorinated biphenyls,
epidemiological, carcinogenicity, and non-carcinogenic. There are also multiple elements of
causality present, from the effects of PCBs on humans to the reason why Congress banned
PCBs.

Passage Elements and Formations Recognition Drill Answer Key

Passage #5:

"Jazz poetry" largely blossomed during the
Harlem Renaissance of the 1920s and 1930s. In
general, jazz poetry attempted to mimic several
aspects of the jazz music that was then in vogue.
(5)   First, the poetry spoke in a uniquely African
American voice. Second, the structure within
individual poems often varied, much like the
music improvised by jazz musicians. Finally,
the writing style and word usage mirrored the
(10)   rhythms and pacing of jazz music.

Dates and Numbers
List

While the passage contains dates and numbers, these are not especially significant, as there is
only one period referenced and no real timeline. The most notable feature of this passage is the
list of items describing how jazz poetry mimicked jazz music.

Passage #6:

Recently, the International Court of Justice in The
Hague ruled that Japan breached international law
when it captured and killed thousands of whales of
certain types and issued permits for the killing of
(5)   other types in an area designated as the Southern
Ocean Whale Sanctuary. The ruling, identified
by many court observers as unprecedented in its
unequivocal rebuke and injunction of whaling
activities by a sovereign nation, was lauded by
(10)   environmentalists. However, many Japanese
fishermen urged their government to fight the
ruling, arguing that whaling is a cultural tradition
that deserves respect. Yet one observer of Japanese
politics noted that the banned whaling activities
(15)   were no longer financially viable, requiring
government subsidies anticipated to soon reach $50
million per year, and that this need for subsidies
explains the Japanese government's almost
immediate decision to abide by the Court's ruling.

Multiple Viewpoints
Trap of Inserted Alternate Viewpoint

The subject matter in this passage excerpt is not difficult. However, there are five viewpoints
presented in four sentences, a circumstance in which the viewpoints become difficult to track.

Passage #7:

Physicists studying super-heavy atomic nuclei
conducted experiments in which they bombarded
a thin layer of americium, an artificial radioactive
metal created when plutonium atoms absorb
(5) neutrons during nuclear reactions, with calcium
ions. This collision produced a new element that
has 115 protons at its center. If approved by an
international committee of physicists and chemists,
this new element will be placed on the periodic
(10) table with the atomic number 115. Temporarily
named "ununpentium," this artificial element would
be the latest super-heavy element to be created
through accelerator based experimentation. Of the
elements found naturally occurring on Earth,
(15) the heaviest is uranium, which has 92 protons in
its nucleus, although the heaviest stable element,
meaning an element that does not decay, is lead,
which has 82 protons in its nucleus.

Challenging Topic and Terminology

The difficulty in this passage comes from its scientific topic, as well as from the use of
unfamiliar terms and concepts.

Passage #8:

Immediately after pleadings are filed, or at some
other time during the pendency of the suit, a trial
court may appoint a Guardian ad Litem (GAL) to
represent a child in matters of custody and
(5)   visitation. GALs are appointed under the theory
that the child's parents, embroiled in difficult
litigation, may put their own needs above those
of the child when making strategic and tactical
decisions related to the contest. The decision
(10) regarding whether and when to appoint a GAL
for a child is almost universally a matter within
the plenary discretion of the trial court, and that
decision is given considerable deference by the
appellate courts. This wide-ranging discretion
(15) has produced great disparity in how trial judges
appoint and use GALs. Some judges appoint them
by default, even when the parties are sophisticated
and represented by counsel, a situation in which
GALs are commonly considered to be unnecessary.
(20) Other judges will appoint a GAL only upon formal
motion by a party, and even then only when a party
has demonstrated a particularized need for the
child to have independent counsel. A new survey
indicates that this disparity in appointment results
(25) in substantial practical implications for family law
practitioners.

Difficult Words and Phrases
Challenging Writing Style

Some may find this passage difficult because of its stilted tone and word choice. This writing
style is designed to slow and distract the reader; when you are forced to wade through
unnecessarily complicated wording, you are able to devote fewer mental resources to actually
understanding the argument being made. Understanding the ideas in the passage is not
difficult, but requires that you see beyond the stylistic complications in the text.

Passage #9:

Fearing the emergence of a new, pandemic zoonotic disease—a contagious disease transmitted from animals to humans and caused by bacteria, viruses, parasites and fungi carried by animals and insects—
(5)   scientists recently created a new pathogen (i.e., a bacterium, virus, or other microorganism that can cause disease) that is 97 percent similar to the 1918 Spanish Flu, which is thought to have originated in birds and which killed approximately 50 million
(10) people. The scientists constructed the new virus by cobbling together wild bird flu fragments. To make the pathogen easier to spread from one animal to another, the scientists mutated it, making it airborne. Some have labeled the project "insane,"
(15) stressing the tremendous danger involved in intentionally creating a virus that could potentially kill millions of people if released into the general population, either accidentally, or deliberately, as a terrorist act, for example. Moreover, the threat of
(20) such a virus emerging naturally from the animal population is too low to justify the risk posed by the research. The researchers have defended their work by pointing to the possibility that a disease similar to the Spanish Flu could spontaneously emerge
(25) without warning from the animal population. By creating such a pathogen in a secure, laboratory environment, they argue, health officials can better prepare to detect and treat a naturally occurring outbreak.

Challenging Topic and Terminology
Challenging Writing Style

The difficulty in this passage comes from the scientific subject matter and challenging terminology ("zoonotic," "pandemic," etc.). The opening sentence has a particularly complicated structure, purposefully designed to slow you down. Regardless, we can summarize the passage quite simply: Researchers have developed a potentially lethal virus in an effort to better detect and treat unexpected outbreaks of certain diseases. Critics believe that the researchers' work is very dangerous and that the risk it poses outweighs the much lower risk of naturally occurring outbreaks.

Passage Elements and Formations Recognition Drill Answer Key

Passage #10:

In an era of corporate downsizing, large law firms have renewed their insistence that law schools focus less on academia and more on the production of the "practice-ready lawyer." However, some law
(5) professors argue that their institutions should reject what they view as a misguided and short-sighted attempt by the firms to shift their training expenses to the law schools. While firms urge law schools to offer more clinics, externships, and practitioner-
(10) specific courses, these professors argue that such an approach is impractical. The first hurdle involves identifying the proper standard for determining what a practice-ready lawyer is. If the standard is minimal competence, professors argue, then
(15) the state-level bar examination already ensures that level of preparedness. Next is the issue of specialization: should law students try to determine a field of practice prior to graduation, the professors ask? If they do not, then the scope of the private
(20) legal market would be too broad for law schools to provide significant practical experience in even the major sub-categories of legal work. Finally, law professors point out that much of what makes legal practice unique is the confluence of institutional
(25) structures, power dynamics, economic incentives, and complex ethical obligations that is impossible to replicate in the law school setting.

Multiple Viewpoints
Lists and Enumerations

The convoluted structure of this passage makes it more challenging to read. By combining the competing perspectives of the law firms and the law professors with multiple lists, the author has created an environment in which students will over-mark the passage in an attempt to keep track of many separate items of information. Here's the passage in a nutshell: Law firms would like legal education to focus on producing "practice-ready" lawyers; however, law professors reject this view as impractical and misguided.

Passage #1: SLE and Dendritic Cells

Question #1: GR, Must, P. The correct answer choice is (C)

Answer choice (A) is incorrect, because it only describes the function of the first paragraph, not the passage as a whole.

Answer choice (B) is incorrect, because the main question in this passage is why SLE is difficult to *treat*, not cure. Furthermore, even if the issue of pDC resistance represents a difficulty that must be overcome in order to find a cure for SLE, this answer choice does not address the function of the first paragraph.

Answer choice (C) is the correct answer choice, because it summarizes the function of each paragraph, as well as of the passage as a whole—to describe the origination of SLE (first paragraph) and explain why glucocorticoid therapy fails to provide lasting relief (second paragraph).

Answer choice (D) is incorrect, because the author does seek to invalidate or challenge the explanation involving pDC.

Answer choice (E) is incorrect, because the author merely introduces the hypothesis that pDC resistance might explain why glucocorticoid therapy fails to provide lasting relief in SLE patients. No evidence supporting this hypothesis has been evaluated.

Question #2: GR, Must. The correct answer choice is (B)

Answer choice (A) is incorrect. Understanding how pDC resistance occurs is probably helpful, but by no means a necessary condition for identifying a cure for SLE. This answer choice falls outside the scope of the passage.

Answer choice (B) is the correct answer choice, because the innate immune system is stimulated in patients with SLE, even though an infection with a pathogen is not present (lines 5-9).

Answer choice (C) cannot be true. Given that SLE is characterized by the proliferation of antibody-immune complexes that cause damage to the kidneys, blood vessels, and skin (lines 9-12), we can assume that any successful course of treatment *does* require reducing these harmful effects.

Answer choice (D) is incorrect, because the passage does not provide sufficient information to help us determine whether the risks of high-dose methylprednisolone pulse therapy outweigh the benefits. All we know is that this type of therapy is more aggressive—and potentially harmful—than glucocorticoid therapy.

Science Mini-Passage Drill Answer Key

Answer choice (E) is false, because cytokines cause inflammation in patients with SLE even though an infection is not present (lines 5-9). Clearly, infection is not required for an inflammatory response.

Question #3: SR, Must, P. The correct answer choice is (D)

Answer choice (A) is incorrect, because the precise mechanism by which pDCs develop resistance to glucocorticoid therapy is unknown (lines 32-33)

Answer choice (B) is incorrect. The fact that pDCs produce key cytokines involved in SLE pathogenesis may be a distinguishing characteristic of pDCs, but the author does not *intend* to show that pDCs are unique. The purpose of this observation is to explain why pDCs are so important in SLE pathogenesis, and why their resistance to glucocorticoid therapy is such a big problem in treating SLE.

Answer choice (C) is incorrect. The fact that pDCs produce the key cytokines involved in SLE pathogenesis highlights their importance in the treatment of SLE, not in fighting infection. SLE is an autoimmune disease, not an infectious disease.

Answer choice (D) is the correct answer choice. The author describes the role of pDCs in SLE pathogenesis in order to explain why their resistance to glucocorticoid therapy causes symptoms to relapse: the level of pDC-produced cytokines does not decrease with treatment.

Answer choice (E) is incorrect. Glucocorticoid therapy does not fail *because* pDCs produce the key cytokines involved in SLE pathogenesis, but rather *in spite of* that fact. Therapy fails because the pDCs are resistant to glucocorticoids.

Science Mini-Passage Drill Answer Key

Passage #2: T-cells and Tumors

Question #1: CR, MustX. The correct answer choice is (D)

Answer choice (A) is incorrect, because the author mentions studies using experimental rodent models, which have replicated the findings described in the first paragraph (lines 16-18).

Answer choice (B) is incorrect, because the author describes the presence of tumor-infiltrating T-cells in tumors as an indication that tumors can elicit cell-mediated immunological responses (lines 12-16).

Answer choice (C) is incorrect, because cell-mediated immunity refers to the activation of antigen-specific T-cells (line 5-6). The author specifically mentions the ability of tumors to express antigens capable of eliciting cell-mediated immunological responses (lines 15-16).

Answer choice (D) is the correct answer choice. Although the inability of T-cells to destroy the tumor is the major paradox in tumor immunology (lines 19-21), this observation is not mentioned in support for the hypothesis that cancer elicits a cell-mediated antitumor immune response in humans.

Answer choice (E) is incorrect, because the relevant research was conducted in the 1990s (line 10).

Question #2: CR, Must. The correct answer choice is (E)

Answer choice (A) is incorrect, because the lytic function is inhibited by the tumor itself (line 35), and not by the specific ability of tumors to escape T-cell surveillance. Also, note that the author would not necessarily agree that tumors have this ability, as it represents the views of the scientists mentioned in line 22.

Answer choice (B) is incorrect. Although tumors clearly disrupt the lytic function of tumor-infiltrating T-cells, there is no evidence that this can be attributed to tumor-specific antigens.

Answer choice (C) is incorrect, because it contains an exaggeration ("critical component"), for which no evidence is provided.

Answer choice (D) is incorrect. While cell-mediated immunity is directed *primarily* at microbes (lines 8-9), it is entirely possible that the lytic function of tumor-infiltrating T-cells is directed only at tumors, and not at microbes.

Science Mini-Passage Drill Answer Key

Answer choice (E) is the correct answer choice. In the second paragraph, the author notes that the lytic defect of tumor-infiltrating T-cells is *exclusive* to T-cells residing in the tumor microenvironment, since similar cells that reside elsewhere in the body do not exhibit the same defect. The author also notes that the defect is also transient, because the lytic function is restored outside the tumor. Thus, we can conclude that the lytic function of these T-cells is dependent, at least in part, upon the environment in which the T-cell resides.

Question #3: Weaken. The correct answer choice is (A)

To weaken the hypothesis described in lines 43-45, we need to present an alternative explanation as to why tumor-infiltrating T-cells exhibit lytic defects.

Answer choice (A) is the correct answer choice. If many tumors are caused by viruses that can also disrupt the normal function of T-cells, this suggests an alternative cause for the lytic defect observed in tumor-infiltrating T-cells:

<u>*Cause*</u>   <u>*Cause/Effect*</u>   <u>*Effect*</u>

Virus   ⟶   *Tumor*   ⟶   *Lytic defect*

By suggesting that viral infections are a common cause for *both* tumors and the lytic defects of tumor-infiltrating T-cells, this answer choice proposes an alternative interpretation for the correlation observed by Genart. This weakens the hypothesis that the lytic function of tumor-infiltrating T-cells is inhibited by the tumor itself.

Answer choice (B) is incorrect. The disruption of T-cell's nonlytic functions at the tumor site has no bearing on the question of why their *lytic* function is disrupted. Our job is to identify an alternative cause for the observed effect, not an additional effect of the purported cause.

Answer choice (C) explains how tumors can avoid T-cell recognition in the first place, not why the lytic function of T-cells is inhibited after these cells have infiltrated the tumor. The former has no bearing on the issue at hand.

Answer choice (D) is incorrect, because the author never argued that the lytic function of T-cells is perfect outside the tumor microenvironment.

Answer choice (E) is attractive, but incorrect. At first glance, this answer choice appears to present an alternative cause for the lytic defect in T-cells: pathogens. However, we need to explain why *tumor-infiltrating* T-cells exhibit lytic defects, not why T-cells in general do. Furthermore, the author never suggested that *only* tumors can disrupt the lytic defect in T-cells. Even if pathogens can inhibit the lytic function of T-cells by integrating into the cell's genome, that does not explain why the lytic function of tumor-infiltrating T-cells is disrupted exclusively at tumor sites.

Passage Set #1

Both passages discuss the complex interaction between humans and bacteria. The author of the first passage focuses on the pathogenic nature of some types of bacteria, while the author of the second argues that bacteria are essential for life. There is no overt disagreement on any factual issue per se; the authors merely focus on two opposing sides of the same issue.

Question #1: GR, Must. The correct answer choice is (C)

Answer choice (A) is incorrect, because we only know how many human deaths are caused by waterborne diarrheal disease, not how many human deaths are caused by bacterial infections in general.

Answer choice (B) is incorrect, because we only know the number (not the percentage) of "good" bacteria that live in the human body.

Answer choice (C) is the correct answer choice, because each passage provides sufficient information to determine that harmful pathogens are sometimes present in the human body. In passage A, the author observes that, "waterborne diarrheal disease...causes about 1.8 million human deaths annually, most of them a direct result of bacterial infections with any number of disease-causing pathogens." Likewise, the author of passage B mentions the discovery that "there are disease-causing bacteria in each of us." Clearly, then, both authors would agree that harmful pathogens are sometimes present in the human body.

Answer choice (D) is incorrect, because we do not know the number of prokaryotic organisms that live in a millimeter of fresh water (we only know the approximate number of bacteria in it). Note that the previous sentence clearly defines bacteria as a *type* of prokaryotic organism: there may be other types of non-bacterial prokaryotes living in fresh water.

Answer choice (E) is incorrect, because the examples provided in passage A are not of bacteria that live inside the human body without harming it.

Comparative Reading Mini-Passages Answer Key

Question #2: CR, Must, AP. The correct answer choice is (B)

Answer choice (A) is incorrect, because passage A contains no evidence to suggest that its author would agree with this statement.

Answer choice (B) is the correct answer choice. The author of passage A would agree with this statement ("In a single milliliter of fresh water…harmless to humans or other animals."). The author of passage B would also agree ("Instead of making us ill… peacefully among their neighbors").

Answer choice (C) is incorrect, because passage B makes no mention of socioeconomic costs.

Answer choice (D) is incorrect, because only passage A discusses the biomass of bacteria.

Answer choice (E) is incorrect, because the author of passage A does not discuss the evolution of organisms.

Passage Set #2

There is no overt disagreement between the two authors. The first author discusses the pros and cons of using sugar substitutes, arguing that ultimately the benefits outweigh the costs. The second author discusses the pros and cons of banning sugary drinks in New York City, also concluding that the benefits of having such a ban outweigh the costs ("the city's ban is a step in the right direction"). Both authors examine a particular solution to a given problem, and after considering some potential objections to its implementation, both endorse a course of action that favors the solution.

Question #1: GR, Must. The correct answer choice is (D)

Answer choice (A) is incorrect. Even though the author of passage B describes the NYC soda ban as controversial, passage A offers no evidence suggesting that the nutritional safety of sugar substitutes is a similarly controversial issue. Furthermore, just because some still worry about the long-term side effects of sugar substitutes does not mean that reaching *scientific* consensus regarding their safety was particularly difficult.

Answer choice (B) is incorrect, because passage B makes no mention of any scientific studies concerned with nutritional safety.

Answer choice (C) is incorrect, because passage A does not analyze the effects of sugar consumption on obesity; it merely alludes to the fact that the health benefits of consuming less sugar outweigh the costs.

Answer choice (D) is the correct answer choice. Passage A defends the FDA endorsement of sugar substitutes. Similarly, passage B argues that the NYC ban on the sale of large sugary drinks is a "step in the right direction."

Answer choice (E) is incorrect, because neither passage questions the feasibility of curbing obesity. This view belongs to the critics of the NYC ban.

Question #2: CR, Must. The correct answer choice is (A)

Answer choice (A) is the correct answer choice. Passage A provides evidence corroborating the safety of making certain nutritional choices, such as replacing sugar with sugar substitutes. Meanwhile, the evidence provided in passage B suggests that sweetened drinks are directly responsible for up to half of the increase in obesity rates in the city. In other words, the evidence in passage B attests to the dangers of *not* making similarly beneficial nutritional choices, such as lowering one's overall sugar consumption.

Answer choice (B) is incorrect, because each author acknowledges that that his or her preferred nutritional strategy is somewhat controversial. Furthermore, it remains unclear whether the controversial nature of these strategies represents an obstacle to their adoption.

Answer choice (C) is incorrect, because the evidence presented in passage A only attests to the safety of using sugar substitutes, which the author of passage B does not need to assume to be true.

Answer choice (D) is incorrect, because each passage considers the costs of adopting the nutritional strategy it recommends: passage A acknowledges (and rejects) the potential dangers of using sugar substitutes. Likewise, passage B acknowledges that the city's actions might be perceived as unfair or overly paternalistic.

Answer choice (E) is incorrect. Although passage B does examine the consequences of making bad nutritional choices (e.g. obesity), passage A does not seek to explain *why* people make such choices.

Comparative Reading Mini-Passages Answer Key

Passage Set #3

The two authors are in sharp disagreement over the benefits of standardized testing, its fairness, and impact on teaching and student achievement. There are virtually no points of agreement, save for the observation that some correlation between student testing and test score improvements does exist.

Question #1: GR, Must. The correct answer choice is (C)

Answer choice (A) is a Reverse answer. It is passage B, not A, that shows more skepticism towards the possibility of quantifying student achievement by means of standardized testing.

Answer choice (B) is incorrect, because there is no evidence suggesting that passage A is any more supportive of ongoing research related to the reliability of standardized testing than passage B. Both authors seem equally intent on determining the reliability of standardized tests (or lack thereof).

Answer choice (C) is the correct answer choice. According to passage A, the use of standardized testing to monitor student progress is "strongly associated with significant and sustained gains on national and international assessments of cognitive ability." By contrast, passage B argues that the correlation is temporary and unreliable, adding that standardized tests measure only a small portion of what makes education meaningful.

Answer choice (D) is incorrect, because there is no evidence suggesting that the author of passage A is any more willing to accept a variety of metrics in assessing cognitive ability than the author of passage B. passage B rejects the metrics of standardized testing, but offers no alternative means of assessing student progress.

Answer choice (E) is incorrect, because passage A clearly refuses to acknowledge that standardized tests are inherently biased, which is a central premise in passage B.

Comparative Reading Mini-Passages Answer Key

Question #2: GR, Weaken/Strengthen. The correct answer choice is (E)

Answer choice (A) is incorrect. The fact that standardized tests are not unique in their ability to cause severe stress among students does not weaken the argument in passage B that such tests are detrimental to student learning.

Answer choice (B) is incorrect, because the relative importance of test scores in college admissions has no bearing on either argument. Even if their importance were lower than expected, standardized tests can still have a detrimental effect on student learning. This answer choice does not cast doubt on the argument in passage B and has no effect on the argument in passage A.

Answer choice (C) is incorrect, because there is no reason to suspect that spending more time preparing for standardized tests is pedagogically desirable. In fact, this may bolster the argument made in passage B that such tests detract from teaching higher-order skills.

Answer choice (D) is incorrect, because the relative difficulty of following each type of curriculum has no bearing on the question of whether either is pedagogically preferable.

Answer choice (E) is the correct answer choice. If standardized tests, when combined with other metrics, have an unusually high level of predictive validity in estimating the academic potential of most students, this would bolster the argument in passage A that such tests provide useful information about student abilities. It would also undermine the argument in passage B that standardized tests measure only a small portion of what makes education meaningful.

Passage Set #4

The author of the first passage firmly believes that video games cause violent behavior. The author of the second passage does not reject the possibility that such a correlation does exist, but presents a more nuanced and cautious outlook. The second author resists making a definitive conclusion as to whether violent video games encourage aggressive behavior, and mentions that even if a correlation is found to exist, it can be explained by reversing the alleged causal relationship between video games and violent behavior.

Question #1: CR, Must, AP. The correct answer choice is (C)

Answer choice (A) is incorrect, because the author of passage B provides no reason to believe that he or she tacitly agrees with the argument presented in passage A.

Answer choice (B) is incorrect. Even though passage B approaches the possibility that video games cause violent behavior with caution, this does not mean that this author's attitude is purely neutral.

Comparative Reading Mini-Passages Answer Key

Answer choice (C) is the correct answer choice. Passage B questions the studies looking for a correlation between violent video games and violent behavior, but cautions against interpreting their flaws as a validation of the safety of video games. In other words, passage B displays cautious reservation toward the argument presented in passage A, requiring additional evidence to weigh in on the issue.

Answer choices (D) and (E) are incorrect, because the author of passage B is neither dismissive of, nor morally outraged by, the possibility of a causal relationship between violence and video games.

Question #2: SR, Must, P. The correct answer choice is (D)

Answer choice (A) is incorrect, because the author of passage B does not seek to highlight the addictive nature of video games.

Answer choice (B) is incorrect, because a purely hypothetical claim cannot serve to undermine evidence that is factual in nature. Passage B only questions the extent to which the evidence presented in passage A can serve to justify a causal conclusion.

Answer choice (C) is the Opposite answer. Evidence that violent youth may seek out violent entertainment would substantiate the correlation between the two, not disprove it.

Answer choice (D) is the correct answer choice. By suggesting that violent youth may seek out violent entertainment in the form of video games, passage B implies that the correlation cited in passage A may allow for the possibility of a reverse cause and effect relationship.

Answer choice (E) is incorrect, because passage B questions the argument outlined in passage A, rather than provide additional evidence in its support.

Comparative Reading Mini-Passages Answer Key

Passage Set #5

The author of the first passage attempts to explain why Locke's work has become part of the transatlantic canon of Western constitutional democracy, holding that history itself may have occasioned this transformation. By contrast, the author of the second passage seeks to situate Locke's work in its own historical context. While the author of the first passage would argue that Locke's treatise is a timeless classic that offers the means to interpret and understand a wide range of seemingly disparate issues, the author of the second passage offers a less enthusiastic endorsement, cautioning against any interpretation that does not take into account the historical context of the treatise.

Question #1: CR, Must. The correct answer choice is (E)

Answer choice (A) is an Opposite answer, because it is passage B—not passage A—that seeks to situate Locke's work in its own historical context.

Answer choice (B) is incorrect, because neither passage provides sufficient evidence to evaluate its author's personal commitment to the principles of liberalism espoused by Locke.

Answer choice (C) is an Opposite answer, because the author of passage B is not as concerned with the canonical value of Locke's work as the author of passage A is.

Answer choice (D) is also an Opposite answer, because the author of passage B considers the prospect of extrapolating broader social implications from John Locke's treatise to be "intellectually dishonest and politically dangerous."

Answer choice (E) is the correct answer choice. By situating Locke's treatise in its own historical context, the author of passage B undermines modern historians' willingness to extrapolate broader social implications from that treatise, calling their efforts "intellectually dishonest and politically dangerous." In other words, the author of passage B is considerably more cautious about viewing Locke's work as a timeless classic than is the author of passage A, who explicitly labels it as such.

Comparative Reading Mini-Passages Answer Key

Question #2: GR, Must. The correct answer choice is (C)

Answer choice (A) is incorrect, because passage A alludes to the fact that Locke's treatise was motivated by a desire to justify a particular constitutional revolution in late seventeenth-century England.

Answer choice (B) is incorrect, because the role of history in transforming Locke's work into a canonical treatise is discussed in passage A but not in passage B.

Answer choice (C) is the correct answer choice. The events described in passage B serve to explain why Locke considered the private man to be the ultimate arbiter of social dispute. Today, this arbiter is the modern constitutional state—making Locke's viewpoint no longer relevant.

Answer choice (D) is an Opposite answer, because passage B considers the prospect of extrapolating broader social implications from John Locke's treatise to be "intellectually dishonest and politically dangerous."

Answer choice (E) is incorrect, because the implications of communism for the liberal state are only mentioned in passage A.

Passage Set #6

The author of the first passage examines several benefits of social networking sites, while the author of the second passage examines a particular downside. Both authors would agree that the Internet lowers social inhibitions; however, the first author regards this in a positive light, whereas the second author believes that it incites cyberbullying.

Question #1: CR, Point of Agreement. The correct answer choice is (C)

Answer choice (A) is incorrect, because passage A makes no mention of cyberbullying or any other form of harassment.

Answer choice (B) is incorrect, because passage B makes no mention of the effects of social networking sites on face-to-face interactions.

Answer choice (C) is the correct answer choice (lines 12-13 in passage A; lines 24-25 in passage B).

Answer choice (D) is incorrect, because passage B makes no mention of the increasing popularity of social networking sites.

Comparative Reading Mini-Passages Answer Key

Answer choice (E) is incorrect, because neither author weighs the benefits of social networking sites against their costs. Answer choice (E) represents a statement we may be able to infer from the two passages taken together, but it is not a position with which each author, individually, would agree.

Question #2: GR, Must, P. The correct answer choice is (B)

Answer choice (A) is incorrect, because it contains an exaggeration: the author of passage B does not criticize the argument made in passage A directly. Furthermore, passage B provides no evidence suggesting that there are dangers inherent in *all* social interactions on the Internet.

Answer choice (B) is the correct answer choice. The author of passage A sees social networking sites in a positive light, whereas the author of passage B argues that they facilitate cyberbullying—a downside.

Answer choice (C) is incorrect, because the author of passage B does not challenge the sources of information relied upon in passage A.

Answer choice (D) is a half-right, half-wrong answer. While the author of passage B questions the value of social networking sites, this author never explicitly weighs the cost of cyberbullying against the benefits provided by these sites.

Answer choice (E) is incorrect, because the argument made in passage A is not logically suspect.

Passage #1: Carbon Footprint

VIEWSTAMP Analysis:

The only **Viewpoint** presented here is that of the author (lines 21-22 and 36-43).

The **Structure** of the passage is as follows:

Paragraph One: Define what a carbon footprint is, and explain why it is frequently underestimated.

Paragraph Two: Propose ways to reduce our carbon footprint.

Paragraph Three: Criticize the U.S. for not taking the steps necessary to reduce its greenhouse emissions.

Tone: While the author is confident that effective measures could be taken to reduce the size of our carbon footprint, she is skeptical regarding the political prospects of implementing these measures.

There is one central **Argument** in the passage: taking small steps to reduce our carbon footprint is not terribly difficult (second paragraph), but it is unlikely to happen anytime soon (third paragraph).

The **Main Point** of the passage is that, despite the alarming size of our carbon footprint and the feasibility of efforts to reduce it, a comprehensive framework for adopting the necessary environmental policies lacks political support.

The **Purpose** of the passage is to outline a problem and suggest that while a solution is possible, it may not be politically feasible.

Prephrasing Drill Answer Key

Question #1: SR, Must, P. The correct answer choice is (A)

Prephrase: The author mentions the distance that produce grown in North America travels from source to point of sale in order to explain why certain activities, such as purchasing out-of-season produce, leave a larger footprint than we would typically expect.

Answer choice (A): This is the correct answer choice. Grocery shopping for out-of-season produce is an example of a "less obvious" activity (line 9) that contributes to a person's carbon footprint. The author mentions how far food can travel from source to point of origin in support of the argument that such activities unexpectedly contribute to global warming. This prephrase agrees with answer choice (A). To thoroughly understand the function of the cited claim, you often need to consult other sections of the passage. The key, as always, is context: if all you do is return to the Specific Reference mentioned in the stem, you may not have the contextual understanding necessary to answer such a Purpose question correctly!

Answer choice (B): The carbon footprint of imported produce is never overtly compared to that of produce grown in North America. Both leave a large carbon footprint.

Answer choice (C): The precautionary measures we can take to reduce the size of our carbon footprint are described in the second paragraph, not in the first.

Answer choice (D): Although this answer choice may seem reasonably attractive, consuming locally grown produce does not always leave a small carbon footprint (lines 16-20). As long as we buy out-of-season produce—whether grown locally or imported—we increase our carbon footprint.

Answer choice (E): This answer choice would seem attractive if you assumed that greenhouse gas emissions actually contribute to global warming. Reasonable as such an assumption may be, the author neither suggested nor implied any causal relationship between greenhouse emissions and global warming.

Prephrasing Drill Answer Key

Question #2: CR, Tone. The correct answer choice is (E)

Prephrase: The author seems fairly skeptical about the prospect of reducing our carbon footprint, but the obstacles seem predominantly political (lines 42-43), not technological or economic.

Answer choice (A): The author clearly believes that reducing our carbon footprint is not terribly difficult (lines 21-22), so technological feasibility does not seem to be a major concern.

Answer choice (B): This answer choice is too optimistic, and would only be attractive if you did not read through the entire passage.

Answer choice (C): While the author is clearly skeptical about the prospect of reducing our carbon footprint, her skepticism is driven by considerations that are strictly political, not economic (lines 36-43).

Answer choice (D): This answer choice may seem attractive, as it correctly highlights the fact that the author is skeptical for political reasons. However, the exaggerated language here ("ever") makes it a non-starter.

Answer choice (E): This is the correct answer choice. From the second paragraph, we know that the author does not consider the prospect of reducing our carbon footprint to be terribly difficult (lines 21-22). The obstacles are mostly political (lines 42-43), suggesting disappointment with the political process that delays its realization.

Question #3: CR, Must. The correct answer choice is (B)

Prephrase: From the discussion in the first and second paragraphs, we know that while consumers underestimate the size of their carbon footprint, certain practical steps can be taken to reduce it.

Answer choice (A): This answer choice contains an exaggeration that is impossible to validate ("never").

Answer choice (B): This is the correct answer choice (lines 7-9).

Answer choice (C): In the last paragraph, the author observes that the U.S. (as a country) is the second largest source of *total* greenhouse emissions in the world after China, not that the *average* U.S. citizen has a carbon footprint that is second only to that of the average Chinese. In fact, from the previous sentence we know that the average U.S. citizen holds the world record in this regard (lines 32-36).

Answer choice (D): We do not know *why* consumers fail to take the steps necessary to reduce their carbon footprints. Such a causal claim cannot be validated with the information contained in the passage.

Prephrasing Drill Answer Key

Answer choice (E): As with answer choice (D), it is impossible to know whether consumers are oblivious to the environmental damage caused by their lifestyle, or whether they are aware of it but simply do not care.

Question #4: CR, Must. The correct answer choice is (D)

Prephrase: From the discussion in the last paragraph, it is clear that the author blames the political climate for the delay in adopting the necessary environmental policies.

Answer choice (A): Consumers are not necessarily viewed as "reluctant" to adopt an environmentally healthy lifestyle. While author alludes to the fact that we all share a personal responsibility to reduce our carbon footprint (second paragraph), the most troublesome barrier facing countries that aim to reduce their carbon footprint is a systemic, political reluctance to adopt the necessary environmental policies (third paragraph).

Answer choice (B): The author never mentions the economic cost of environmental reform.

Answer choice (C): Although the author herself clearly does not trust the current political climate to implement the necessary environmental policies, we have no reason to suspect that this skepticism is so widespread as to represent a barrier facing countries that aim to reduce their carbon footprint.

Answer choice (D): This is the correct answer choice. The author clearly views environmental policies aimed at curbing greenhouse gas emissions as a necessary precondition for any meaningful reduction in such emissions (lines 36-41). In the last sentence, she blames the current political climate for the "dubious distinction" of being second only to China as a source of total greenhouse emissions.

Answer choice (E): The discussion in the second paragraph suggests that taking small steps to reduce our carbon footprint can be quite effective. There is no reason to suspect that people are skeptical about the feasibility of such measures, let alone argue that their skepticism is the most troublesome barrier facing countries that aim to reduce their carbon footprint.

Question #5: CR, MustX. The correct answer choice is (A)

Prephrase: Prephrasing the correct answer to a MustX question is virtually impossible. Instead, try to predict what sort of answer will be incorrect. Here, four of the answer choices will describe decisions that could result in reducing one's carbon footprint. The first two paragraphs will be critical in validating such decisions.

Answer choice (A): This is the correct answer choice, because any produce that is out of season—whether local or imported—is likely to increase one's carbon footprint (lines 9-20). Thus, if both types of produce are out-of-season, choosing local, rather than imported, produce will not be a terribly effective means of reducing one's carbon footprint.

Answer choice (B): The practice of disconnecting electrical appliances when not in use is discussed in lines 29-31.

Answer choice (C): Forfeiting bottled water for the sake of filtered water is discussed in lines 22-29.

Answer choice (D): The consumption of produce that is not in season is described as environmentally damaging (lines 9-20). Thus, refusing to purchase such food is likely to be an effective strategy towards reducing one's carbon footprint.

Answer choice (E): In lines 6-7, the author mentions refueling at the gas station as an activity that increases one's carbon footprint. It is reasonable to assume that doing less nonessential driving is a decision that could reduce one's carbon footprint.

Prephrasing Drill Answer Key

Passage #2: Judicial Solicitations

<u>VIEWSTAMP</u> Analysis:

The primary **Viewpoint** presented here is that of the author (line 11 and lines 27-41). A secondary viewpoint belongs to the proponents of the exception to the solicitation ban applicable to campaign committees (lines 21-26).

The **Structure** of the passage is as follows:

<u>Paragraph One</u>:	Explain why judges are prohibited from personally soliciting funds for their election campaigns.
<u>Paragraph Two</u>:	Outline the scope of the solicitation ban, and introduce a possible exception to the targeted conduct.
<u>Paragraph Three</u>:	Argue that the solicitation ban should apply to both personal and committee solicitations.

The author's **Tone** is critical towards the viewpoint outlined in the second paragraph, and confident in the recommendations presented in the third paragraph.

There are two central **Arguments** presented in the passage: The proponents of the exception to the solicitation ban believe that campaign committees do not place the judge's reputation at risk when asking for campaign donations (second paragraph). The author's counterargument is that they do, because the two solicitations are similar in form as well as substance (third paragraph).

The **Main Point** of the passage is that the ban on personal solicitation requests should extend to solicitations by a candidate's campaign committee, as long as the public perceives the judge to be beholden to a specific individual or corporation.

The **Purpose** of the passage is to outline and critique the scope of a legal doctrine.

Prephrasing Drill Answer Key

Question #1: GR, Main Point. The correct answer choice is (A)

Prephrase: The solicitation ban that Caledonia justifiably applied to judges and judicial candidates should be extended to solicitations by a candidate's campaign committee.

Answer choice (A): This is the correct answer choice. The author agrees that judicial candidates should not personally solicit campaign donations (lines 9-13), but wishes to extend this ban to solicitations by a candidate's campaign committee (lines 27-41).

Answer choice (B): This answer choice is incorrect, because the author does not argue that campaign committees *should* act solely on behalf of the candidates they represent: this is a stated fact (lines 28-29), which the author uses to support her view that campaign solicitations, whether direct or indirect, may undermine the public's confidence in the integrity of the judiciary.

Answer choice (C): This answer choice is incorrect, because it expresses the views of those who support the legality of solicitations by a judicial candidate's campaign committee. The author regards their reasoning as "absurd" (line 27).

Answer choice (D): While the author would certainly agree that judges should not act in a manner that creates an appearance of impropriety (lines 32-36), the main point of the passage has to do with the scope of the solicitation ban during an election campaign. Answer choice (D) expresses a general principle that supports the main conclusion of the passage, and as such serves as a premise for that conclusion.

Answer choice (E): This answer choice captures the content of the first paragraph, but not of the passage as a whole.

Prephrasing Drill Answer Key

Question #2: CR, Must. The correct answer choice is (D)

Prephrase: Because the public has difficulty distinguishing between the actions of a campaign committee and those of the judicial candidate, the committee should probably not solicit individuals for money.

To answer this Concept Reference question, a suitable prephrase is key. So is your understanding of Passage Structure, as the correct answer choice must be proven by reference to the third paragraph.

Answer choice (A): The author clearly believes that campaign committees act solely on behalf of the candidate (lines 28-29), not as impartial third parties (line 28). There is no reason to believe, as answer choice (A) suggests, that the author would object to this arrangement. In fact, it is precisely *because* committees act on behalf of their candidates that the author believes the solicitation ban should apply to both.

Answer choice (B): This is the Opposite answer, as the author regards this line of reasoning as "absurd" (line 27).

Answer choice (C): We cannot determine the *main* objective of the campaign committee given the information provided. This answer choice contains an exaggeration.

Answer choice (D): This is the correct answer choice. Solicitations are actions that may create the appearance of impropriety (lines 34-35), i.e. they can damage the reputation of the candidate. Note that our prephrase had a somewhat different scope than the correct answer choice, which is perfectly normal: prephrasing need not be exact to be useful.

Answer choice (E): This answer choice may be attractive, but incorrect. Even though the author regards an appeal for money from a campaign committee to be "similar in form as well as substance" (line 30) to a personal solicitation, we cannot infer that the actions of campaign committees are indistinguishable from those of the judge. This statement contains a generalization, as the only actions under discussion are monetary solicitations. Unlike answer choice (D), which states a mere possibility ("its actions *can* damage…"), here we are faced with a certainty of outcome ("its actions *are* indistinguishable"), which is impossible to prove. Just because two things are similar does not mean that they are indistinguishable from each other.

Prephrasing Drill Answer Key

Question #3: SR, Must, P. The correct answer choice is (B)

Prephrase: Discuss the scope of the solicitation ban, and present a viewpoint defending an exception to that ban.

Answer choice (A): This answer choice may be attractive, because the author ultimately disagrees with the proponents of the exception mentioned in lines 20-21. However, the mere fact of this disagreement does not necessarily mean that the *purpose* of the second paragraph is to raise an objection to the author's views.

Answer choice (B): This is the correct answer choice. The first part of the second paragraph discusses the type of conduct targeted by the solicitation ban (a "legal doctrine"), whereas the second part of the paragraph introduces a possible exception, and the rationale behind it. In short, the paragraph outlines the *scope* of the solicitation ban.

Answer choice (C): The second paragraph outlines the viewpoint of those who favor the exception (lines 21-26), but the function of that paragraph is not to argue on their behalf. In fact, the author explicitly disagrees with the proponents of the exception in the next paragraph.

Answer choice (D): This answer choice outlines the purpose of the third paragraph, not the second.

Answer choice (E): This answer choice may seem attractive, because the author briefly summarizes the reasoning behind allowing campaign committees to solicit funds on behalf of judicial candidates towards the end of the second paragraph. However, the function of the second paragraph *as a whole* is not to present this line of reasoning. This answer choice stops short of capturing the overall purpose of the paragraph.

Prephrasing Drill Answer Key

Question #4: CR, MustX. The correct answer choice is (A)

Prephrase: The author will probably approve of a solicitation request that does not create the appearance of impropriety, i.e. a request that does not make the judge beholden to a specific individual or corporation.

Answer choice (A): This is the correct answer choice. Since the TV ad encourages all supporters to make small donations to the campaign, the public is unlikely to perceive the judge as being beholden to a specific individual or corporation. Such a solicitation will probably not cause the public to lose confidence in the integrity of the judiciary.

Answer choice (B): This answer choice is incorrect, as the author clearly approves of the existing ban on personal solicitations (first paragraph).

Answer choice (C): A fundraiser event is, by definition, an event where the attendees are asked to donate money to a candidate. Given the targeted nature of the invitations (auto industry executives), such an event can easily create the appearance of impropriety, as the judge can be perceived as beholden to that industry.

Answer choice (D): The fact that the solicitation targets a long-time supporter has no bearing on the issue at hand. The ban applies to all personal solicitations (lines 9-13), regardless of the manner in which they are made (lines 17-19).

Answer choice (E): If a judicial candidate asks a wealthy donor to fundraise on her behalf, this would clearly implicate the judge's reputation and create the appearance of impropriety. The public can easily perceive the judge as being beholden to that donor, whether or not the donor herself donated money to the election campaign.

Chapter Two:
Individual
Passages

Chapter Two: Individual Passages

Chapter Notes

This section contains ten individual Reading Comprehension Passages. You can use these passages in a variety of ways, but perhaps the best approach is to complete each passage as a time trial, and then check your work against the complete setup and explanation provided at the end of this section. We do *not* recommend that you do all ten passages in a row as this will defeat the purpose of learning from your mistakes and improving your performance. We also do not recommend that you section these passages out and try to make them into Reading Comprehension sections. The next section of the book contains complete LSAT Reading Comprehension sections, and those should be done as full timed exercises.

To properly time yourself on these individual passages, keep in mind the timing guidelines dictated by the 35-minute format of each LSAT section. The following table displays the amount of time that should be allotted to each passage, depending on how many you plan to attempt in a section:

# Passages Attempted in a Section	Time per Passage Attempted
2	17 minutes and 30 seconds
3	11 minutes and 40 seconds
4	8 minutes and 45 seconds

Thus, if your overall goal in the Reading Comprehension section is to complete all four passages, then you should look to complete each individual passage in this section in 8 minutes and 45 seconds. If you only expect to complete three passages per test, then you should look to finish each individual passage in this section in 11 minutes and 40 seconds (although, of course, you should always look to go faster—part of the goal with this book is to give you practice with our methods and techniques in an effort to help you work more quickly and efficiently).

Stay focused, be positive, and good luck!

Passage #1

The Fourth Amendment to the United States Constitution protects "the people" against unreasonable searches and seizures. The right to be free from unreasonable searches and seizures is an individual
(5) right, uniquely held by each person, regardless of whether that person is a citizen. Yet, in the area of criminal law and procedure, there is no individual remedy available to a person subjected to an arrest, a type of seizure, that may be unlawful. Rather, the only
(10) remedy available for a Fourth Amendment violation is the "exclusionary rule." Pursuant to this rule, the courts may suppress—or exclude from use in a later prosecution—evidence obtained as a result of an arrest based on neither a warrant nor probable cause that
(15) a crime has been committed, i.e., an unreasonable seizure. However, the exclusionary rule is not routinely applied and, in fact, is considered by courts to be an "extreme sanction" for police misconduct.

No individual has the right to demand automatic
(20) imposition of this extreme sanction, despite its role as the sole remedy for violations of the individual rights guaranteed by the Fourth Amendment. Instead, it is a judge-made rule, limited in application by a narrow interpretation of its economic rationale. The purpose
(25) of the rule is to deter police misconduct by imposing a sanction for intentional, reckless, or systematically negligent violations of the Fourth Amendment, in which the officer knew or should have known that the action being taken would result in a violation
(30) of an individual's constitutional rights. Courts have consistently held that only in such flagrant cases of police misconduct, where the conduct is susceptible to appreciable deterrence, do the benefits of deterrence outweigh the significant costs of exclusion, which can
(35) result in the release of dangerous and guilty defendants. Under this view, many individuals who suffered violations of their Fourth Amendment rights through mere negligence (for example, police failing to remove a withdrawn arrest warrant from a law enforcement
(40) database, resulting in the warrantless arrest of a suspect without probable cause) have no remedy for the violation, and are subjected to criminal convictions dependent upon the use of unlawfully obtained evidence, at times resulting in fines, imprisonment,
(45) or even another type of extreme sanction, the death penalty.

Recently, dissenting opinions crafted by influential jurists have argued that the established interpretation of the exclusionary rule is improperly restrictive. These
(50) jurists argue that the rule is an inextricable corollary to the Fourth Amendment. After all, asking of what use is an individualized constitutional safeguard for which there is no individualized enforcement mechanism in place?
(55) Under this alternative view, the exclusionary rule should not merely be a deterrent for future misconduct by police, but rather should return the government to the same evidentiary position it would have held absent

the constitutional violation. This approach would
(60) shift the focus of the rule from generalized deterrence to an individualized remedy with a consequential deterrent effect. Interestingly, the predominant effect of the proposed interpretation would arise in cases involving mere negligence, rather than intentional
(65) police misconduct, because the exclusionary rule would still apply to suppress evidence obtained through intentional violations of the constitution. Ultimately, despite the fact that some guilty defendants may go free if the application of the exclusionary rule is
(70) expanded in accordance with the alternative view, such expansion is necessary to preserve the freedom from unreasonable searches and seizures promised by the Fourth Amendment.

1. Which one of the following most accurately expresses the main point of the passage?

(A) The Fourth Amendment permits unreasonable searches and seizures only when the police act in a way that is merely negligent, rather than reckless.

(B) The expanded interpretation of the exclusionary rule proposed in recent dissenting opinions better protects against unreasonable searches and seizures than does the traditional interpretation consistently applied by the courts.

(C) Only the alternative view of the exclusionary rule protects individuals against unreasonable searches and seizures.

(D) The application of the exclusionary rule is costly, because it can result in the release of a dangerous defendant who is guilty of the crime with which he is charged.

(E) The traditional interpretation of the exclusionary rule was established soon after the adoption of the Fourth Amendment.

2. Based on the passage, which one of the following can be most reasonably inferred about an arrest made without a warrant?

    (A) The arrest is a violation of the Fourth Amendment.
    (B) The exclusionary rule, as traditionally interpreted, would require that all evidence obtained as a result of the arrest be suppressed at trial.
    (C) A warrantless arrest must result from either police negligence or intentional police misconduct.
    (D) Unless police had probable cause at the time of the arrest that the defendant may have committed a crime, the warrantless arrest is an unreasonable seizure in violation of the Fourth Amendment.
    (E) An arrest made without a warrant typically occurs when a law enforcement agency fails to update its database.

3. The passage mentions which one of the following as a potential cost of excluding evidence at trial?

    (A) an increase in the number of wrongful convictions
    (B) a loss of respect for the judiciary
    (C) the release of guilty defendants
    (D) increased prevalence of police misconduct
    (E) increase in the amount of violent crime

4. A judge upholding the traditional interpretation of the exclusionary rule is most likely to agree with which one of the following statements?

    (A) The protection against unreasonable searches and seizures guaranteed by the Fourth Amendment is not an individual right.
    (B) The primary purpose of the exclusionary rule is punitive, because it is designed to punish police officers for their past misconduct.
    (C) The cost of suppressing evidence is too great to justify application of the exclusionary rule to cases of systematically negligent police misconduct, as opposed to intentional police misconduct.
    (D) The exclusionary rule is not an extreme sanction for police misconduct.
    (E) The exclusionary rule should not be interpreted to require the suppression of evidence in isolated cases of police negligence, because the cost of suppressing evidence in those cases outweighs the benefits of deterrence.

5. Which one of the following principles, if true, would do most to justify the author's argument in support of the alternative interpretation of the exclusionary rule?

    (A) If one knows that one will be responsible for harm resulting from carelessness or inattention in conducting an activity, then one can take steps to minimize the likelihood of such harm.
    (B) One can only prevent foreseeable harm, and harm resulting from negligence is rarely foreseeable.
    (C) Holding individuals responsible for inadvertence cannot, by itself, encourage them to make better choices.
    (D) It is more important to convict guilty defendants than to protect the constitutional rights of innocent ones.
    (E) An individual right should not be protected if the social cost of protecting it is too high.

6. The primary purpose of the passage is to

    (A) examine the history of the Fourth Amendment
    (B) criticize the traditional view of the exclusionary rule and argue for the adoption of an alternative interpretation
    (C) reexamine the standards required for police to obtain an arrest warrant
    (D) defend the traditional view of the exclusionary rule
    (E) examine the social impact of implementing the alternative view of the exclusionary rule

Passage #2

The Osage people were Native Americans who, prior to the arrival of Europeans to the region, lived and hunted over a broad swath of territory that would eventually become the states of Oklahoma, Kansas,
(5) Arkansas, and Missouri. They were fierce and cunning warriors but were also known to have a deep respect for life, avoiding direct attacks in order to minimize casualties whenever possible. This strategic approach to conflict was manifest in the actions of the Osage
(10) both before and after the United States expansion into the West.

One tactic long employed by the Osage to defeat their enemies while avoiding direct conflict was that of "bluff war," which they would wage when facing an
(15) enemy encamped in a well-fortified position. Bluff war consisted of baiting the enemy to leave the fortified encampment for terrain more favorable to the Osage. In some cases, the "bait" would be a seemingly vulnerable member of the Osage war party, ostensibly cut off
(20) from the main force. In other instances, the Osage baited their enemies by taunting them, using calls and hand gestures designed to offend the particular enemy being engaged. The objective: To elicit an emotional response from the enemy force, so that they would lose
(25) control and attack—individually or in groups, but with less than a strategically optimal force. In this way, the Osage used guile to defeat a larger, stronger enemy force while avoiding direct attacks and minimizing full-scale combat.

(30) After the expansion of the United States into what had been Osage territory, the Osage were ultimately removed from their lands and eventually resettled onto the Osage Nation reservation in Oklahoma. While the resettlement brought terrible hardships to the Osage,
(35) the location of their eventual settlement included lush grasslands, ideal for grazing cattle.

At first, the Osage had difficulty managing the lands of their reservation, as cattlemen continually violated Osage sovereignty by driving herds of cattle
(40) onto Osage lands to graze. For a time, this exploitation continued as the Osage feared retaliation by the United States Army in response to any attack on the encroaching cattlemen, many of whom supplied the Army with beef. Facing a stronger enemy—cattlemen
(45) backed by the U.S. Army—the Osage were again able to find a strategic solution that allowed them to emerge victorious while avoiding direct conflict. Rather than engage the various cattlemen directly, the Osage used the law to their advantage, entering into valuable grass
(50) leases with individual cattlemen, whom they permitted to fence in their respective leased lands. Careful to guard their financial investment against encroachment by others, the owner of each herd fenced in his own land and patrolled its borders. In the same way, the
(55) Osage leased all of the lands that it wanted fenced and patrolled, creating a border whose builders and guards paid the Osage for the privilege of doing so.

1. Which one of the following most accurately states the main point of the passage?

(A)   The Osage were a fierce and cunning people who lived in what is now Oklahoma, Arkansas, Kansas, and Missouri.

(B)   The Osage were improperly forced by the United States government to leave their ancestral lands and relocate to a reservation in Oklahoma.

(C)   After their forced relocation to a reservation in Oklahoma, the Osage were not able to adapt to their new reality.

(D)   A cunning people, the Osage were able to adapt their traditional strategy of bluff war to the new challenges posed by the westward expansion of the United States.

(E)   The cattlemen who grazed their stock on land bordering the Osage Nation demanded that the Osage fence in their lands, so that the Osage herds of cattle would not wander into the bordering lands.

2. Which one of the following most accurately represents the primary function of the third paragraph?

(A) It connects two different periods of Osage history by showing how the Osage were able to use a traditional strategy against a new enemy.

(B) It bridges earlier events in the history of the Osage to later events, while signaling that something positive would happen to the Osage.

(C) It connects historical events affecting the Osage to post-resettlement events in a way that highlights the ferocity of the Osage.

(D) It indicates that, despite the devastation levied against the Osage, the post-resettlement future of the Osage had the potential to be positive.

(E) It describes the respect for human life that greatly influenced the development of Osage strategy during the pre-relocation era.

3. The author mentions each one of the following EXCEPT:

(A) The Osage baited their enemies by taunting them with offensive hand gestures.

(B) The cattlemen who encroached on the Osage reservation land supplied beef to the United States Army.

(C) The Osage were known to be a fierce people whose primary military strategy involved defeating their enemy by using swift, ambush attacks carried out by overwhelming numbers of Osage warriors.

(D) The Osage convinced cattlemen to pay them for the privilege of fencing and patrolling their borders.

(E) The Osage were forcibly removed from their ancestral lands by the United States government and relocated to a reservation in what is now the state of Oklahoma.

4. Which one of the following titles would be most appropriate for this passage?

(A) "Osage Military Strategy Adapted to Post-Relocation Realities"

(B) "Osage Military Predominance in the Pre-Relocation Era"

(C) "Bluff War: The Osage's Cunning Use of Terrain in Military Strategy"

(D) "The Role of the United States Army in the Expansion of Commercial Beef Production"

(E) "The Fortuitous Landscape of Forced Osage Relocation"

5. The passage suggests that the author would be most likely to agree with which one of the following claims about the Osage?

(A) They were unable to maintain their cultural heritage after their forced relocation.

(B) They routinely forced their enemies to retreat to fortified positions during war.

(C) They thrived in the post-relocation era.

(D) They were, as a people, gifted strategists who were able to adapt their techniques to new environments.

(E) They primarily lived during the pre-relocation era in the territory that would become the state of Kansas.

INDIVIDUAL PASSAGES

Passage #3

① Biologists have long suspected that vegetal behavior is exceptionally sensitive, responsive, and complex, but such hypotheses were impossible to test due to limited technical resources. We assumed, for
(5) instance, that plants are able to interpret and adaptively respond to external stimuli, but were unable to test our assumptions. Similarly, we observed that plants can process informational input on humidity, light, and gravity, but could not analyze the physiological
(10) mechanisms allowing them to do so. Until recently, it was impossible to compare the neural architecture that gives rise to animal cognition to biologically plausible forms of learning in plants. Consequently, no one suspected that plants could anticipate imminent
(15) hazards, let alone communicate these hazards through biochemical cues. Today, with the advent of plant neurobiology, scientists can finally shed light on the incredible complexity that underlies vegetal behavior.

② Plant neurobiology is a relatively new discipline, Def P. neuro
(20) incorporating knowledge from well established areas of research such as cell biology, molecular biology, and plant electrophysiology. The primary focus of plant neurobiologists—to study the complex patterns of behavior of plants through information-processing
(25) systems—is inherently interdisciplinary. Research in plant neurobiology has not only deepened our knowledge of vegetal behavior, but has also prompted a critical reevaluation of "cognition" as an operative term in a variety of seemingly unrelated fields, such
(30) as linguistics, philosophy, and anthropology. Thanks to plant neurobiologists, we now have definitive proof that plants possess cognitive capacities even though they lack the neural or synaptic structures that give rise to animal cognition. Clearly, our very understanding
(35) of "cognition" has evolved into a more thorough appreciation of the sophisticated signal-interaction behavior commonly observed in plants.

③ The accelerated pace of discoveries involving plant intelligence warrants significant institutional
(40) commitment, which can only be provided by establishing a Department of Plant Neurobiology at our university. Some of my colleagues worry that this department would have no clear rationale, because its academic objectives are in principle achievable by plant
(45) physiologists. This is not true. By assembling leading scientists to study vegetal behavior under one roof, a department dedicated solely to plant neurobiology will be uniquely capable of addressing issues far beyond the scope of plant physiology, including—but
(50) not limited to—plant memory and learning, adaptive behavior in plants, hormonal signaling pathways and communication, and plant intelligence. Not before long, we will discover that plants—just like animals—are capable of experiencing pain, of differentiating
(55) between positive and negative experiences, and of employing complex cost-benefit analysis to adapt and learn from their mistakes. Our understanding of the natural world will be not only incomplete, but also

(60) somewhat distorted, without proper appreciation of vegetal behavior. Such an appreciation is undoubtedly attainable if, but only if, we recognize the value of plant neurobiology as an autonomous discipline worthy of institutional support.

1. Which one of the following most accurately expresses the main point of the passage?

   (A) Plant neurobiology has deepened our understanding of the incredible complexity that underlies vegetal behavior.
   (B) Thanks to recent advances in plant neurobiology, our understanding of cognition has evolved.
   (C) Advances in the field of plant intelligence require establishing an autonomous department dedicated to the study of plant neurobiology.
   (D) Plant neurobiology has accelerated the pace of scientific discoveries involving vegetal behavior.
   (E) Plants possess cognitive capacities even though they lack the neural architecture that gives rise to animal cognition.

2. Each one of the following is mentioned in the passage as an example of known vegetal behavior, EXCEPT:

   (A) to process environmental input
   (B) to communicate information
   (C) to experience pain
   (D) to interact through signals
   (E) to use biochemical cues

3. The author observes that plants "lack the neural or synaptic structures that give rise to animal cognition" (lines 33-34) mainly in order to

   (A) indicate a necessary precondition for cognitive function
   (B) differentiate the cognitive abilities of plants from those of animals
   (C) explain why scientists find it difficult to attribute cognitive abilities to plants
   (D) show that certain physiological attributes are no longer sufficient to prove cognitive function
   (E) suggest a way in which our understanding of cognition has changed over time

INDIVIDUAL PASSAGES

4. Which one of the following most accurately describes the relationship between the second paragraph and the final paragraph?

(A) The second paragraph anticipates the objections raised in the final paragraph.

(B) The second paragraph helps to justify the course of action recommended in the final paragraph.

(C) The final paragraph supports the argument made in the second paragraph by clarifying the potential significance of an academic initiative.

(D) The second paragraph describes a controversial view that the author defends in the final paragraph.

(E) The final paragraph debates the significance of a biological phenomenon, which is described in the second paragraph.

5. The passage provides information that answers each of the following questions EXCEPT:

(A) How can research in plant physiology contribute to our future understanding of vegetal behavior?

(B) How has plant neurobiology altered our conception of cognition?

(C) What impact has the study of plant neurobiology made on other academic fields?

(D) Which fields of study have paved the way for the advances made in plant neurobiology?

(E) What are some of the directions for future research in vegetal behavior?

6. Given its tone and content, from which one of the following was the passage most likely drawn?

(A) a textbook on plant neurobiology

(B) a grant application for an experimental study

(C) an editorial published in a national newspaper

(D) a strategic initiative proposed by an academic dean

(E) a study focusing on vegetal behavior

7. Which one of the following, if true, would most call into question the author's assertion in the last sentence of the passage?

(A) Earlier work in plant physiology has paved the way for most of the recent advances in plant neurobiology.

(B) If plant neurobiology becomes established as an autonomous academic field, its interdisciplinary focus is likely to be compromised.

(C) Since pharmaceutical companies are likely to benefit from any future research in plant neurobiology, it is incumbent upon them to support such research.

(D) In the course of their research, plant neurobiologists frequently rely on methods and techniques developed for use in other disciplines.

(E) Plant neurobiology is not the only academic field conducting research in vegetal behavior.

8. Which one of the following is most analogous to the position discussed in lines 42-45?

(A) A car manufacturer refuses to develop a new type of electric car, because the currently existing hybrid model is environmentally friendly.

(B) A car manufacturer refuses to develop a new type of electric car, because the cost of research and development is far greater than the potential earnings from the sale of such cars.

(C) A car manufacturer refuses to develop a new type of electric car, because such cars merely exchange one form of pollution for another, equally destructive form.

(D) A car manufacturer refuses to develop a new type of electric car, because there is no scientific consensus on the issue of global warming.

(E) A car manufacturer refuses to develop a new type of electric car, because the infrastructure required to support such cars is not yet available.

Passage Set #4

Passage A

The topic of criminality in Andrew Kerr's work is a commonly pursued one. Its richness lies as much within the thematic framework of Kerr's prose as it does within the author's own scandalous life. Not
(5) surprisingly, scholars frequently examine Kerr's fictional world for clues that could reveal the "real" story of their author. While the verdict of such critiques traverses the entire spectrum of moral judgments, from wholehearted compassion to reluctant absolution
(10) and dismissive condemnation, they all share a certain smugness that prevents them from appreciating the poetic brilliance of their *objet de critique*.

At the less commendable end of this critical spectrum is Mark Newman's 1989 study titled, *Andrew*
(15) *Kerr: Biography of Deceit*. In his book, Newman undertakes the formidable challenge of correcting and clarifying certain aspects of Kerr's biography. The study, a detective narrative in its own right, seeks to expose Kerr not only as a petty thief, but also as bad
(20) playwright. Newman holds no punches in condemning Kerr's plays as disturbing, distasteful, even disgusting. He even dislikes the playwright's penchant for meta-theater, arguing that only a highly skilled dramaturge can interweave multiple plays-within-a-play and still
(25) maintain a coherent narrative structure. The implication being, of course, that Kerr was far from being a skilled dramaturge.

Passage B

On the Porch (1957), Andrew Kerr's final meta-theatrical production, tells the story of an experimental
(30) theater set in Weimar Germany. Under the guidance of what appear to be professional actors, audience members (who are also actors) suspend the pretense of reality to assume a variety of loosely scripted roles. The production is bound to be a flop, of course, but
(35) the cast manages to stay afloat by turning the theater into a brothel. Role-playing assumes a decidedly more prurient, but no less experimental, form.

The play was first performed in London, then subsequently in New York, Paris and Berlin. Despite
(40) its success, Kerr was highly critical of the manner in which it was directed. He eventually included an introduction that gave lengthy instructions on "How to Play *On the Porch*." The playwright was also displeased with the directors' attempts to simplify the
(45) plot line and turn the play into a satire, which they did primarily in order to appeal to middle-class audiences. Mockery, they realized, offers an unexpected comfort from the more incoherent—and offensive—aspects of the plot.
(50) Unfortunately, the dramatic effects of the satirical genre were inconsistent with Kerr's philosophy of truth and illusion, which revels in ambiguity. In a letter he later wrote to a friend, Kerr remarked that "The only truths worth exalting are those that cannot be proven
(55) and that, in fact, are false."

1. Which one of the following best describes the main point of passage A?
   (A) By judging Andrew Kerr's personal life rather than the quality of his work, critics fail to accord him the appreciation he deserves.
   (B) Some of the themes that inhabit Andrew Kerr's fictional world are drawn from his criminal past.
   (C) Mark Newman's biography of Andrew Kerr is well-informed, but the judgments it reaches are overly harsh.
   (D) Andrew Kerr's fictional world provides a valuable insight into his personal life.
   (E) Andrew Kerr's moral failings have prevented him from reaching his true artistic potential.

2. Which one of the following pairs would be most appropriate as titles for passage A and passage B, respectively?
   (A) "Who is Andrew Kerr?" "Meta-theater *On the Porch*"
   (B) "Life Edited: The Tarnished Brilliance of Andrew Kerr" "Truth and Illusion *On the Porch*"
   (C) "Andrew Kerr: A Playwright or a Criminal?" "*On the Porch*: A Flop!"
   (D) "Once a Criminal, Always a Genius: Andrew Kerr and the Dubious Honor of Being a Thief" "Meta-theater in Weimar Germany"
   (E) "The Real Story of Andrew Kerr" "True or False? Find Out *On the Porch!*"

3. Both passages explicitly mention which one of the following?
   (A) role-playing
   (B) narrative structure
   (C) theatrical plot
   (D) meta-theater
   (E) moral judgments

INDIVIDUAL PASSAGES

4. It can be inferred from passage B that Andrew Kerr
    would be most likely to agree with which one of the
    following statements about the views described in lines
    4-12 of passage A?

    (A) They are inconsequential, because such opinions
        are inherently subjective.
    (B) They are condescending, because their proponents
        assume a position of moral superiority.
    (C) They are hypocritical, because no one is morally
        blameless.
    (D) They are misguided, because their proponents
        seem preoccupied with provable truths.
    (E) They are unnerving, because they seek to gratify
        prying curiosity.

5. It can be inferred from passage A that Mark Newman
    and the kind of director described in passage B would
    be most likely to agree with which one of the following
    statements about the work of Andrew Kerr?

    (A) It is too complex for a regular audience.
    (B) It is not the product of a skilled dramaturge.
    (C) It is offensive to all viewers.
    (D) It is incoherent but potentially amusing.
    (E) It is troubling and disjointed.

6. Which one of the following most accurately expresses
    how the use of the phrase "fictional world" in passage A
    (line 6) relates to the use of the word "illusion" in passage
    B (line 52)?

    (A) The former refers to a body of work produced by
        an artist, whereas the latter refers to position held
        by that artist.
    (B) The former refers to a true belief that something
        is objectively false, whereas the latter refers to a
        false belief that something is objectively true.
    (C) The former refers to an artistic concept, whereas
        the latter refers to a philosophical one.
    (D) The former refers to a potentially deceptive work,
        whereas the latter refers to the expected effects of
        that work.
    (E) The former refers to a product requiring
        imagination, whereas the latter refers to a figment
        of that imagination.

7. Each one of the following inferences about Andrew Kerr
    is supported by one or both of the passages, EXCEPT:

    (A) In at least some instances, his work was used as
        evidence to cast a moral judgment on him.
    (B) The subject matter of his work bore at least some
        similarity to aspects of his life.
    (C) Some of his theatrical productions did not receive
        popular acclaim.
    (D) Some of his work was altered against his will.
    (E) His philosophical beliefs were at odds with the
        reputed preferences of his audience

Passage #5

Responsible mining of natural resources can be a sustainable way to eradicate poverty in developing nations. In many of these nations, however, indigenous populations have developed complex relationships
(5) with their ancestral lands. Significant conflicts have arisen from recent governmental takings of such lands in, even when the land was taken for beneficent purposes. These conflicts raise an important question: What constitutes adequate compensation for the
(10) governmental taking of indigenous lands?

Often, the developing nation performing the taking has adopted the landowner compensation practices of developed nations. Under these schemes, compensation focuses on the fair market value of the land, with
(15) no consideration given to the subjective meaning of the land to the property owner. Early studies into the efficacy of this approach in developing nations has focused on four areas of conflict: ownership of the land; compensation for the taking; impact of the
(20) economic activity on the environment; and distribution of the ultimate economic benefit of the activity.

A recent study of the governmental taking of private lands in the Kenyan city of Kwale for the purpose of proposed titanium mining has powerfully exposed the
(25) failure of prior research to account for ethnoecological factors relevant to the issue of adequate compensation. Ethnoecology is an interdisciplinary study focusing on how established groups of people perceive and relate to their respective environments. In the context of fair
(30) compensation for governmental takings of ancestral, indigenous lands, an ethnoecological approach expands the traditional compensation analysis to include the subjective value of the land to the property owner, a value that must be included in any truly adequate
(35) compensation.

The Kenyan study offers much support for this view. In that study, the author detailed the value of the coconut tree to a group of landowners, a value only partly accounted for by the government agency that
(40) authorized the "adequate" compensation payment for the confiscated land. The coconut tree is a multigenerational asset that can bear fruit for hundreds of years. The Mijikenda community, members of the Bantu ethnic group, made use of every part of the tree,
(45) from its roots to its fruits and fronds. The author points out that the tree provides not only a respite from the heat, but also milk and meat for sustenance. Centuries-old standing trees represent historical markers of great cultural significance, while a tree may be felled to
(50) produce a *kigango*, or grave post.

Beyond these and other valuable uses, most of which may be purchased even by one who does not own the tree, the actual ownership of the coconut tree has great significance to the social hierarchy of the community.
(55) After their land was taken by the government, farmers who had nurtured their coconut tree groves were reduced to buying coconuts at market, or *ukunda*. To the farmers, this was a shameful act that lowered their

(60) social status, and thus restricted their participation in socio-cultural activities. Even more destructive to the community was the impact of the loss of the coconut trees on the ability of some Mijikenda women to marry. Mijikenda tradition requires that the father of the bride
(65) present gifts to the groom's family made from coconuts owned by the father himself. Among the necessary gifts is a cask of *mnazi*, a milky palm wine, made from the father's own trees. To substitute purchased *mnazi* would not only be shameful for the father, but
(70) would also permanently reduce the bride's standing within her new family. Replacing the trees taken to produce enough *mnazi* for the traditional bridal gift required a minimum of five years, during which time the daughters could marry, but only in shame. No
(75) compensation for the taking of these ancestral lands could be adequate without full recognition of the complex relationships of such indigenous groups with their land.

1. Which one of the following most accurately expresses the main point of the passage.

(A) Developing nations increasingly use governmental authority to take land from indigenous landowners for the purpose of mining natural resources.

(B) The mining of natural resources is a sustainable way to eradicate poverty in developed nations.

(C) Landowner compensation for governmental takings of indigenous lands would not be adequate unless it takes ethnoecological principles into account.

(D) The subjective value of land includes the cultural relevance of certain crops, such as coconut trees, to the landowner.

(E) Ethnoecological principles are important to determining an adequate compensation mechanism for governmental takings of land in most developed nations.

2. The primary function of the third paragraph in relation to the second paragraph is to

(A) describe an issue related to the valuation of land which the approach described in the second paragraph does not consider

(B) indicate a third approach to the valuation of land not referenced in either paragraph

(C) describe how the impact of coconut tree ownership on marriage rituals is accounted for under the procedures detailed in the second paragraph

(D) describe four areas of conflict in the valuation of land in the community identified in the second paragraph

(E) support the position that the approach described in the second paragraph is ultimately a fair method for determining the true value of land

3. Which one of the following is most strongly supported by the information in the passage?

(A) The *kigango* is a species of coconut tree grown predominately in Kenya.

(B) Under the ethnoecological approach, it is important to distribute the economic benefit of the activity for which land is being taken.

(C) Although some affected landowners may lose their privately owned coconut trees, this loss can be entirely compensated by a payment that equals the fair market value of the trees.

(D) The complete loss of her family's coconut trees may cause a Mijikenda woman to be less likely to marry for a period of at least two years from the date of loss.

(E) Some developed nations have embraced the addition of ethnoecological factors to the traditional fair market analysis of land value.

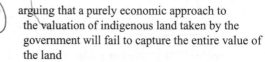
co3
ec prod;
B
w wat

4. The passage mentions each of the following as an area of conflict in the governmental taking of indigenous lands EXCEPT:

(A) the environmental impact of the economic activity for which the land is being taken

(B) the distribution of the economic benefit resulting from the activity for which the land is being taken

(C) the likelihood that the proposed economic activity underlying the taking would help eradicate poverty in that region

(D) the ownership of the land

(E) the monetary compensation for the land being taken

5. The author of the passage is primarily concerned with

(A) arguing that a purely economic approach to the valuation of indigenous land taken by the government will fail to capture the entire value of the land

(B) suggesting that the areas of conflict identified in the second paragraph are overstated by those who oppose the ethnoecological approach

(C) defending the traditional valuation approach against claims that it focuses too narrowly on market-based factors

(D) observing that the economic value of coconut trees renders the ethnoecological analysis of subjective value inapposite to the case of the Mijikenda community

(E) defending the value of coconut trees to the Mijikenda community

6. The author's attitude toward the traditional, fair market value approach to determining adequate compensation can most accurately be described as

(A) reasoned disapproval
(B) grudging acceptance
(C) optimistic advocacy
(D) frustrated confusion
(E) uneasy ambivalence

Passage 5-8

x21/24

Passage A

Even though state employment law generally
disfavors anticompetitive agreements—restrictive
covenants that tend to prevent an employee from
pursuing a similar vocation after termination of
(5) employment—courts are likely to enforce such
agreements as long as they are necessary to protect
the legitimate needs of the employer. Courts typically
limit the cognizable employer interests to the extent
necessary to prevent the disclosure of trade secrets,
(10) or where an employee's services are so unique and
extraordinary that losing such services would cause
irreparable harm to the employer.

Courts have been reluctant to enforce broader
noncompete clauses, in part because such clauses
(15) are said to have a stifling effect on entrepreneurship
and innovation. Once the term of an employment
agreement has expired, the argument goes, employers
should not be allowed to insulate themselves from
competition. Nevertheless, noncompete clauses are
(20) becoming increasingly common in such far-ranging
fields as technology, media relations, marketing,
manufacturing, and education. Their proponents
justifiably argue that such clauses are uniquely capable
of protecting trade secrets and other proprietary
(25) information vital to the long-term well-being of the
company. In a sense, noncompete agreements act as a
form of insurance policy against unfair competition. By
limiting the risk of possible loss, they also encourage
companies to invest in their employees.

Passage B

(30) Even if an employer can demonstrate that a former
employee's services are sufficiently unique to provide
a legitimate basis for protection, courts should not
enforce a noncompete clause solely on the basis of
uniqueness of services. Doing so would take into
(35) account only the harm sustained by the employer,
not by the employee. Since compliance with a
severely restrictive covenant can cause the employee
significant financial hardship, courts must weigh the
cost of breaching the agreement against the cost of not
(40) breaching it. Consequently, for noncompete clauses to
pass judicial muster, they must be reasonable in time,
area, and scope of activities being restricted.

Even if the court determines that some kind of
restraint is warranted, the terms of the covenant must
(45) be clear and precise. If they are not, the court must
reduce the scope of the covenant to a reasonable
level and enforce it to that extent. Such a "pairing
down" approach should not be used, however, if the
noncompete clause is unrestricted in both time and
(50) area. Such imprecision suggests that the parties have
not made *bona fide* attempts to impose reasonable
limitations and, consequently, have not justified an
attempt at judicial rewriting. In that case, the decision
rendered should favor the employee.

1. Which one of the following is mentioned in passage B but not in passage A?

   (A) the need to protect the legitimate interests of the employer
   (B) the harm caused by noncompete clauses on free enterprise
   (C) the potential benefits employees might derive from being bound by noncompete agreements
   (D) the economic harm sustained by employees bound by noncompete agreements
   (E) the conditions under which a noncompete clause is likely to pass judicial muster

2. It can be inferred that both authors would be likely to agree with which one of the following statements regarding noncompete clauses?

   (A) They benefit employees.
   (B) They benefit employers.
   (C) They benefit employers more than they benefit employees.
   (D) They benefit employers and employees equally.
   (E) They benefit neither employers nor employees.

3. In terms of what it alludes to, "possible loss" (line 28) is most closely related to which one of the following phrases in passage B?

   (A) uniqueness of services (line 34)
   (B) harm sustained by the employer (line 35)
   (C) significant financial hardship (line 38)
   (D) cost of not breaching it (lines 39-40)
   (E) reduce the scope (line 46)

4. Which one of the following most accurately characterizes a difference between the two passages?

    (A) Passage A defends a controversial employment practice, whereas Passage B clarifies the conditions under which the practice should be legally permissible.
    (B) Passage A discusses a problem in employment law, whereas Passage B defends a resolution of that problem.
    (C) Passage A justifies the need for a contractual provision, whereas Passage B suggests that the provision is based on a mistaken rationale.
    (D) Passage A describes the harm that results from breaching a contractual obligation, whereas Passage B describes the harm that results from not breaching it.
    (E) Passage A objectively reports on a divisive contractual provision, whereas Passage B subjectively takes issue with a particular aspect of that provision.

5. With regard to their respective attitudes toward noncompete clauses, passage B differs from passage A in that passage B is more

    (A) radical and opinionated
    (B) informative but confrontational
    (C) impartial and skeptical
    (D) judicious and prescriptive
    (E) apprehensive but hopeful

6. Based on the information contained in both passages, which one of the following describes a restrictive covenant that is LEAST likely to be deemed legally enforceable?

    (A) To protect sensitive information relevant to national security, a defense contractor prohibits its lead engineers from accepting job offers at foreign companies.
    (B) A broadcast network disallows its evening anchor from accepting job offers at competing networks for 2 years after termination of employment.
    (C) To harm their main competitor, a cable company forbids all entry-level customer service associates from pursuing jobs in the telecommunications industry after termination of employment.
    (D) To safeguard their biotechnological patents, a pharmaceutical company disallows its principal scientists from pursuing positions of similar responsibility at other companies in that state.
    (E) A hair salon forbids its celebrity hairdresser from opening a hair salon within a 10-mile radius of his previous place of employment.

7. Based on information contained in both passages, each one of the following is a factor relevant to the determination of whether a noncompete clause is legally enforceable, EXCEPT:

    (A) the employee's length of employment with the company seeking to enforce the agreement
    (B) the specificity of the language used in the covenant
    (C) the employee's probable access to proprietary information
    (D) the employer's ability to easily replace the employee
    (E) the undue burden imposed by the covenant on the employee

Passage #7

①   Gund Hall, home to Harvard's Graduate School
of Design and the Frances Loeb Library, was built
between 1968 and 1972. It is situated at the corner
of Cambridge and Quincy Streets, only steps away
(5)   from Harvard Yard, and yet its non-traditional design
seems miles away from Harvard's red-brick Georgian
architecture. Gund Hall is a modern building, and
unabashedly so. It features a reinforced concrete flat
slab structure, with massive overhangs precariously
(10) supported by eleven cylindrical columns. A quasi-alien
green fiberglass covers the roof. The grassy forecourt
typical of Harvard buildings is entirely omitted in
an attempt to create a more "urban" look, while the
ground floor is wrapped in a glass bandage of doors
(15) more reminiscent of a shopping arcade than a library.

②   Critics have compared the building to a "medieval-
modern" fortress, admitting uneasiness—even
repulsion—at Gund Hall's stark monumentality.
Such claims are missing the point. It is no secret
(20) that John Andrews, head of the building's design
team, made little effort to fit the building into its
architectural milieu. Such an integration was not his
intent. By designing a central studio space extending
across all four floors in a step-like fashion, Andrews
(25) envisioned an environment that could foster academic
collaboration and social contact. Gund Hall's unified
studio space was certainly ahead of its time, conceived
decades before "interdisciplinarity" became a mainstay
of academic jargon.

③ (30)   Unfortunately, design innovations sometimes come
at the expense of practical considerations. An open,
multi-tiered studio space embodied a progressive
idea, but it also denied students visual and acoustic
privacy. By forcing its occupants to work under one
(35) roof, Gund Hall could not cater to their increasingly
divergent design and architectural needs. Meanwhile,
fire regulations forced the erection of concrete walls
between the faculty studios and the central studio
space, effectively restoring the institutional barriers
(40) Andrews so keenly sought to destroy. Similarly, the
entrance lobby—designed as a transitional space
between exterior and interior—had to be enclosed
by a glass screen in order to protect the interior from
adverse weather conditions. To add insult to injury,
(45) officials had to install a guard post in response to an
increase in the crime rate.

④   While these modifications stemmed from practical
necessities, they could have been foreseen and
integrated into the building's original design without
(50) compromising its modernist aesthetic. They were
not. Likewise, open-space architecture need not be
antithetical to privacy, as many other architects have
since demonstrated. It was Andrews' absolutist,
unapologetic adherence to modernist ideals that
(55) eventually compromised their execution, resulting in
a building that is neither purely modern, nor entirely
practical.

(handwritten margin notes: "mods", "Desp. prevmember", "Andrew's absolutism → design failure")

1. Which one of the following best summarizes the main
point of the passage?

  (A)   In designing Gund Hall, John Andrews did not
       intend a seamless integration with the rest of
       Harvard's campus.

  (B)   Gund Hall's progressive ideals notwithstanding,
       its architectural design was undermined by
       foreseeable practical considerations.

  (C)   Gund Hall's modernist design anticipated the
       interdisciplinary approach that would become a
       mainstay in academia.

  (D)   Despite its imperfections, Gund Hall was able to
       successfully fulfill its academic mission.

  (E)   The modernist aesthetic embodied by Gund Hall
       is incompatible with the practical requirements of
       most academic buildings.

2. It can be inferred from the passage that the author would
be most likely to view the critics mentioned in line 16 as

  (A)   essentially correct, even if their claims might
       initially appear to be somewhat exaggerated

  (B)   making a reasonable claim that is nonetheless
       based on a mistaken rationale

  (C)   somewhat misguided, because they misinterpret
       the aesthetic motivations behind the object of
       their critique

  (D)   making a questionable claim that ignores the
       practical necessities of academic buildings

  (E)   fundamentally mistaken, because no reasonable
       support is provided for their claims

3. The passage suggests which one of the following about
the kind of academic spaces typically found on Harvard's
campus?

  (A)   They were more compartmentalized than Gund
       Hall.

  (B)   They were better suited to meeting the needs of
       design and architecture students than was Gund
       Hall.

  (C)   Unlike Gund Hall, they were admired by the
       critics.

  (D)   They were a reaction against the type of
       architecture typified by Gund Hall.

  (E)   They were rarely found outside Harvard Yard.

4. Which one of the following words employed by the author is most indicative of the author's attitude toward John Andrews' modernist ideals?

(A) uneasiness
(B) transitional
(C) divergent
(D) compromised
(E) practical

5. In the passage the author is primarily concerned with doing which one of the following?

(A) arguing that Gund Hall's modernist aesthetic was incompatible with students' academic needs
(B) explaining why Gund Hall did not receive the appreciation it deserves
(C) criticizing the design of Gund Hall for its failure to blend in with the rest of Harvard's architecture
(D) defending Gund Hall from accusations for which there is no reasonable basis
(E) evaluating the degree to which Gund Hall's aesthetic was suited to its academic mission

6. Each of the following is identified in the passage as part of Gund Hall's original architectural design EXCEPT:

(A) green fiberglass covering the roof
(B) reinforced concrete flat slab structure
(C) multi-tiered studio space
(D) a glass screen enclosing the entrance lobby
(E) glass bandage of doors

Passage #8

Edith Maude Eaton was born in 1865, one of fourteen children born to her English father and Chinese mother. Though her family was financially secure at the time of her birth, their fortunes
(5) changed during her childhood, forcing the family to emigrate to Canada in search of work. The Eatons arrived in Canada soon after the discovery of gold in California, which produced a massive influx of Chinese immigrants. From the start, these immigrants
(10) faced great prejudice, based on their distinct physical appearance, their "peculiar" customs, their frugality, and their willingness to perform hard, dangerous work for low wages.

As a child living in Canada, Eaton contracted
(15) rheumatic fever, which left her with an enlarged heart and poor health for the rest of her life. Because she was incapable of sustained physical activity but needed to contribute to her family's income, Edith became a stenographer, which required her to write down words
(20) spoken by someone else. After some time, Eaton began to work for local newspapers, which came to recognize the quality of her own words.

In her 30s, Eaton moved to California and began an increasingly peripatetic period of her life. She traveled
(25) back and forth among San Francisco, Los Angeles, Seattle, and Montreal, connecting with the Chinese community in each city. Although Eaton's Chinese heritage was not physically apparent, meaning she could protect herself from anti-Chinese bigotry, she
(30) rejected the safety of Western conformity. During this period of her life, Eaton accepted writing assignments from newspapers in the various cities, typically writing about events in the Chinese community. In completing these assignments, Eaton developed closer bonds with
(35) the Chinese community, learning more about both her own heritage and the plight of Chinese immigrants who were subjected to racial insensitivity and a discriminatory bureaucracy. Eaton discovered that Chinese women were at an even greater disadvantage,
(40) because they were often isolated and were not given the opportunity to learn English or adjust to the culture of their new home.

To combat this inequality, Eaton further embraced her own Chinese heritage and adopted the pseudonym
(45) Sui Sin Far (Chinese for "narcissus"). She began to write articles and short stories that focused on the problems faced by the Chinese in the United States and Canada. Because she was a member of both the Chinese and the Western communities, Eaton was able
(50) to write in a realistic way about the situation of the Chinese, and to do so in a way that could effectively communicate that reality to the newspapers' Western readers. Eaton continued to advocate for the Chinese community for the rest of her life, despite the toll her
(55) work took on her. In her autobiography, she wrote, "I give my right hand to the Occidentals and my left to the Orientals, hoping that between them they will not utterly destroy the insignificant 'connecting link.'" Ironically, it was Eaton's physical infirmity,
(60) an enlarged heart, that put her in a position to help so many others find a voice and a place within the broader society. Eaton's supposed weakness enabled her to develop the strength to bridge together two communities and honor the heritage of her beloved
(65) mother.

1. Which one of the following most accurately states the main point of the passage?

(A) Edith Eaton, a woman of Chinese and English descent, became a writer after beginning her career as a stenographer.

(B) Edith Eaton was a Chinese-English writer who overcame the anti-Chinese bigotry to which she was subjected on account of her physical appearance.

(C) Despite her poor health, Edith Eaton became an advocate for Chinese people in the United States and Canada, leveraging her connection to both the Chinese and the Western communities to communicate the situations confronting the Chinese on Western soil.

(D) The Chinese who immigrated to the United States in the 1860s faced discrimination for several reasons, and Edith Eaton was instrumental in advocating for legislation aimed at eliminating certain discriminatory bureaucratic procedures.

(E) Edith Eaton's non-fiction writing, which consisted of reviews of Western theatrical productions that depicted Chinese themes, sought to educate Western audiences about the authentic Chinese experience.

2. Which one of the following most accurate describes the meaning of the word "peripatetic," as it is used in line 24 of the passage?

A (A) The quality of changing residences frequently, particularly in connection with work.

(B) The quality of living within a limited budget, spending money only sparingly.

(C) The quality of living dangerously, taking unnecessary risks.

(D) The quality of existing in a continuing state of emotional turmoil.

(E) The quality of gaining advanced knowledge or skill in a particular area.

3. Which one of the following most accurately represents the primary function of the second paragraph?

B (A) It describes the reasons why the Eatons moved to Canada when Edith Eaton was a young child.

(B) It establishes what started Eaton on the professional path that lead to her becoming a writer.

(C) It describes the source of Eaton's passionate advocacy for the Chinese living in the United States and Canada.

(D) It provides the cause underlying Eaton's ability to write realistically about the problems facing the Chinese community in the United States and Canada.

(E) It gives evidence supporting the author's position that Eaton was physically stronger than her family assumed.

4. Which one of the following is a statement with which the author would most likely agree?

A (A) The more a person learns about a certain community, the more that person may be able to realistically portray the problems faced by that community.

(B) People should not subject themselves to discrimination and bigotry if they can avoid doing so.

(C) Eaton was highly confident that she could continue her pro-Chinese advocacy for as long as necessary to achieve meaningful reforms.

(D) Women in immigrant communities always face a higher level of discrimination than men do.

(E) Eaton's enlarged heart, which developed as a result of a childhood illness, was a weakness that she was never able to overcome.

5. The passage mentions each of the following as a reason why Chinese immigrants were discriminated against, EXCEPT:

(A) physical features that distinguished the Chinese from their Western counterparts

D (B) a good work ethic

(C) customs that Western people found to be strange

(D) Chinese views on the ownership of personal property

(E) willingness to work for low wages

Passage #9

Nutritional biologists have long argued that sugar should be classified as a toxin. Indeed, excessive consumption of simple carbohydrates, especially fructose, has been definitively linked to an increased
(5) risk of cardiovascular disease, diabetes, and cancer. However, to classify sugar as a "toxin" would be a misnomer. Almost any otherwise benign nutritional substance can be toxic if ingested in quantities sufficiently large to cause harm. Moreover, our
(10) obsession with sugar is itself harmful, as it detracts from focusing on an equally important part of any balanced diet: sodium.

Just like sugar, excessive consumption of sodium represents a significant health risk, especially for those
(15) suffering from hypertension. Everyone needs some sodium in his or her diet to replace routine losses. But while an adequate and safe intake of sodium for healthy adults is 1,100 to 3,300 milligrams a day, most processed foods exceed the upper limit of that range
(20) at least two-fold. It is likely that excessive sodium intake plays a role in the etiology of hypertension, additionally elevating the risk of stroke, coronary heart disease, and renal disease. Furthermore, since the salt used in the preparation of processed foods is generally
(25) refined, its consumption fails to satisfy the organism's need for other salts and minerals, which induces further craving. The excessive consumption of sodium can therefore enhance caloric overconsumption, and—just like dietary fructose—contribute to weight gain.
(30) Unfortunately, by limiting the intake of sugar, many of today's "fad diets" inadvertently increase the consumption of sodium. This is because diets low in sugar are often tasteless, and salt increases their palatability. Of course, substituting one harmful
(35) additive for an equally harmful one is nothing new: manufacturers were quick to promote "low-fat" foods in the 1980's when fat was viewed as the enemy, but increased the sugar content to keep consumers happy. Good nutrition, just like good health, is best viewed
(40) holistically. A well-balanced diet does not focus on any single nutritional additive in isolation. Instead, it uses natural foods to satisfy the body's need for macronutrients (carbohydrates, proteins, fat) while also taking into account the role of vitamins, minerals and
(45) fiber.

1. The primary purpose of the passage is to

(A) argue that excessive consumption of sodium is more harmful than is excessive consumption of sugar
(B) explain why low-carb diets may induce an undesirable dietary habit
(C) call attention to the undesirable effects of sodium intake
(D) reject the view that sugar should be classified as a toxin
(E) compare and contrast the effects of two harmful nutritional substances

2. The author mentions the fact that diets low in carbohydrates are often tasteless (line 33) primarily in order to

(A) distinguish low-carbohydrate diets from low-fat diets
(B) indicate a way in which low-carbohydrate diets promote unhealthy eating habits
(C) explain why low-carbohydrate diets often fail to achieve their primary objectives
(D) illustrate a potential downside unique to low-carbohydrate diets
(E) suggest why an alternative dietary regimen is superior to low-carbohydrate diets

3. Based on the passage, the author would be most likely to agree with which one of the following statements about sodium intake?

(A) It is a necessary component of any diet.
(B) It interferes with the body's ability to absorb nutrients.
(C) It is just as toxic as sugar.
(D) It represents a significant health risk.
(E) In large amounts, it invariably exacerbates hypertension.

4. The author would be most likely to regard low-carbohydrate diets as

    (A) somewhat beneficial, because added sugar has no nutritional value
    (B) clearly healthful, because they limit the consumption of a potentially toxic substance
    (C) overly restrictive of an important macronutrient
    (D) inconsistent with the tenets of a well-balanced diet
    (E) harmful, because they require an increased consumption of sodium   *Causal, or Conditional*

5. Which one of the following best describes the function of the second paragraph of the passage?

    (A) It outlines the structure of the author's central argument.
    (B) It provides the rationale for correcting a misconception described in the first paragraph.
    (C) It explains why an outlook suggested in the first paragraph is potentially harmful.
    (D) It presents research that undermines the argument presented in the first paragraph.
    (E) It supports a course of action recommended in the first paragraph.

6. Which one of the following statements would most appropriately continue the discussion at the end of the passage?

    (A) Clearly, food cannot be judged one component at a time.
    (B) Thus, no single dietary regimen is likely to be completely harmless.
    (C) Nor surprisingly, our evolving views on nutrition are reflected in the dietary choices we make.
    (D) Therefore, manufacturers must strive for greater consistency in their dietary recommendations.
    (E) Otherwise, if one waits long enough, almost any food will be reported as healthful.

Passage #10

(1)

To modern-day actors and their instructors, Russian actor-director Constantin Stanislavski (1863—1938) developed one of the most influential systematic approaches to training actors. The eponymous
(5) "Stanislavski method," succinctly summarized in his first book on acting—*An Actor Prepares* (1936) represents a point of departure for most contemporary acting theories. As with any modern theoretical text in the humanities, however, especially those whose
(10) pedagogical theory originates in the autobiographical or the experiential, full understanding of the Method requires more than a cursory read. Actors quickly realize that Stanislavski's theory needs to be lived (through), acted (out), and experienced both
(15) cognitively and emotionally.

(2)

Stanislavski understood better than anyone else that acting is an inherently relational art. When preparing for a role, an actor is told to draw upon her own emotional recall to recreate a character, but without
(20) ever blurring the boundary between herself and her character. Stanislavski cautions actors to be less concerned with their public appearance than with their own internal dialogue, avoiding self-consciousness at all cost. The central focus of the Method, after all, is to
(25) develop realistic characters.

(3)

Like most intellectuals of his generation, Stanislavski developed a methodology rooted in the metaphysical and the positivistic. As such, his Method presumed a fundamental and seemingly irreducible
(30) difference between actor and spectator, character and self, reality and fantasy. A closer look, however, reveals a far more complex relationship. According to Stanislavski's motto, "an actor does not act, but lives." If so, then his Method has *already* placed life squarely
(35) on stage: actors cannot conceive of the creative process as anything *but* life. As Sharon Carnicke points out in *Stanislavski in Focus* (2008), Stanislavski inadvertently equates experiencing with creating, identifying time on stage with real time. Indeed, one
(40) cannot demand emotional recall from the actor's real life experience without also admitting that acting and living are two sides of the same proverbial coin. The reality of emotions may well be the ultimate source of representational technique, but only insofar as the
(45) boundary between what is "real" and what is "acted" is already blurred. This is precisely why his Method has been such a success: not because of the barriers it sets out to built, but rather because of the barriers it subtly destroys.

1. Which one of the following best summarizes the main point of the passage?

    (A) To help actors develop realistic characters, Stanislavski uses real-life emotions as a source of representational technique.

    (B) By requiring actors to draw upon their own emotional recall in recreating a character, Stanislavski's Method unsettles the fundamental distinctions upon which it is premised.

    (C) In developing his Method of acting, Stanislavski misunderstood the relationship between acting and living.

    (D) Despite its imperfections, Stanislavski's Method is foundational to most contemporary acting theories.

    (E) The primary objective of Stanislavski's Method is to develop characters who display real emotions.

2. It can be inferred from the passage that the author would be most likely to view Stanislavski's Method as

    (A) impressive not merely as a pedagogical theory, but also as a modern theoretical text.

    (B) decidedly successful, despite some questionable presuppositions.

    (C) a pedagogical theory unique in its autobiographical and experiential origins.

    (D) very valuable in theory, but not quite as valuable in practice.

    (E) fundamentally misunderstood by Stanislavski himself.

3. Which one of the following most accurately describes the organization of the material presented in the passage?

    (A) A methodology is described, its theoretical presuppositions are scrutinized, and a counterargument is made.

    (B) A theory is outlined, its drawbacks and advantages are contrasted, and an opinion is ventured.

    (C) The significance of an artistic development is evaluated, conditions that brought about the development are explained, and a judgment of its merits is made.

    (D) A pedagogical approach is evaluated, its central predicament is explained, and a tentative resolution of the predicament is recommended.

    (E) A system is analyzed, its historical relevance is debated, and the assumptions upon which it is premised are undermined.

4. Which one of the following is most analogous to an actor's use of Stanislavski's Method, as described in the passage?

    (A) A physics professor conducts research in string theory in order to question the central tenets of theoretical physics.
    (B) A painter studies Renaissance art in order to make a faithful reproduction of an original painting.
    (C) An runner trains at high altitude in order to prepare for a competitive race, which is held at a lower altitude.
    (D) A pianist digresses from the printed notes in order to introduce a feeling of spontaneity into the performance.
    (E) A photographer takes pictures of her own hometown in order to convey a more vivid sense of nostalgia.

5. The author mentions Sharon Carnicke (line 36) primarily in order to

    (A) illustrate a central tenet of the Method of acting
    (B) emphasize the degree to which the Method demands emotional recall from an actor's real life
    (C) support a critical observation made elsewhere in the passage
    (D) contrast the theory behind the Method of acting with its practical value
    (E) support Stanislavski's understanding of the relationship between acting and living

6. The passage suggests that Stanislavski would be most likely to agree with which one of the following statements?

    (A) Experiencing and creating are virtually indistinguishable from each other.
    (B) An actor can only recreate a character if she is aware of the emotional recall required to do so.
    (C) To recreate a character's emotional state, an actor must have subjectively experienced that state.
    (D) Internal dialogue is antithetical to good acting.
    (E) An actor cannot develop a realistic character without blurring the boundary between herself and her character.

7. The author would be most likely to agree with which one of the following statements about Stanislavski?

    (A) He failed to understand why actors must experience the emotions they perform on stage.
    (B) He was not fully aware of the complex relationship between experiencing and acting.
    (C) He believed that a true actor can never stop acting, even when off stage.
    (D) He intentionally blurred the boundary between acting and living.
    (E) He was convinced that actors are, in some sense, also spectators.

Passage #1 Analysis: Fourth Amendment

This passage discusses two competing views of the proper interpretation of the exclusionary rule, a judge-made rule by which unconstitutionally obtained evidence may be suppressed at trial.

Paragraph One:

The passage begins with a description of the Fourth Amendment right to be free from unreasonable searches and seizures. Next, the author introduces the exclusionary rule, and explains that it is a rarely applied, "extreme sanction" for police misconduct.

Paragraph Two:

In the second paragraph, the author outlines the limitations of the exclusionary rule, as the rule has traditionally been interpreted. According to that interpretation, unlawfully obtained evidence can only be suppressed if the police acted in an intentional, reckless, or repeatedly negligent manner. Mere negligence by the police does not justify suppression of evidence, because the costs of exclusion (defendants go free) outweigh the benefits of deterrence (negligence is not as susceptible to deterrence as reckless or intentional conduct). The cost/benefit analysis favors applying the exclusionary rule only in situations where the unlawful police behavior is generally deterrable.

Paragraph Three:

The author introduces a trend of dissenting judicial opinions arguing for a more expansive interpretation of the exclusionary rule.

Paragraph Four:

In the final paragraph, the author expands on the alternative interpretation of the exclusionary rule, according to which the primary goal of the rule is to provide an individualized remedy for Fourth Amendment violations. While intentional misconduct would still be deterred under this interpretation, the rule would apply to a broader range of cases involving police misconduct, potentially excluding evidence that was obtained through mere negligence.

The passage concludes with the author's assertion that the alternative view is required to protect individuals from unlawful searches and seizures.

VIEWSTAMP Analysis:

There are three **Viewpoints** presented in the passage: the traditional interpretation of the exclusionary rule (lines 16-18 and 24-46); the alternative interpretation of the rule (lines 46-67), and the author's (67-72).

The **Structure** of the passage is as follows:

Paragraph One: Introduce the Fourth Amendment and the exclusionary rule.

Paragraph Two: Explain the limited application of the rule under the traditional interpretation. Describes the cost associated with the decision to suppress, or not to suppress, unlawfully obtained evidence.

Paragraph Three: Introduce the recent trend of dissenting judicial opinions, which comprise an alternative view.

Paragraph Four: Discuss the objectives of the alternative interpretation of the exclusionary rule, and argue that this interpretation should be the one adopted.

The **Tone** of the passage is negative toward the traditional interpretation of the exclusionary rule and positive toward the alternative view. By the end of the passage, the author definitively states that adoption of the alternative view is necessary to safeguard Fourth Amendment liberties.

There are two main **Arguments** advanced in the passage: one defending the traditional interpretation of the exclusionary rule, and the other advocating for an alternative, more expansive interpretation. Each argument weighs the cost of suppressing potentially valuable, but unlawfully obtained evidence at trial (a guilty defendant goes free) against the benefits of deterring unlawful police conduct.

According to the traditional interpretation, the cost/benefit analysis favors applying the exclusionary rule only in situations where the unlawful police behavior is generally deterrable. The dissenting view supports a more expansive interpretation that would also exclude evidence obtained through negligent police behavior. The author supports this view by observing that the primary goal of the exclusionary rule is to provide an individualized remedy for Fourth Amendment violations.

The **Main Point** of the passage is that the alternative, more expansive interpretation of the exclusionary rule is better suited to protect against the liberties guaranteed by the Fourth Amendment than is the traditional interpretation.

Question #1: GR, Main Point. The correct answer choice is (B)

The main point of the passage is prephrased in our VIEWSTAMP analysis above.

Answer choice (A): According to the passage, the Fourth Amendment prohibits any unreasonable search or seizure, regardless of whether it results from intentional or merely negligent behavior. Although the traditional view of the exclusionary rule provides no *remedy* for an unreasonable search or seizure that results from negligent behavior, such a search or seizure is nonetheless prohibited by the Fourth Amendment.

Answer choice (B): This is the correct answer choice, because it restates the author's main point. Here, the "expanded interpretation of the exclusionary rule proposed in recent dissenting opinions" is a reference to the alternative view the author thinks provides a proper, individualized remedy for Fourth Amendment violations.

Answer choice (C): Although the alternative interpretation of the exclusionary rule is better suited to protect against Fourth Amendment violations than is the traditional interpretation, the latter still protects against intentional or flagrant violations. This answer choice contains an exaggeration and misses a key nuance of the debate.

Answer choice (D): Although excluding evidence from trial does carry certain costs, this is not the main point of the passage.

Answer choice (E): While courts have consistently held that the traditional view is the proper interpretation of the exclusionary rule, the author does not discuss *when* this view was first established.

Question #2: CR, Must. The correct answer choice is (D)

From the discussion in the first paragraph, we know that an arrest based on neither a warrant nor probable cause constitutes a violation of the Fourth Amendment that triggers application of the exclusionary rule (lines 9-16). From this, we can infer that a warrantless arrest is unconstitutional if the arresting officer had no probable cause to make the arrest.

Answer choice (A): An arrest constitutes "unreasonable seizure" if the arresting officer had neither a warrant nor probable cause to perform the arrest (lines 9-16). Clearly, then, a warrantless arrest would not necessarily violate the Fourth Amendment if the police had probable cause to make the arrest.

Answer choice (B): This answer choice is incorrect for two reasons: First, as previously discussed, a warrantless arrest is not necessarily a Fourth Amendment violation, and so the exclusionary rule may not be implicated by the arrest. Second, even if the arrest is deemed unconstitutional, the exclusionary rule is applied only when the police misconduct is intentional, reckless, or systematically negligent (under the traditional view). Without knowing this level of culpability on the part of the police, we cannot say whether the exclusionary rule would necessarily require the suppression of evidence.

Answer choice (C): The author stated that police may lawfully arrest a person even without a warrant, so long as the officer had probable cause to believe the person may have committed a criminal offense. So, the fact the arrest was made without a warrant does not by itself imply that any police misconduct was involved.

Answer choice (D): This is the correct answer choice, as it is consistent with our prephrase above.

Answer choice (E): While it is true that the parenthetical example provided in the third paragraph (lines 38-41) described a warrantless arrest that resulted from the failure of police to remove a withdrawn arrest warrant from the agency's database, this one example does not establish that a warrantless arrest *typically* occurs for this reason.

Question #3: CR, Must. The correct answer choice is (C)

To answer this question correctly, it is critical to understand the rationale behind narrowly interpreting the exclusionary rule (second paragraph): the costs of suppressing evidence might outweigh the benefits. So what are those costs? The possibility of guilty defendants going free (lines 34-35). This prephrase agrees with answer choice (C).

Answer choice (A): The phrase "wrongful convictions" implies that a person was convicted of something the person did not do. The cost of suppressing evidence at trial is that the guilty might escape justice, not that the innocent would be convicted.

Answer choice (B): The author never addressed the issue of respect for the judiciary.

Answer choice (C): This is the correct answer choice, as it agrees with our prephrase above.

Answer choice (D): This is an Opposite answer choice. The purpose of the exclusionary rule is to deter, not encourage, police misconduct.

Answer choice (E): This answer choice would only be attractive if you assumed that the release of guilty defendants would lead to an increase in the amount of violent crime. Reasonable as such an assumption might be in the real world, the question stem clearly states that the correct answer choice must be a cost *mentioned in the passage*. Since an increase in the amount of violent crime is never discussed as a cost associated with the application of the exclusionary rule, answer choice (E) is incorrect.

Question #4: GR, Must, SP. The correct answer choice is (E)

As with Question #3, passage Structure and Argumentation are once again key. The traditional interpretation of the exclusionary rule is discussed in the second paragraph, which will prove useful in validating the correct answer choice to this Subject Perspective question.

Answer choice (A): While the traditional view does not recognize an individualized *remedy* for a violation of the Fourth Amendment, all sides agree that the protection against unreasonable searches and seizures is an individual *right*.

Answer choice (B): It is clear from the second paragraph that the primary purpose of the exclusionary rule is to deter future police misconduct, not to punish past misconduct.

Answer choice (C): This is an attractive, but incorrect, answer choice. Although merely negligent conduct does not trigger application of the exclusionary rule, *systematically* negligent conduct does (lines 24-30). This is because systematic negligence, just like reckless or intentional conduct, is considered "susceptible to appreciable deterrence" (lines 30-35).

Answer choice (D): This is an Opposite answer, because the exclusionary rule is considered by courts to be an "extreme sanction" for police misconduct (lines 16-18).

Answer choice (E): This is the correct answer choice. According to the traditional interpretation of the exclusionary rule, unlawfully obtained evidence can only be suppressed if the police acted in an intentional, reckless, or repeatedly negligent manner. Mere negligence by the police does not justify suppression of evidence, because the costs of exclusion (defendants go free) outweigh the benefits of deterrence.

Question #5: CR, Strengthen—PR. The correct answer choice is (A)

To answer this question correctly, you need to identify a principle that would strengthen the argument offered in support of the alternative interpretation of the exclusionary rule. If you understood the Structure of this passage, you can quickly locate this argument in the fourth paragraph.

In that paragraph, the author suggests that the primary goal of the exclusionary rule is to provide an individualized remedy for Fourth Amendment violations. While deterrence of intentional or reckless conduct is still important, the rule would need to implicate cases involving negligent police misconduct. Skeptics would probably counter this argument by noting that negligence is not susceptible to deterrence, and so the cost of exclusion outweighs the benefits of deterrence (lines 30-35). To strengthen the author's argument, you need to show that negligence can, in fact, be successfully deterred.

Answer choice (A): This is the correct answer choice. This principle clearly suggests that negligent conduct can be deterred: if a police officer knows that he will be responsible for violating an individual's constitutional rights, then that officer can take steps to minimize the likelihood of such violations. If true, this principle suggests that the benefits of deterrence in cases of negligence might actually outweigh the cost of excluding potentially valuable evidence, bolstering the author's argument.

Answer choice (B): This answer choice suggests that harm resulting from negligence is not deterrable, which corroborates the traditional interpretation of the exclusionary rule, not the alternative view.

Answer choice (C): As with answer choice (B), this principle suggests that negligent police conduct is not deterrable, bolstering the traditional view.

Answer choice (D): If the conviction of guilty defendants takes precedence over the protection of individual liberties, then why have an exclusionary rule at all? Clearly, this principle supports a vastly different position from the one adopted by the author.

Answer choice (E): This principle establishes a caveat for protecting individual rights - such protection is justified as long as the social cost of doing so is not too high. How high is "too high" remains unclear. If the release of a guilty defendant elevates the cost beyond what is reasonable, one can easily argue that this principle would strengthen the traditional interpretation of the exclusionary rule.

Question #6: GR, Must, P. The correct answer choice is (B)

If you are short one time, you may want to tackle this question first. At the most general level, the purpose of this passage is to outline the limitations of a legal doctrine for safeguarding a constitutional right, and argue in favor of lifting some of these limitations.

Answer choice (A): The passage provides some background information regarding the Fourth Amendment, but does not discuss its history.

Answer choice (B): This is the correct answer choice, as it is consistent with our prephrase above.

Answer choice (C): The passage does not address the standards required for police to obtain a warrant.

Answer choice (D): This is an Opposite answer choice, as the author is critical of the traditional view of the exclusionary rule.

Answer choice (E): The social cost of implementing the alternative view is alluded to in the last paragraph (some guilty defendants may go free), but this is clearly not the primary purpose of the passage.

Passage #2 Analysis: Osage

Paragraph One:

The passage begins with an introduction to the Osage, a Native American people for whom the author clearly has much respect. Though the Osage were fierce and cunning, the author points out, their respect for human life and desire to minimize bloodshed could be seen in the Osage approach to conflict, both before and after the United States westward expansion.

This introduction sets the stage for the remainder of the passage, in which the author discusses the Osage use of bluff war before the expansion, as well as the tactics they employed after their resettlement.

Paragraph Two:

As an example of a military strategy that reflects the Osage people's desire to minimize loss of life, the author introduces the tactic of "bluff war." Bluff war, we learn, consisted of Osage warriors baiting their enemy away from their encampments toward terrain more favorable to the Osage. The goal was to make the enemy lose control and attack without planning ahead. By using guile, the Osage were able to defeat stronger enemy forces while minimizing the loss of life.

Paragraph Three:

The third paragraph performs a transitional role, as we learn of the U.S. expansion into the West and the eventual resettlement of the Osage in Oklahoma. The author suggests that the resettlement brought great hardship to the Osage people, but also mentions that their new location may have hidden benefits.

Paragraph Four:

In the closing paragraph, the author discusses how the Osage adapted their traditional strategies to the new challenges that emerged as encroaching cattlemen, with the implicit support of the United States Army, drove their own herds of cattle to Osage lands to graze. Rather than engage a larger, stronger enemy forces in direct conflict, the Osage figured out a way to lease their land to the cattlemen who needed it. Since each herd owner would now guard his own parcel against encroachment by others, the Osage essentially "outsourced" the task of patrolling their land. They avoided military conflict, and also got paid for it.

VIEWSTAMP Analysis:

The only **Viewpoint** specifically presented in this passage is that of the author, who clearly respects and admires the Osage people. The passage also provides insights into the perspective of the Osage who, despite being fierce and cunning warriors, sought to minimize loss of life whenever possible.

The **Structure** of the passage is as follows:

Paragraph One: Introduce the Osage as cunning warriors who nonetheless avoided direct attacks in an effort to minimize loss of life.

Paragraph Two: Outline the concept of bluff war, and show how the tactic could be used to secure a strategic advantage while successfully avoiding full-scale conflict.

Paragraph Three: Discuss the resettlement of the Osage and foreshadow a potential benefit conferred by that resettlement.

Paragraph Four: Describe how the Osage adjusted to their new circumstances, specifically adapting their traditional tactics to the new type of conflict that emerged as a result of their resettlement.

The author's **Tone** is quite favorable toward the Osage, a traditionally underrepresented group. The author is critical of the encroaching cattlemen and, less explicitly, of the United States government who resettled the Osage.

The main **Argument** in the passage is that the Osage were a cunning people who developed the tactic of bluff warfare, and were able to adapt the strategy to an entirely new context following their resettlement.

The **Main Point** of the passage is that the Osage were a fierce and cunning people whose respect for human life could be seen in their approach to conflict both before and after their forced resettlement.

Question #1: GR, Main Point. The correct answer choice is (D)

The VIEWSTAMP analysis above provides a readily prephrased answer to this Main Point question: the Osage were cunning warriors whose "bluff war" military strategy not only showed respect for human life, but also allowed the Osage to face certain challenges during the post-resettlement period.

Answer choice (A): While undeniably true, this answer choice only reflects the content of the first paragraph, not of the passage as a whole.

Answer choice (B): This answer choice provides information that was referenced in the third paragraph. While it passes the Fact Test, this answer choice is certainly not the main point of the passage.

Answer choice (C): This is an Opposite Answer. The author clearly admires the Osage, and underscores the fact that they were able to adapt to their new reality quite well.

Answer choice (D): This is the correct answer choice, as it agrees with our prephrase above.

Answer choice (E): From the last paragraph, we know that it was actually the Osage who managed to set up a system in which cattlemen fenced in Osage grasslands to protect their own interests and those of the Osage. This answer choice is factually false, and certainly does not capture the main point of the passage.

Question #2: SP, Must, P. The correct answer choice is (B)

A prephrased answer to this question can be found in the Structure portion of the VIEWSTAMP analysis above. The third paragraph introduces the unfortunate fact that the Osage were forcibly resettled, but also alludes to the possibility that the new lands would potentially provide some benefit.

Answer choice (A): As discussed above, the author uses the third paragraph to transition from an earlier point in Osage history to their resettlement, and to allude to the potential benefits associated with their new lands.

This is a clever wrong answer choice, because it is true that the third paragraph links together two periods of Osage history. They did not, however, use bluff war against encroaching cattlemen, so this choice fails the Fact Test and cannot be the right answer to this Must Be True question.

Answer choice (B): This is the correct answer choice. As discussed above, the author uses the third paragraph to transition from an earlier point in Osage history to their resettlement, and also to allude to the potential benefits associated with their new lands.

Answer choice (C): The passage is not intended to highlight the ferocity of the Osage, but rather their cleverness and respect for life. Further, this choice fails to mention the reference to the new, potentially beneficial lands, suggested at the end of the third paragraph.

Answer choice (D): Although this choice mentions the author's reference to the potentially beneficial grasslands on which the Osage were settled, there is nothing about the paragraph's transition from pre- to post-relocation eras.

Answer choice (E): The author does discuss the Osage respect for human life, but this discussion takes place in the first paragraph rather than the third. Furthermore, this answer choice fails to mention the central purpose of the third paragraph, as explained in our prephrase above.

Question #3: GR, MustX. The correct answer choice is (C)

The answer to this Global Reference, MustX question would be difficult to prephrase. The four incorrect answer choices will contain statements that were mentioned in the passage; the correct answer will not contain such a statement.

Answer choice (A): How the Osage baited their enemies is discussed in lines 15-23.

Answer choice (B): The fact that some of the encroaching cattlemen supplied the U.S. army with beef is mentioned in lines 43-44. This is presented as a reason why the Osage did not want to attack the encroaching cattlemen.

Answer choice (C): This is the correct answer choice, Although the Osage were known as a fierce and cunning people, the only fighting strategy discussed in the passage is that of bluff war. A military strategy of ambush attacks carried out by overwhelming numbers is not mentioned anywhere in the passage, making answer choice (C) the correct answer choice to this MustX question.

Answer choice (D): The fact that the Osage convinced cattlemen to pay them for the privilege of patrolling their borders is mentioned in the last paragraph. It show how the Osage were able to cleverly leverage their position and navigate the challenging terrain entailed by their relocation.

Answer choice (E): This answer choice can easily be confirmed by reference to the third paragraph of the passage, so it cannot be the correct answer to this MustX question.

Question #4: GR, Must, Expansion. The correct answer choice is (A)

This Expansion question asks us to identify the most appropriate title for the passage. Such questions typically reflect the Main Point, albeit in a more succinct way. Here, the author is primarily focused on the ability of the cunning Osage to adapt and advance their own interests while minimizing major conflict and bloodshed.

Considering that the correct answer choice might reference some or all of the points prephrased above, the answer can be difficult to prephrase with precision. So, proceed by the process of elimination, and try to narrow down the range of possible contenders before selecting the answer choice that best relays the focus of the passage.

Answer choice (A): This is the correct answer choice, as it is the only answer choice that highlights both the military strategy of the Osage (second paragraph) and their ability to adapt to changing circumstances (fourth paragraph).

Answer choice (B): Although the Osage may have been able to use clever tactics to fight their enemies, there is no suggestion that they achieved military predominance in the pre-relocation era. As such, this choice does not provide an appropriate title for the passage.

Answer choice (C): The author mentions the fact that the Osage would sometimes bait their enemy in order to draw them from their fortified encampments, but the passage is not centrally focused on that point.

Answer choice (D): In the last paragraph of the passage, the author mentions that some of the cattlemen who were encroaching on Osage land enjoyed the implicit protection of the United States Army, whom they supplied with beef. This is certainly not a main focus of the passage, however, so it cannot be the right choice.

Answer choice (E): In the third paragraph, the author mentions the fact that the eventual Osage settlement included lush grasslands ideal for grazing. However, this is clearly not the main point of the passage.

Question #5: GR, Must, AP. The correct answer choice is (D)

To answer this Global Reference question correctly, we need to identify an answer choice with which the author would most likely agree. The lack of specificity makes the answer difficult to prephrase, but the right answer choice is likely to reflect the author's positive attitude towards the Osage people.

Answer choice (A): While we know that the Osage were able to adjust their tactics after resettlement, there is no reason to suspect that they were unable to maintain their cultural heritage.

Answer choice (B): This is an Opposite answer. In the second paragraph, the author states that the Osage would sometimes bait their enemy away from fortified positions, not forced them to retreat to those positions.

Answer choice (C): This answer choice may seem attractive given the lush grasslands and the success with which the Osage seem to have adapted to their new environment. However, there is no evidence that the Osage actually "thrived" in the post-relocation era. This answer choice is too broad to be provable and contains an exaggeration.

Answer choice (D): This is the correct answer choice. The passage clearly supports this assertion, as evidenced by the discussion in the second and fourth paragraphs.

Answer choice (E): In the first paragraph, the author states that the Osage lived and hunted across a territory that now includes the states of Oklahoma, Kansas, Arkansas, and Missouri. However, the passage provides no support for the claim that the Osage lived primarily in the territory that would become the state of Kansas.

Passage #3 Analysis: Vegetal Behavior

Paragraph One:

Most science passages begin by outlining some unexplained phenomenon or unresolved question, and this one is no exception. Here, the question is how vegetal behavior manages to be so sensitive and complex. The author presents various observations about the incredible complexity of plant behavior, none of which could be verified (until now). The paragraph concludes by introducing plant neurobiology as the field likely to provide an answer to all of the aforementioned questions, and we can expect to learn more about it later on in the passage.

Paragraph Two:

As predicted, this paragraph defines the academic scope of plant neurobiology, highlighting the significance of its contributions to the scientific community. The author emphasizes the field's interdisciplinary focus, noting not only the various disciplines that have influenced its development, but also the way in which it forced scientists in other fields to reevaluate their conception of "cognition."

Paragraph Three:

The third paragraph presents the author's main point: advances in plant intelligence require institutional support, which can only be provided by establishing a Department of Plant Neurobiology. The author acknowledges some of the arguments against this recommendation, but defends it by predicting a variety of research directions that can only be pursued by a department dedicated solely to plant neurobiology.

VIEWSTAMP Analysis:

There are four **Viewpoints** outlined in this passage: those of the biologists mentioned in the first paragraph; the neurobiologists discussed in the second paragraph; the opponents of establishing a department of plant neurobiology in the third paragraph; and the author's—also in third paragraph.

The **Structure** of the passage is as follows:

> Paragraph One: Describe instances of vegetal behavior that were either unknown, or impossible to prove, before the advent of plant neurobiology.

> Paragraph Two: Define the scope of plant neurobiology and highlight the significance of its contributions.

> Paragraph Three: Recommend the establishment of a department dedicated solely to research in plant neurobiology, and counter some of the possible arguments against it.

The author's **Tone** is enthusiastic about the promise held by plant neurobiology, and forceful in his recommendation that the discipline is worthy of institutional support.

There are two **Arguments** presented here: one in favor of establishing a department dedicated solely to plant neurobiology, and one against it. The first argument is supported observations made in the second and third paragraphs.

The **Main Point** of the passage is the recent advanced in the field of plant intelligence warrant establishing a Department of Plant Neurobiology (lines 38-42). The passage as a whole supports that recommendation. Broadly speaking, the purpose of the passage is to recommend a future course of action.

Question #1: GR, Main Point. The correct answer choice is (C)

The answer to the Main Point question should always be prephrased. See VIEWSTAMP analysis above.

Answer choice (A) is incorrect. While plant neurobiology may have deepened our understanding of the incredible complexity that underlies vegetal behavior (lines 16-18), this observation merely supports the appeal made in the final paragraph of the passage.

Answer choice (B) is attractive, because it represents the main point of the second paragraph. However, the extent to which our understanding of cognition has evolved is not the main point of the passage as a whole.

Answer choice (C) is the correct answer choice, because the passage as a whole is intended to support the recommendation offered in the third paragraph: plants possess cognitive capacities that can only be appreciated through the autonomous study of plant neurobiology (lines 38-42 and 60-63).

Answer choice (D) is incorrect, because—while true—it is not the main point of the passage.

Answer choice (E) is also incorrect, because it only captures a point made in the second paragraph of the passage (lines 30-34), which is not the main point of the passage as a whole.

Question #2: CR, MustX. The correct answer choice is (C)

To answer this Must Be True/EXCEPT question, proceed by the process of elimination: four of the answer choices will contain examples of known vegetal behavior, and will be incorrect. Questions of this type are usually time-consuming, because the correct answer choice must be the one we *cannot* prove by referring to information contained in the passage.

Answer choice (A) is incorrect, because the ability of plants to process informational input is discussed in line 8.

Answer choice (B) is incorrect, because the ability of plants to communicate danger, which is a type of information, is discussed in line 15.

Answer choice (C) is the correct answer choice, because experiencing pain is not an example of *known* vegetal behavior. Instead, it is discussed in lines 52-57 as an example of something scientists are bound to discover *in the future*.

Answer choice (D) is incorrect, because the author describes the sophisticated signal-interaction behavior observed in plants in lines 36-37. The passage also contains evidence suggesting that plants can communicate hazards through biochemical cues (lines 15-16), which is an example of signal-interaction behavior.

Answer choice (E) is incorrect, because the ability of plants to use biochemical cues is discussed in line 16.

Question #3: SR, Must, P. The correct answer choice is (E)

This Specific Reference/Purpose question asks us to explain why the author observes that "plants lack the neural or synaptic structures that give rise to animal cognition" in lines 33-34. Such questions almost always require a more thorough understanding of the context in which the quoted reference appears, and their answers should always be prephrased.

Answer choice (A) is the Opposite answer. The author argues that plants possess cognitive capacities even *without* exhibiting neural or synaptic structures, suggesting that such structures are *not* a necessary precondition for cognitive function.

Answer choice (B) is incorrect, because the author does not seek to *differentiate* between plant and animal cognition. On the contrary: she argues that both possess cognitive capacities, despite their physiological differences.

Answer choice (C) is incorrect, because the difficulty of attributing cognitive abilities to plants is not discussed in the second paragraph of the passage.

Answer choice (D) is incorrect, because it confuses a necessary condition for a sufficient one. The author observes that plants lack the neural or synaptic structures that give rise to animal cognition in order to show that certain physiological attributes are no longer *necessary* to prove cognitive function. The author never discusses what conditions might be sufficient to prove cognitive function.

Answer choice (E) is the correct answer choice. The author mentions the fact that plants lack neural structures in order to show that such physiological attributes are no longer necessary to establish cognitive function. This, in turn, supports the author's contention that our understanding of cognition has evolved over time (lines 34-37).

Question #4: GR, Must, O. The correct answer choice is (B)

Again, we should seek to prephrase an answer based on our understanding of Passage Organization: by discussing the various contributions already made by the field of plant neurobiology, the second paragraph provides support for the recommendation offered in the third paragraph.

Answer choice (A) is incorrect. The final paragraph raises the issue of whether a department of plant neurobiology has a clear rationale (lines 42-44), given that its academic objectives can be achieved by plant physiologists. Nowhere in the second paragraph does the author anticipate such an objection, and no indication is given as to whether or not neurobiology is uniquely qualified to answer questions concerning vegetal behavior.

Answer choice (B) is the correct answer choice. By explaining why research in plant neurobiology is scientifically significant, the second paragraph helps justify the recommendation in favor of establishing a department of plant neurobiology outlined in the third paragraph.

Answer choice (C) is half-right, half-wrong. The final paragraph clearly suggests that establishing an autonomous department of plant neurobiology is potentially significant; however, this is the main point of the passage, not a premise in support of the argument made in the second paragraph.

Answer choice (D) is incorrect. The second paragraph does not describe a controversial view, as the cognitive capacity of plants is not under debate. The issue is whether research in plant neurobiology warrants establishing a separate academic department dedicated to that field—an issue raised in the third paragraph, not in the second.

Answer choice (E) is also half-right, half-wrong. The second paragraph describes the biological phenomenon of plant cognition, but its significance is not debated in the final paragraph. The controversy only concerns whether or not a department of plant neurobiology has a clear rationale.

Question #5: GR, MustX. The correct answer choice is (A)

To answer this Must Be True/EXCEPT question, proceed by the process of elimination: four of the answer choices will contain examples of known vegetal behavior, and will be incorrect.

Answer choice (A) is the correct answer choice, because the author only enumerates those areas of research that fall *outside* the scope of plant physiology (lines 49-52). No information is given as to how research in plant physiology can contribute to our future understanding of vegetal behavior.

Answer choice (B) is incorrect, because the question is answered in lines 26-37.

Answer choice (C) is incorrect, because the question is answered in lines 26-29.

Answer choice (D) is incorrect, because the question is answered in lines 19-22.

Answer choice (E) is incorrect, because the question is answered in lines 52-56.

Question #6: GR, Must, Expansion. The correct answer choice is (D)

To answer this Expansion question correctly, you need to understand both the purpose and the tone of the passage. The two are prephrased in our discussion of VIEWSTAMP above.

Answer choice (A) is incorrect because the author's tone is not as descriptive as we would expect from a textbook. Indeed, the final paragraph advocates a course of action that is unlikely to be found in an educational source.

Answer choice (B) is incorrect, because the passage makes no mention of any experimental studies for which the author could conceivably seek funding.

Answer choice (C) is attractive, but incorrect. The polemic tone in the final paragraph may well belong to an editorial, but a national newspaper is unlikely to urge establishing a department of plant neurobiology "at our university" (lines 41-42), let alone refer to other scientists as "my colleagues" (line 42). Editorials are opinion pieces written by senior editorial staff of a newspaper, not by contributing writers.

Answer choice (D) is the correct answer choice. The reference to "our university" in lines 41-42 suggests that the author is most likely a senior university administrator or a professor, whose job is to convince his or her "colleagues" (line 42) that a certain strategic initiative is worthy of institutional support. The author makes this appeal only after describing the scientific contributions made by plant neurobiologists, suggesting that the first and second paragraphs are meant to support the proposal outlined in the third paragraph.

Answer choice (E) is incorrect. The author is clearly convinced that vegetal behavior is incredibly sensitive and complex (lines 1-3), a belief she supports with observations involving plant cognition, signal-interaction, biochemical communication, etc. However, the purpose of the passage is not purely descriptive, as would be the case if the passage were drawn from a study on vegetal behavior. The third paragraph clearly advocates a particular course of action, which is inconsistent with the objectives typically associated with scientific studies.

Question #7: SR, Weaken. The correct answer choice is (B)

Here, we need to weaken the author's argument that establishing a department of plant neurobiology as an autonomous discipline is both a sufficient, and a necessary condition for appreciating vegetal behavior. While arriving at a precise prephrase might be difficult to do, think about the ways in which such a department would compromise the objectives it sets out to reach.

Answer choice (A) is incorrect, because the author acknowledges the contributions made by other fields of study to plant neurobiology (lines 21-22). Just because earlier work in plant physiology has paved the way for most of the recent advances has no bearing on the issue of whether or not plant neurobiology should be regarded as an autonomous discipline *in the future*.

Answer choice (B) is the correct answer choice. If turning plant neurobiology into an autonomous field detracts from its interdisciplinary focus, then at least some of the research directions outlined in the final paragraph may not come to fruition. Note that in the second paragraph the author describes the primary focus of the field as "*inherently* interdisciplinary" (line 25). It is reasonable to conclude that any action threatening to compromise a central feature of plant neurobiology would also compromise the quality of its research.

Answer choice (C) is incorrect, because the author never argues that universities represent the *only* source of institutional support for plant neurobiology.

Answer choice (D) is incorrect, because the potential overlap between plant neurobiology and other disciplines is taken into account in the second paragraph. Even if plant neurobiologists rely on methods and techniques developed for use in other disciplines, it is still possible that neurobiologists are uniquely capable of understanding the complexity of vegetal behavior.

Answer choice (E) is incorrect. Even if plant neurobiology is not the only academic field conducting research in vegetal behavior, it is still possible that plant neurobiology is the only field whose contributions are both necessary, and sufficient, for appreciating the complexity of vegetal behavior.

Question #8: SR, Parallel. The correct answer choice is (A)

Although a prephrased answer to this Parallel Reasoning question would be difficult to produce, examine the opponents' position closely: they object to the establishment of a department in plant neurobiology, primarily because it would be redundant—the same objectives, in principle, can be achieved by plant physiologists. Apply the Test of Abstraction: your job is to identify an analogous situation, in which a course of action is rejected because its objectives can be achieved by an existing process or product.

Answer choice (A) is the correct answer choice. A car manufacturer refusing to develop a new type of electric car is analogous to a scientist who refuses to support a department dedicated to plant neurobiology. The rationale in both cases is roughly the same: the objectives of plant neurobiology can arguably be achieved by plant physiologists, just like the environmental benefits of electric cars can be attained by hybrid models. In both instances, the new product or entity is made redundant by a currently existing product.

Answer choice (B) is incorrect, because the argument described in lines 42-45 does not weigh the benefits of establishing a department in plant neurobiology against its costs. No analogous relationship is presented in the passage.

Answer choice (C) is incorrect, because here the manufacturer questions the environmental benefits of electric cars, which no clear parallel to the position discussed in lines 42-45. The value of the scientific contributions made by plant neurobiology is never under debate.

Answer choice (D) is attractive, but incorrect. Here, as well as in the passage, a course of action is rejected because of a faulty rationale. However, the premises supporting the conclusion differ. In answer choice (D), the manufacturer suspects that there is no scientific consensus on the issue of global warming, implying that electric cars may be offering a solution to an inexistent problem. No analogous argument is made in the passage, as the opponents never argue that plant neurobiologists are studying a phenomenon that may not, in fact, exist. The existence of plant intelligence or cognition is not under debate.

Answer choice (E) is incorrect, because the lack of required infrastructure to support electric cars has no analogous premise in the argument outlined in the beginning of the third paragraph. The opponents never argue, for instance, that a department dedicated to plant neurobiology should not be established because of limited technical or financial resources.

Passage Set #4 Analysis: Andrew Kerr

Passage A

The author of passage A outlines the critical reception of Andrew Kerr's work, elaborating on a particularly unfavorable critical view.

Paragraph One:

In the first paragraph, we learn that Andrew Kerr is a writer with a criminal past, which seems to bear some resemblance to the subject matter of his work. We also learn that Kerr's scholars use his fictional world to find clues about his life. Most importantly, the first paragraph provides an insight into the author's own views regarding Kerr and his critical reception: the judgmental attitude shared by his critics has prevented them from appreciating the "poetic brilliance" of Andrew Kerr.

Paragraph Two:

This paragraph elaborates on Mark Newman's particularly negative critical view of Kerr and his work. Newman regards Kerr as a thief as well as a bad playwright, and seems particularly bothered by the latter's penchant for meta-theater. While "meta-theater" is not explicitly defined here, we can infer that—in its ideal form—it interweaves multiple plays-within-a-play and still maintains a coherent narrative structure. Notably, according to Newman, Kerr failed to achieve this artistic objective.

Passage B

Passage B focuses on the content and critical reception of *On the Porch*, Andrew Kerr's final meta-theatrical production.

Paragraph One:

The passage opens with a description of the plot line of *On the Porch*. It is important to realize that *On the Porch* is not an experimental theater in itself; rather, its plot is *about* an experimental theater, which flops and is replaced by a brothel. Both performances entail role-playing, though the latter assumes a more prurient (i.e. indecent) form.

Paragraph Two:

This paragraph suggests that *On the Porch* received popular acclaim, but only at the expense of turning it into a satire in order to appeal to a broader audience.

Paragraph Three:

In conclusion, the author offers a glimpse into Andrew Kerr's own philosophical beliefs about truth and illusion, which revel in ambiguity. This is the only section of the passage that provides any explicit information about Kerr's own viewpoints, which is why it should be highlighted.

Passage Similarities and Differences

Both passages discuss aspects of Andrew Kerr's work. Additionally, both mention meta-theater, although only passage B elaborates on a particular example of it. Both authors appear to have a favorable view of Kerr.

While the passages have similar topics and express similar views, their function and scope differ. Passage A focuses on Kerr's critical reception, which the author illustrates by discussing the views of Mark Newman. Meanwhile, passage B focuses on the reception of a particular play—*On the Porch*—focusing on a different set of viewpoints (the directors' and their audience). The tone in passage A is somewhat defensive, while the tone in passage B is more detached and academic. Kerr's own viewpoints are expressly stated in passage B, but not in A.

Question #1: GR, Main Point. The correct answer choice is (A)

The answer to this question is prephrased in the VIEWSTAMP analysis above.

Answer choice (A) is the correct answer choice. The first paragraph of passage A outlines the negative critical reception of Andrew Kerr's work, and the second paragraph supports this view by describing one study that exemplifies this reception. The author's own position is revealed in lines 11-12, in which she expresses regret the critics have not appreciated Kerr's "poetic brilliance." This prephrase agrees with answer choice (A).

Answer choice (B) is incorrect. The author neither illustrates nor elaborates on the idea that some of the themes that inhabit Andrew Kerr's fictional world are drawn from his criminal past. Even if true, this is not the main point of the passage.

Answer choice (C) is incorrect for two reasons: First, we have no evidence that the author regards Newman's study as "well-informed." As an avid fan of Andrew Kerr's work, the author would have little appreciation for the views expressed in the study. Second, the main point of the passage is not to discuss Mark Newman's biography of Andrew Kerr, which is merely mentioned as an example meant to substantiate a broader claim.

Answer choice (D) is incorrect, because it describes an assumption of the "scholars [who] frequently examine Kerr's fictional world for clues that could reveal the 'real' story of their author" (lines 5-7). This is not the author's position, let alone the main point of the passage.

Answer choice (E) is incorrect, because it presents a position most likely shared by some of Kerr's critics, not by the author herself.

Question #2: GR, Must, P. The correct answer choice is (B)

To answer this question correctly, you need to understand the overall purpose and main point of each passage. As discussed in our VIEWSTAMP analysis, the author of passage A admires Kerr's work but regrets its critical reception; meanwhile, passage B focuses on a particular example of his work. Choose a pair of titles consistent with these two ideas.

Answer choice (A) is half-right, half-wrong. Whereas "Meta-theater *On the Porch*" would be a somewhat acceptable title for passage B, passage A does not attempt to answer the question "Who is Andrew Kerr?" It is the scholars whose views are discussed in the passage that are trying to piece together the "real story" of the playwright, not the author herself.

Answer choice (B) is the correct answer choice. The title for passage A is appropriate: "Life Edited" refers to the biographical accounts furnished by Newman and other scholars, whose attempts to "correct and clarify" certain aspects of Kerr's biography show a decidedly moralistic streak. Similarly, the second part of the title alludes to the main point of the passage, which is that Kerr's poetic brilliance did not receive the appreciation it deserves.

The title for passage B is also appropriate: its author is preoccupied with Kerr's meta-theatrical production *On the Porch*, focusing specifically on the interplay between fiction and reality in the first and third paragraphs. Thus, "Truth and Illusion *On the Porch*" would properly reflect the general content of passage B.

Answer choice (C) is incorrect for two reasons: First, the author of passage A is not particularly judgmental about Kerr's past. If anyone is trying to decide whether Kerr is more of a criminal than a playwright, it is Mark Newman et al. Secondly, the author of passage B never suggested that *On the Porch* is a flop. The only thing that "flopped" was the "play within the play" (Note that *On the Porch* itself was successful—see line 40).

Answer choice (D) is half-right, half-wrong. The title "Once a Criminal, Always a Genius: Andrew Kerr and the Dubious Honor of Being a Thief" would be virtually perfect for passage A: it shows not only the author's appreciation of Kerr's artistic talents, but it also acknowledges the legacy of his criminal past. Unfortunately, "Meta-theater in Weimar Germany" misses the point of passage B entirely. There are no claims made about Weimar Germany or its theatrical legacy, except for the fact that Kerr's play was set in Weimar Germany.

Answer choice (E) is incorrect. Passage A makes no effort to tell the "real" story of Andrew Kerr (maybe the critics mentioned in it do). Furthermore, "True or False? Find Out *On the Porch!*" sounds like a Broadway poster, which clearly that does not reflect the purpose of passage B.

Question #3: GR, Must. The correct answer choice is (D)

This question asks us to determine a textual element explicitly mentioned in both passages. While arriving at a suitable prephrase would be difficult, use the process of elimination: any answer choice containing an element not explicitly mentioned in *both* passages will be incorrect.

Answer choice (A) is incorrect, because only passage B mentions role-playing (line 36)

Answer choice (B) is incorrect, because only passage A mentions narrative structure (line 25)

Answer choice (C) is incorrect, because only passage B mentions the theatrical plot of a play (line 44)

Answer choice (D) the correct answer choice. Meta-theater is mentioned in passage A (lines 22-23) as well as passage B (lines 28-29).

Answer choice (E) is incorrect, because only passage A *explicitly* mentions any sort of moral judgments being made (line 8).

Question #4: SR, Must, SP. The correct answer choice is (D)

To answer this question correctly, viewpoint identification and passage structure are both key. Andrew Kerr's views are discussed in the last paragraph of passage B, which would provide a suitable reference point in approaching this Subject Perspective question.

Answer choice (A) is incorrect, because we have no way of knowing whether Andrew Kerr regarded the negative critical reception of his work as inconsequential. Furthermore, even if he might regard it as "inherently subjective," this cannot be proven with the information provided. Remember: when answering Must Be True questions, stay away from answer choices that are impossible to prove, even if—*especially* if—they state claims you might personally agree with.

Answer choice (B) is incorrect for the same reasons as the ones stated above. Just because you might perceive the scholars' views as condescending does not mean that Andrew Kerr did.

Answer choice (C) is incorrect, because there is no evidence suggesting that Kerr believes everyone to be morally blameworthy.

Answer choice (D) is the correct answer choice. In lines 50-55, we learn about Kerr's philosophy of truth and illusion, which is quite different from the scholars' position described in lines 4-12. In particular, the scholars use clues from Kerr's fictional world in order to find the "real truth" about his life, whereas Kerr has no regard for truths that can be proven: "The only truths worth exalting are those that cannot be proven and that, in fact, are false." (lines 53-55). Thus, it is reasonable to infer that Kerr would regard the scholars' perspective as mistakenly preoccupied with provable truths.

Answer choice (E) is incorrect, because there is no evidence that Kerr was in any way bothered by the prying curiosity of his biographers.

Question #5: CR, Must, SP. The correct answer choice is (E)

Viewpoint identification is once again key. Newman's views are discussed in lines 13-27, whereas the directors' position can be found in lines 44-48. You need to refer to both of these sections in reaching a logically provable answer. Make sure to avoid choosing answer choices with which you might subjectively agree, but which are not supported by the information contained in both passages.

Answer choice (A) is incorrect, because only the directors believe that Kerr's work is too complex for middle-class audiences (lines 44-49). Newman believes that Kerr's meta-narrative is incoherent, but not necessarily that it is too complex. Furthermore, Newman never discusses the popular reception of any of Kerr's plays.

Answer choice (B) is incorrect, because only Newman implies that Kerr is not a skilled dramaturge (lines 25-27). The directors never allude to Kerr's abilities as a dramaturge.

Answer choice (C) is attractive, but incorrect. Newman clearly believes that Kerr's work can be "disgusting" (line 21), while the directors worry that *On the Porch* would be "offensive" to middle-class audiences (line 48). However, unless the directors assume that *all* viewers are middle-class, we cannot prove their belief that the work of Andrew Kerr would be offensive to *all* viewers. This answer choice contains an exaggeration that is not supported by the information presented in passage B.

Answer choice (D) is incorrect. Newman would agree that Kerr's work is incoherent, but not necessarily that it is amusing. Similarly, the directors might agree that *On the Porch* is potentially amusing (hence their decision to turn the play into a satire), but not necessarily that it is incoherent. Thus, neither speaker would necessarily agree with both adjectives used here.

Answer choice (E) is the correct answer choice. We have evidence from passage A that Newman would regard Kerr's work as "disturbing, distasteful, even disgusting" (line 21), later implying that it lacks a "coherent narrative structure" (line 25). Thus, Newman would probably agree that Kerr's work is "troubling and disjointed." The directors mentioned in passage B would probably agree as well, given their realization that turning *On the Porch* into a satire would offer "an unexpected comfort from the more incoherent—and offensive—aspects of the plot" (lines 47-49).

Question #6: SR, Must, P. The correct answer choice is (A)

The answer to this Passage Relationship question should be prephrased. In passage A (lines 5-7), the author describes how scholars examine Kerr's fictional world looking for clues that could reveal the "real" story of their author. In this context, "fictional world" refers to the body of work produced by Kerr. Meanwhile, in passage B (lines 50-52) the author remarks that the dramatic effects of the satirical genre were inconsistent with "Kerr's philosophy of truth and illusion." Here, "illusion" most likely refers to a philosophical position held by the artist.

Answer choice (A) is the correct answer choice, as it correctly describes the function of each phrase in the context in which it appears. See discussion above.

Answer choice (B) is incorrect, because neither phrase is used to designate a belief that is either provably false or provably true. Do not be tempted by the use of convoluted language here, unless you can definitively rule out the remaining answer choices.

Answer choice (C) is half-right, half-wrong, because the usage of the phrase "fictional world" in passage A does not refer to an artistic concept as much as an actual body of work produced by an artist.

Answer choice (D) is incorrect, because there is no evidence suggesting that Kerr's artistic work is potentially deceptive (though the critics might have been deceived by it), nor that "illusion" is an *expected* effect of that work.

Answer choice (E) is incorrect, because even if Kerr's work is a product requiring imagination (difficult to prove, but reasonable to assume), the word "illusion" in passage B does not refer to a "figment" of his imagination.

Question #7: CR, MustX. The correct answer choice is (C)

The correct answer to this EXCEPT question would be a statement that is not supported in *either* of the two passages. Use the Fact Test to eliminate the four incorrect answer choices.

Answer choice (A) is incorrect, because it is supported by passage A (lines 7-12).

Answer choice (B) is incorrect, because it is supported by passage A (lines 2-4).

Answer choice (C) is the correct answer choice. While it is true that Kerr's work did not receive the *critical* acclaim it deserves—something we can readily prove by reference to passage A—neither passage suggests the lack of *popular* acclaim. Passage B makes it clear, for instance, that *On the Porch* was a success (line 40). The only thing that "flopped" was the play within the play, not the theatrical production itself.

Answer choice (D) is incorrect, because we have evidence from passage B that the directors simplified the plot line of *On the Porch* and turned the play into a satire (lines 44-46).

Answer choice (E) is incorrect. Note that Kerr's philosophical beliefs were inconsistent with the dramatic effects of the satirical genre (lines 50-52), and also that the directors turned *On the Porch* into a satire in order to appeal to middle-class audiences (line 46). Taken together, these facts suggest a disagreement between Kerr's philosophical views and the reputed preferences of his audience (we say "reputed" because the audience's actual preferences are unknown).

Passage #5 Analysis: Government Appropriation of Private Land

Paragraph One:

The author begins this Diversity passage by introducing a central conflict, which is the determination of adequate compensation for the governmental taking of indigenous lands. Adjectives such as "responsible," "sustainable," and "complex," indicate the author's attitude, which is sympathetic to the impact of the taking on both the environment and the indigenous populations.

The paragraph concludes with an important question, which will probably be answered in subsequent paragraphs: what constitutes adequate compensation for the governmental taking of indigenous lands? Textual questions should be underlined and notated.

Paragraph Two:

In this paragraph, the author provides viewpoint neutral background information concerning a common method of determining landowner compensation (the fair market value approach). This paragraph also provides a list of factors considered by early studies of these compensation practices.

Paragraph Three:

This is the most important paragraph in the passage. In it, the author introduces the principles of ethnoecology and argues that landowner compensation for governmental takings of indigenous lands would not be adequate unless it takes these principles into account. When determining land value under the ethnoecological approach, it is especially important to consider the subjective value of the land to the property owner. To support her views, the author mentions a Kenyan study of governmental takings in Kwale, and we should expect to learn more about that study in the next paragraph.

Paragraph Four:

As predicted, this paragraph describes in greater detail how the Kenyan study supports the ethnoecological principles outlined in the third paragraph.

Paragraph Five:

In this final paragraph, the author expands on the Kenyan study, discussing the cultural importance of owning coconut trees to social status and marriage. The author ends the passage by arguing that any adequate compensation for indigenous lands must take into consideration the relationship of the people to the land.

<u>VIEWSTAMP</u> Analysis:

This passage presents three **Viewpoints**. The first is that of the governments of developing nations, which often adopt the landowner compensation practices of developed nations (the fair market value approach). Next is that of the author of the Kenyan study, who disapproves of the fair market value approach because it does not take into account ethnoecological factors. The author agrees with the ethnoecological view, but appears skeptical toward the notion that adequate compensation can be determined using the fair market value analysis only.

The **Structure** of the passage is a follows:

Paragraph One: Introduce the topic of governmental takings of indigenous land, and question if such takings are adequately compensated.

Paragraph Two: Describe the fair market value analysis for determining compensation, and identify the areas of conflict that arise from the application of this method in developing countries.

Paragraph Three: Mention a recent study of such takings in the Kenyan city of Kwale, and suggest that an ethnoecological approach for determining their value would be preferable.

Paragraph Four: Use the example of a coconut tree to illustrate the importance of subjective value, critical to the ethnoecological approach.

Paragraph Five: Further detail the cultural importance of the coconut tree, and conclude by asserting the Main Point of the passage.

The author's **Tone** is critical of the fair market value analysis adopted by developing nations, and supportive of the use of ethnoecology in determining adequate compensation.

The main **Argument** here is that the ethnoecological approach to determining land value is preferable to the commonly adopted fair market value analysis, because the former takes into account subjective factors that the latter does not. This argument is supported by the example of the coconut tree discussed in the fourth and fifth paragraphs.

The **Main Point** of the passage is that any compensation for the taking of indigenous lands must take into account the subjective value of the land to the landowner, as provided by the ethnoecological approach..

Question #1: GR, Main Point. The correct answer choice is (C)

The main point of the passage is prephrased in the VIEWSTAMP analysis above.

Answer choice (A): This answer choice is incorrect for two reasons. First, the passage does not support the statement that developing nations "increasingly" use their authority to take indigenous lands. The author does not describe a change in the rate at which such land is being taken. Further, even if this answer choice were consistent with the passage, it still would be incorrect because it fails to convey the main point.

Answer choice (B): Although responsible mining can be a sustainable way to eradicate poverty in developing nations (lines 1-3), this answer choice is incorrect for several reasons: it refers to all mining, not just responsible mining; it presents a definitive statement that mining is sustainable, and it also fails to capture the main point of the passage.

Answer choice (C): This is the correct answer choice, because it presents the main point of the passage, namely, that the ethnoecological approach is necessary for adequately compensating landowners whose indigenous land is being taken by the government.

Answer choice (D): This statement is supported by the fourth paragraph of the passage; however, it does not reflect the main point, because it does not address the issue of adequate compensation for the government's taking of land.

Answer choice (E): Ethnoecological principles have little to do with the taking of land in *developed* nations, and so does this passage.

Question #2: SR, Must, P. The correct answer choice is (A)

To prephrase an answer to this question, passage Structure is key. The third paragraph describes the ethnoecological principles of determining indigenous land value that the approach described in the second paragraph (fair market value analysis) does not consider.

Answer choice (A): This is the correct answer choice, and is consistent with our prephrase.

Answer choice (B): This choice is incorrect, because the passage discusses only two approaches to the valuation of land.

Answer choice (C): This answer choice is incorrect, because the issue of marriage rituals does not appear until the fifth paragraph.

Answer choice (D): The third paragraph focuses on the ethnoecological principles of valuation, not on the conflicts that arise under the fair market value analysis.

Answer choice (E): This is an Opposite answer, because the purpose of the third paragraph is to reject the fair market value approach discussed in the second paragraph.

Question #3: GR, Must. The correct answer choice is (D)

Due to the global nature of this question, no specific prephrase is possible. The best approach is to use the Fact Test to eliminate those answer choices that are inconsistent with the passage.

Answer choice (A): The *kigango* is a grave post made from a felled coconut tree (lines 50-51), not a species of coconut tree..

Answer choice (B): This answer choice describes a factor critical to the fair market value approach, not to the ethnoecological approach (lines 18-21).

Answer choice (C): This is an Opposite answer. As described in the last paragraph, Mijikenda culture ascribes social significance to the ownership of coconut trees that cannot be completely compensated for by the fair market value of the trees.

Answer choice (D): This is the correct answer choice, despite the fact that the two-year period was not mentioned in the passage. In the fifth paragraph, the author describes a Mijikenda tradition whereby the father of the bride presents the groom's family with a gift of *mnazi*, a milky palm wine made from the father's own trees. It takes five years to grow the coconut trees in quantities sufficient to produce the necessary amount of *mnazi*. Since marrying without that gift is bound to bring shame on the bride (lines 68-74), we can logically infer that a family's complete loss of coconut trees may cause a Mijikenda woman to be less likely to marry for a period of at least two years from the date of loss.

Answer choice (E): While the passage does not preclude the possibility that some developed nations have adopted ethnoecological factors in the fair market value analysis, the passage does not provide any evidence to support such an assertion.

Question #4: SR, MustX. The correct answer choice is (C)

Because this is an Except question, the four incorrect answer choices will be areas of conflict in the governmental taking of indigenous land. The correct answer choice will state a conflict that was *not* mentioned in the passage.

Once again, passage Structure is key. The areas of conflict implicated by governmental takings of indigenous land are discussed at the end of the second paragraph (lines 16-21), which should prove useful in confirming the four incorrect answer choices.

Answer choice (A): This area of conflict is mentioned in lines 19-20.

Answer choice (B): This area of conflict is mentioned in lines 20-21.

Answer choice (C): This is the correct answer choice. Whether the proposed economic activity will help eradicate poverty in the developing nation is not a mentioned conflict in the second paragraph. Therefore, this is the correct answer choice to this MustX question.

Answer choice (D): This area of conflict is mentioned in lines 18-19.

Answer choice (E): This area of conflict is mentioned in line 19.

Question #5: GR, Must, P. The correct answer choice is (A)

When prephrasing an answer to General Reference, Purpose questions, focus on what the author *does* in the passage. Here, the purpose is clearly to criticize the fairness of a particular method of land valuation, and propose that an alternative method be adopted in cases involving governmental takings of indigenous land. This prephrase agrees with answer choice (A), which is correct.

Answer choice (A): This is the correct answer choice. See prephrase above.

Answer choice (B): This author does not discuss whether the areas of conflict described in the second paragraph are overstated.

Answer choice (C): This is an Opposite answer choice. The author does not defend the traditional approach.

Answer choice (D): This is another Opposite answer. The author clearly states that the ethnoecological approach is required to determine the full value of the ancestral lands to the indigenous populations, which would include the Miijikenda.

Answer choice (E): While the author clearly defends the value of coconut trees to the Mijikenda community, this defense is not the focus of the passage.

Question #6: GR, Tone. The correct answer choice is (A)

Global Reference, Purpose or Attitude questions with brief answer choices are great go-to questions when time is short.

Here, we are asked to consider the author's attitude toward the traditional, fair market value approach. From the discussion in the third paragraph, we know that the author considers this approach inadequate in determining the subjective value of indigenous lands, and unfair to the indigenous populations whose land is being taken. So, we can safely assume that her attitude would be negative, which eliminates answer choices (B), (C), and (E). Answer choice (D) is also incorrect, because there is no evidence that the author is particularly confused about the fair market value approach.

This leaves us with answer choice (A), which is consistent with the author's tone, as prephrased in the VIEWSTAMP analysis earlier.

Passage Set #6 Analysis: Noncompete Agreements

Passage A

The author of passage A describes the terms under which noncompete clauses are typically enforced, and defends their use in industry.

Paragraph One:

The first paragraph introduces noncompete agreements as a type of restrictive covenant generally disfavored by state employment law. However, such agreements are deemed enforceable as long as they serve to protect the legitimate interests of the employer. The author identifies two conditions under which courts typically recognize employer interests: (1) to prevent disclosure of trade secrets, and (2) to protect the employer against the irreparable harm of losing an employee whose services are deemed "unique and extraordinary."

Paragraph Two:

This paragraph outlines the arguments for and against the use of noncompete agreements. Courts dislike them because they stifle entrepreneurship, but their proponents argue that such clauses are uniquely capable of protecting the interests of the employer. The author agrees with the proponents (referring to their argument as "justifiable" in line 23), adding that noncompete agreements also encourage employers to invest in their employees.

Passage B

The author of Passage B argues for a stricter enforcement of noncompete agreements.

Paragraph One:

The author argues that the harm sustained by the employer is not the only factor that courts should take into account when considering the enforceability of noncompete agreements. That harm, the author claims, should be weighed against the harm done to the employee by not breaching the agreement. Courts must therefore also consider the time, area, and scope of noncompete agreements.

Paragraph Two:

The second paragraph further restricts the enforceability of noncompete clauses by requiring their language to be clear and precise. Without such language, judges have the discretion to use a "pairing down" approach and enforce the covenant to a more limited extent, assuming an earnest effort has already been made to restrict the clause in either time or space. Otherwise, the covenant should not be enforced.

Passage Similarities and Differences

The two passages portray somewhat different viewpoints. While they both agree that noncompete agreements can protect the interests of employers, the author of passage B has a less favorable view of such agreements. Passage A defends their enforcement, whereas passage B takes a more nuanced stance, suggesting that employers' interests do not necessarily take precedence over the harm sustained by an employee who is bound by an unreasonably broad noncompete agreement. Compared to the author of passage A, the author of passage B is decidedly more cautious about the benefits of such covenants, and more prescriptive in his tone.

Question #1: GR, Must. The correct answer choice is (D)

Our job in this question is to identify a statement that is mentioned in passage B, but not in passage A. Use the Fact Test to eliminate any answer choice that is either not mentioned in passage B, or mentioned in passage A (or both).

Answer choice (A) is incorrect, because the need to protect the legitimate interests of the employer is discussed in passage A (lines 6-7), but not in passage B.

Answer choice (B) is incorrect, because passage A discusses the harm caused by noncompete clauses on free enterprise (they stifle "entrepreneurship and innovation"—lines 15-16).

Answer choice (C) is incorrect, because only passage A discusses the potential benefits employees might derive from being bound by noncompete agreements: the agreements encourage companies to invest in their employees (line 29).

Answer choice (D) is the correct answer choice. The economic harm sustained by employees bound by noncompete agreements is discussed in passage B (lines 36-37), but not in passage A.

Answer choice (E) is incorrect, because both passages mention certain conditions necessary for noncompete agreements to be legally enforceable (lines 6-12 and 43-50).

Question #2: CR, Must. The correct answer choice is (B)

This question asks us to identify a statement about noncompete clauses with which both authors would agree. This is somewhat tricky, given the different positions held by the two authors. Nevertheless, keep in mind that the correct answer choice will contain a factual statement that passes the Agree/Agree Test, i.e. it must produce responses where both speakers would say, "Yes, I agree with this statement."

Answer choice (A) is incorrect, because only the author of passage A believes that noncompete clauses benefit employees (by encouraging employers to invest in them—lines 27-29). Passage B makes no mention of any potential benefit to the employee.

Answer choice (B) is the correct answer choice. Passage A explicitly agrees with the view that noncompete clauses benefit employers (lines 23-29). The author of passage B implies that such a benefit exists by suggesting that broader enforcement of noncompete agreements would benefit the employer, but not the employee (lines 34-36). Passage B makes a similar point later in the same paragraph, arguing that courts must weigh the cost of breaching the agreement against the cost of not breaching it (lines 38-40). Clearly, the author of passage B acknowledges that restrictive covenants benefit employers by reducing the cost of a contractual breach.

Answer choice (C) is incorrect, because only the author of passage B would agree with this statement. The author of passage A does not explicitly acknowledge the relevant interests of the employee until the last sentence of the passage, in which she claims that noncompete clauses may be of benefit to the employees. She might even agree that noncompete agreements are a win-win for both parties, in disagreement with the claim made in answer choice (C).

Answer choice (D) is incorrect, because the author of passage B would probably disagree with this statement. Furthermore, the author of passage A would not necessarily agree that both parties benefit *equally* from noncompete agreements.

Answer choice (E) is incorrect, given the claims made in passage A about the benefits of noncompete agreements.

Question #3: SR, Parallel. The correct answer choice is (B)

This question tests if you understand the meaning of the phrase "possible loss" in passage A (line 28). Context is key, and so is arriving at a suitable prephrase: In passage A, the author claims the enforcement of noncompete agreements is designed to limit the risk of "possible loss" sustained by the employer. In this context, "possible loss" clearly refers to the harm sustained by the employer if the employee breaches her contractual obligations. This prephrase is consistent with answer choice (B).

Answer choice (A) is incorrect, because the "uniqueness of services" represents a factor relevant to the question of whether or not a noncompete agreement is enforceable. This has no relation to the "risk of possible loss," which refers to the harm an employer might sustain if a former employee discloses trade secrets or uses proprietary information after termination of employment.

Answer choice (B) is the correct answer choice. The "harm sustained by the employer" in case of a breach is precisely the sort of "possible loss" noncompete agreements are meant to prevent.

Answer choice (C) is incorrect, because the "possible loss" mentioned in line 28 refers to the harm caused to the employer, not the employee.

Answer choice (D) is incorrect, because the risk of "possible loss" mentioned in line 28 refers to the harm an employer might sustain from an employee's contractual breach, whereas the "cost of not breaching [the agreement]" (lines 39-40) affects the employee.

Answer choice (E) is incorrect, because the scope of a noncompete agreement has no bearing on the risk of possible loss resulting from its breach.

Question #4: GR, Must. The correct answer choice is (A)

The discussion of Passage Similarities and Differences (above) should be sufficient to help you locate the correct answer choice.

Answer choice (A) is the correct answer choice. The language used in the second paragraph of passage A leaves no doubt that its author advocates the use of noncompete agreements ("their proponents *justifiably* argue…"—lines 22-23). Passage B, meanwhile, attempts to limit the enforceability of such agreements by clarifying the conditions under which noncompete clauses should be legally permissible.

Answer choice (B) is half-right, half-wrong. Passage A can be described as discussing "a problem in employment law;" however, passage B does not defend a resolution of that problem.

Answer choice (C) is also half-right, half-wrong. Passage A clearly attempts to justify the value of noncompete agreements; however, passage B never suggested that these agreements are based on a mistaken rationale. Doing so would be tantamount to rejecting the legality of noncompete clauses altogether, which is neither suggested nor implied in passage B.

Answer choice (D) is attractive, but incorrect. Passage A alludes to the harm sustained by employers when a former employee breaches her contractual obligations (lines 22-27), but the main point of the passage is not to describe that harm. Similarly, passage B acknowledges the potential harm that might result from an employee's *not* breaching his or her contractual obligation (lines 36-40), but—again—its author does not describe this harm in any detail. Simply put, neither passage has a purely descriptive purpose, which makes answer choice (D) less than ideal.

Answer choice (E) is incorrect, because the author of passage A is not entirely objective in his defense of noncompete agreements.

Question #5: GR, Must, Tone. The correct answer choice is (D)

To correctly answer this question, it is essential to understand how the tone of passage A differs from that of passage B. Recall that passage A takes a favorable view of noncompete agreements, whereas passage B is more skeptical about their use.

Answer choice (A) is incorrect, because the arguments presented in passage B are neither radical nor particularly "opinionated."

Answer choice (B) is incorrect, because both passages are somewhat informative, and neither is particularly confrontational.

Answer choice (C) is attractive, but incorrect. It is reasonable to regard passage B as more impartial than passage A, because passage B is not exclusively concerned with protecting the interests of the employer. However, passage B shows no overt skepticism toward the possibility that noncompete agreements can be properly enforced, albeit with caution and judicial restraint.

Answer choice (D) is the correct answer choice. It is reasonable to regard passage B as more "judicious" than passage A, because passage B—unlike passage A—acknowledges the interests of both parties to the noncompete agreement. We can also qualify the attitude of passage B as more normative or "prescriptive," because the author makes a series of recommendations regarding what *should* be done about noncompete agreements.

Answer choice (E) is incorrect. While the author of passage B does appear somewhat apprehensive toward the possibility that noncompete agreements can cause harm, there is no sign that she is "hopeful" in any way.

Question #6: CR, MustX. The correct answer choice is (C)

This question tests your cumulative understanding of the conditions under which noncompete agreements would be legally enforceable. Note that the difference between the two passages is irrelevant: your response must be based on the information contained in *both* passages as if they were a single passage.

Answer choice (A) is incorrect, because it does not describe a restrictive covenant of the type outlined in the two passages. The legal enforceability of a covenant whose goal is to protect national security is entirely unknown.

Answer choice (B) is incorrect, because an evening anchor's services may well be deemed "unique and extraordinary" enough to provide a legitimate basis for protection. Furthermore, the covenant seems limited in duration, which can be used as evidence that it is not unreasonably burdensome to the employee. Thus, the covenant is likely to be found enforceable.

Answer choice (C) is the correct answer choice. First, the covenant is motivated by the desire to harm a competitor, which is frowned upon (lines 13-19). Second, the services of entry-level customer associates are neither unique nor extraordinary. They are also unlikely to possess any trade secrets. Last, the language of the covenant seems unusually broad, as it is unrestricted in time, area, and scope of activities. Thus, the noncompete agreement described in answer choice (C) is likely to be found unenforceable.

Answer choice (D) is incorrect, because the protection of trade secrets or other proprietary information is a cognizable employer interest (lines 7-12). Although the covenant does not appear to be limited in time, it is limited in area as well as scope of activities being restricted, which can be used as evidence that the employee is not especially burdened by it. Thus, the covenant is likely to be found enforceable.

Answer choice (E) is incorrect, because a celebrity hairdresser who opens his own salon in close proximity to his former employer is likely to attract the employer's most valuable clients. The hairdresser's services will probably be deemed "unique and extraordinary," but even if they are not, the court may still decide that the contractual breach would cause irreparable damage to his former employer. The covenant is limited in scope, suggesting that the hairdresser can still practice his profession elsewhere. Such an obligation is unlikely to be seen as particularly burdensome, suggesting that the courts will probably find the covenant to be legally enforceable.

Question #7: CR, MustX. The correct answer choice is (A)

To answer this question correctly, use the process of elimination: any answer choice stating a factor relevant to the enforceability of noncompete clauses will be incorrect. As with Question #6, the difference between the two passages is irrelevant: your response must be based on the information contained in *both* passages as if they were a single passage. The correct answer choice will state a factor that *neither* passage mentions as relevant in this context.

Answer choice (A) is the correct answer choice. The employee's length of employment with the company seeking enforcement is not discussed in either passage.

Answer choice (B) is incorrect, because the specificity of the language used in the covenant is a factor relevant to its enforceability: the terms of the agreement must be "clear and precise" (line 45).

Answer choice (C) is incorrect, because the employee's access to proprietary information is relevant to the question of whether the employer has a legitimate interest in seeking protection (line 24).

Answer choice (D) is incorrect, because the employer's ability to easily replace the employee can help determine whether the employee's services were sufficiently "unique and extraordinary" to provide a legitimate basis for protection (lines 10-12).

Answer choice (E) is incorrect, because for noncompete clauses to pass judicial muster, "they must be reasonable in time, area, and scope of activities being restricted" (lines 41-42). Thus, they cannot impose undue burden on the employee.

Passage #7 Analysis: Gund Hall

Paragraph One:

The passage begins by introducing Gund Hall to the reader, and briefly describes its unique architectural style. The author also compares Gund Hall to the rest of Harvard's campus, noting the apparent differences between the two. The discussion is purely descriptive.

Paragraph Two:

In the second paragraph, the author introduces the critics' objection to Gund Hall's aesthetic, but defends the head of the building's design team, John Andrews, as being "ahead of his time." The author justifies the unique building design by observing that it was meant to foster academic collaboration and social contact.

Paragraph Three:

The third paragraph adopts a somewhat negative view toward Gund Hall and its design ("add insult to injury"—line 44). The author discusses a series of practical flaws and concludes that Gund Hall's design innovations have come at the expense of practical considerations. This is also the main point of the passage.

Paragraph Four:

The last paragraph explains how Andrews' absolutist adherence to modernist ideals compromised both the modernist aesthetic and the practical value of the building.

VIEWSTAMP Analysis:

The primary **Viewpoint** presented here is that of the author, who respects Andrews' modernist ideals but feels ambivalent towards their execution. Two additional viewpoints are suggested: the critics' (line 16), who felt uneasy about Gund Hall's design, and John Andrews', who envisioned an environment that could foster academic collaboration (lines 24-25).

The **Structure** of the passage is as follows:

> Paragraph One: Describe Gund Hall's architectural style and juxtapose it with the rest of Harvard's campus.
>
> Paragraph Two: Introduce the critics' objections to Gund Hall's aesthetic, and defend it by explaining the architectural motivations behind its design.
>
> Paragraph Three: State the main point of the passage and support it by enumerating the practical flaws inherent in Gund Hall's design.
>
> Paragraph Four: Explain how Andrews' modernist vision undermined its execution.

Initially, the author exhibits a **Tone** that is somewhat deferential towards Andrews, whose aesthetic vision is largely defended in the second paragraph. The last two paragraphs reveal a much more critical perspective on the extent to which Gund Hall was able to fulfill that vision.

The only **Argument** is that of the author, who is critical towards the extent to which Gund Hall was able to fulfill its academic mission. As evidence, the author introduces a number of examples in the third paragraph.

It is not until the third paragraph that we find out what the *author* thinks of Gund Hall: the **Main Point** of the passage is that Gund Hall's design innovations came at the expense of practical considerations (lines 30-31). This statement is supported by examples in the third paragraph, and elaborated upon in the fourth. The author provides a critical evaluation of Gund Hall's design aesthetic, and analyzes the extent to which that aesthetic was compatible with the academic mission of the building.

Question #1: GR, Main Point. The correct answer choice is (B)

The answer to a Main Point question should always be prephrased. See VIEWSTAMP analysis above.

Answer choice (A) is incorrect, because it does not represent a summary of the passage. The claim that Andrews never intended to integrate Gund Hall with the rest of the campus is stated as a fact in the second paragraph, and no additional support is given for this claim.

Answer choice (B) is the correct answer choice. The author acknowledges Andrews' progressive ideals (second paragraph), but ultimately holds that the architectural design of the building did not take into account practical considerations central to its academic purpose (third and fourth paragraphs).

Answer choice (C) is incorrect, because it is not the main point of the passage. While Gund Hall's design was certainly ahead of its time (lines 26-27), the rest of the passage does not seek to support this claim.

Answer choice (D) is incorrect, because Gund Hall was not necessarily successful in fulfilling its academic mission (the building was "neither purely modern, nor entirely practical"—lines 56-57).

Answer choice (E) is incorrect, because it contains an exaggeration. Although Gund Hall's design certainly did not take into account certain practical considerations, the author never suggested that modernist aesthetic (in general) is incompatible with the practical requirements of *most* academic buildings.

Question #2: SR, Must, AP. The correct answer choice is (C)

The critics mentioned in line 16 clearly dislike Gund Hall (they admit "uneasiness, even "repulsion"). The author attributes their views to the fact that Gund Hall does not fit into its architectural milieu (lines 21-22), but defends Andrews for having no intent to achieve such an integration. In other words, the author is likely to view the critics' position as somewhat misguided, because they fail to appreciate Andrews' aesthetic motivations. Answer choice (C) agrees with this prephrase, and is therefore correct.

Answer choice (A) is incorrect, because the author does not share the critics' uneasiness (or repulsion) at the building's aesthetic qualities.

Answer choice (B) is attractive, but incorrect. While it is true that the author criticizes Gund Hall for different reasons than the critics mentioned in line 16, she remarks that they are "missing the point" (line 19). Thus, she would not necessarily regard their claims as "reasonable."

Answer choice (C) is the correct answer choice. See discussion above.

Answer choice (D) is incorrect, because it is Andrews—not the critics—who ignored the practical necessities of a building such as Gund Hall.

Answer choice (E) is incorrect, because it contains an exaggeration ("fundamentally mistaken"). Furthermore, the author does not accuse the critics of making unsupported claims.

Question #3: CR, Must. The correct answer choice is (A)

To answer this Concept Reference question, passage organization is key. Gund Hall is juxtaposed with the rest of Harvard's campus in the first paragraph, and the comparison is elaborated upon in the second.

Answer choice (A) is the correct answer choice. In line 22, the author remarks that integration with Harvard's campus was not Andrews' intent, a claim illustrated by the description of Gund Hall's central studio space in lines 22-26. In the same paragraph, the author also remarks that "Gund Hall's unified studio space was certainly ahead of its time," suggesting that the academic spaces *typically* found on Harvard's campus are more compartmentalized than Gund Hall.

Answer choice (B) is attractive, but incorrect. Just because Gund Hall "could not cater to [students'] increasingly divergent design and architectural needs" (lines 35-36) does not mean that the rest of Harvard's campus was *better* suited to meeting those needs.

Answer choice (C) is incorrect, because the critics' views on buildings other than Gund Hall were neither suggested nor alluded to.

Answer choice (D) is incorrect, because Harvard's traditional buildings were not a reaction against the type of architecture typified by Gund Hall. The reverse, in fact, is more likely to be true.

Answer choice (E) is incorrect, because no information is provided as to whether the kind of academic spaces typically found on Harvard's campus can be found outside Harvard Yard.

Question #4: CR, Must, AP. The correct answer choice is (D)

From the second paragraph, we know that the author respects Andrews' modernist ideals. That said, the discussion in the third and fourth paragraphs suggests that these ideals were ultimately compromised by Andrews' "absolutist, unapologetic adherence" to them (lines 53-55). Answer choice (D) best reflects this line of criticism, and is therefore correct.

Answer choice (A) is incorrect, because it was the critics—not the author—who felt uneasiness with Gund Hall's architectural design.

Answer choice (B) is incorrect, because Andrews' modernist ideals cannot be described as "transitional." The author refers to them as "progressive" (line 32).

Answer choice (C) is incorrect. The author labels as "divergent" the needs of design students (line 36), which could not be met by a modernist building such as Gund Hall. It would be improper, however, to employ the same adjective in describing the author's attitude towards Gund Hall itself.

Answer choice (D) is the correct answer choice (lines 53-55).

Answer choice (E) is the Opposite answer. Andrews' modernist ideals were certainly not practical; in fact, they came at the expense of practical considerations (lines 30-31).

Question #5: GR, Must, P. The correct answer choice is (E)

The answer to a Purpose question should always be prephrased, and is directly related to your understanding of Argumentation. See VIEWSTAMP analysis above.

Answer choice (A) is incorrect, because it is not the main purpose of the passage. The author certainly believes that Gund Hall could not cater to students' "increasingly divergent design and architectural needs" (lines 35-36), but this is not the central argument in the entire passage. No additional evidence is introduced to substantiate this point, and most of the passage has no bearing on it.

Answer choice (B) is incorrect for two reasons: First, it is not entirely certain that the author would regard Gund Hall as deserving of appreciation, given the critical tone of the last two paragraphs. Secondly, although the author alludes to some of the reasons why Gund Hall was initially disliked by the critics (second paragraph), this is not the main point of the passage as a whole.

Answer choice (C) is incorrect, because it represents a concern of the critics', not the author's.

Answer choice (D) is attractive, but incorrect. While the author defends Andrews' modernist vision from the critics' accusations in the second paragraph, the rest of the passage is overtly critical of the manner in which his vision compromised the academic objectives the building was meant to achieve.

Answer choice (E) is the correct answer choice. As explained in the VIEWSTAMP analysis above, the purpose of the passage is to provide a critical evaluation of Gund Hall's design aesthetic (first two paragraphs), and analyze the extent to which that aesthetic was compatible with the academic mission of the building (last two paragraphs).

Question #6: CR, MustX. The correct answer choice is (D)

To answer this Except question, passage organization is key. The author describes Gund Hall in the first two paragraphs, which are bound to be helpful in eliminating at least a few of the answer choices.

Answer choice (A) is incorrect, because a green fiberglass covering the roof is part of Gund Hall's original design (line 11).

Answer choice (B) is incorrect, because Gund Hall features a reinforced concrete flat slab structure (lines 8-9).

Answer choice (C) is incorrect, because a multi-tiered open studio space is part of the original design (lines 23-24 and 32).

Answer choice (D) is the correct answer choice. The glass screen enclosing the lobby was added in order to protect the interior from adverse weather conditions (line 40). Thus, it is not part of the building's original design.

Answer choice (E) is incorrect, because the ground floor is wrapped in a glass bandage of doors (line 14).

Passage #8 Analysis: E. Eaton

Paragraph One:

The first paragraph tells us about Eaton's birth and emigration to Canada, and also establishes the historical context of the passage. We also learn more about the underrepresented group under discussion—Chinese immigrants to North America who arrived in Canada and the U.S. soon after the discovery of gold in California.

Paragraph Two:

Here, the author describes the results of Eaton's childhood illness, which lead to her working as a stenographer. It was Eaton's work as a stenographer that exposed her to opportunities to become a writer, a transition that was critical to Eaton's transformation into an activist.

Paragraph Three:

This paragraph discusses Eaton's increasing contact with the Chinese immigrant community, her discovery of their plight, and her acquisition of an increased communication platform through her work with newspapers in various cities in California and Canada.

Paragraph Four:

In the final paragraph, the author describes how Eaton came to more fully embrace her Chinese heritage, and used her platform as a newspaper writer and novelist to communicate the problems faced by the Chinese immigrant community to a Western audience. This is also the main point of the passage.

VIEWSTAMP Analysis:

The **Viewpoints** presented in this passage are those of Edith Eaton, who refused to hide her Chinese heritage and sought to speak out for the Chinese community; the Westerners, who feared certain aspects of the Chinese that they did not understand (i.e., their appearance and their customs); and the author's, who has a favorable view of Eaton and her work.

The **Structure** of the passage is as follows:

Paragraph One: Situate Edith Eaton in a historical context and mention the discrimination faced by a minority group.

Paragraph Two: Provide a brief biographical account of Eaton's early years, and explain how her physical condition led her to become a stenographer and then a writer.

Paragraph Three: Continue the biographical account of the preceding paragraph by focusing on Eaton's work and life while in her 30s. Discuss Eaton's bond with the Chinese immigrant community.

Paragraph Four: Outline Eaton's development as an advocate for Chinese immigrants and her sense of identity. The main point can be found here.

The **Tone** of the passage is highly favorable toward Eaton, negative toward the Westerners, and both positive and sympathetic toward the Chinese immigrants.

The author's main **Argument** is that Eaton's physical infirmity set her on a path to new experiences that helped her develop into an advocate for Chinese immigrants.

The **Main Point** of the passage is that Eaton, a Chinese-English woman who lived in the late 19th century, overcame physical and cultural adversity to become an influential advocate for Chinese immigrants.

Question #1: GR, Main Point. The correct answer choice is (C)

Our prephrase to this Main Point question is provided in the VIEWSTAMP analysis above.

Answer choice (A): Although a true statement, this answer choice fails to capture the content of the third and the fourth paragraphs.

Answer choice (B): This answer choice is inconsistent with the passage, because Eaton's Chinese heritage was not physically apparent, which allowed her to protect herself from anti-Chinese bigotry (lines 26-29).

Answer choice (C): This is the correct answer choice, as it alludes to points made in each of the four paragraphs of the passage.

Answer choice (D): This answer choice contains information that is not supported by the passage. Although Eaton was a tireless advocate for the Chinese residents of the United States, there is no indication that her writings played any role in advocating for anti-discriminatory legislation.

Answer choice (E): This answer choice is tempting, because it describes the type of scenario that is sometimes seen in Diversity passages (the underrepresented group corrects the overrepresented group). However, we have no reason to believe that Eaton's non-fiction writing consisted of reviews of Western theatrical productions depicting Chinese themes.

Question #2: SR, Must. The correct answer choice is (A)

The passage does not explicitly define the term "peripatetic", because is not jargon or specialized knowledge. Although it is a rarely used word, we can look to the context of the passage to define it. In the clause immediately following the word "peripatetic", Eaton is described as moving from one city to the next. So, we can prephrase that the word "peripatetic" means something like moving from place to place.

Answer choice (A): This is the correct answer choice, because it states the meaning of the word "peripatetic," as described above. Although our prephrase did not discuss work, the passage does indicate that Eaton would take assignments from newspapers in the various cities.

Answer choice (B): This answer choice better fits the meaning of the word "frugality," used in line 11 of the passage.

Answer choice (C): This answer choice might be tempting because the paragraph in which the word "peripatetic" is used states that Eaton declined to hide her Chinese heritage. However, there is no reason to suspect that she lived dangerously or took unnecessary risks as a result of living as a Chinese immigrant.

Answer choice (D): Here, the answer choice is inconsistent with the passage, which indicates that this period of Eaton's life was characterized by positive growth, both for Beaton personally and in terms of her relationships with the Chinese community.

Answer choice (E): Eaton certainly learned a great deal about herself and the Chinese community, but there is no support for the view that the word "peripatetic" relates to this type of growth.

Question #3: SR, Must, P. The correct answer choice is (B)

The function of the second paragraph is prephrased in our VIEWSTAMP analysis above: in the second paragraph, the author provides a brief biographical account of Eaton's early years, and explains how her physical condition led her to become a stenographer and then a writer. Answer choice (B) agrees with this prephrase, and is therefore correct.

Answer choice (A): The reasons for Eaton's family moving to Canada are outlined in the first paragraph, not in the second.

Answer choice (B): This is the correct answer choice. See discussion above.

Answer choice (C): This answer choice is incorrect, because the author describes how Eaton developed her passion for pro-Chinese advocacy in the third paragraph, not in the second..

Answer choice (D): This answer choice describes a role played by the *fourth* paragraph.

Answer choice (E): Whether Eaton was physically stronger than her family assumed is neither asserted nor alluded to. The author focuses on her moral, not physical, fortitude.

Question #4: GR, Must, AP. The correct answer choice is (A)

To solve this Author Perspective question, apply the Fact Test and proceed by the process of elimination: any answer choice that cannot be proven by reference to the information contained in the passage will be incorrect.

Answer choice (A): This is the correct answer choice. From the discussion in the fourth paragraph, we know that Eaton was able to realistically communicate the problems faced by the Chinese immigrant community at least in part because of her ties to that community (lines 48-53). While such a causal relationship need not always exist, it is certainly possible that it *sometimes* exists. One of the central tenets of the Fact Test to solving Must Be True questions is that a possibility is easier to prove than certainty. This is precisely why this answer choice is provably true: it only states that such a relationship *may* exist, not that it *must* exist.

Answer choice (B): Although the author stated that Eaton *could* have avoided experiencing anti-Chinese bigotry by keeping her Chinese heritage a secret, there is no indication that the author would agree that Eaton, or anyone else for that matter, *should* do so. In fact, if Eaton had hidden her Chinese heritage in order to avoid discrimination, should would have been less able to perform the advocacy that the author finds laudable.

Answer choice (C): We have no way of knowing how confident Eaton was that she would continue her pro-Chinese advocacy for as long as possible. In fact, judging from the autobiographical quote used in the fourth paragraph (lines 56-59), she worried being torn apart by her efforts to act as a bridge between the Chinese and Western communities.

Answer choice (D): While it is true that Chinese women were placed at a greater disadvantage than their male counterparts (lines 38-42), we cannot extrapolate that this dynamic occurs in every immigrant population. This answer choice contains a generalization.

Answer choice (E): This answer choice directly contradicts the author's description of Eaton's "*supposed* weakness" in the final sentence of the passage (lines 62-65).

Question #5: CR, MustX. The correct answer choice is (D)

To answer this MustX question quickly and efficiently, understanding passage Structure is once again key! The reasons why the Chinese immigrants were being discriminated against are discussed in the first paragraph, which should prove useful in confirming the four incorrect answer choices.

Answer choice (A): The distinct physical appearance of the Chinese was mentioned as a basis for discrimination (lines 10-11).

Answer choice (B): The willingness of the Chinese to work hard was mentioned as a basis for discrimination (line 12).

Answer choice (C): The peculiar customs of the Chinese were mentioned as a basis for discrimination (line 11).

Answer choice (D): This is the correct answer choice, because the Chinese views on ownership were never discussed in this passage.

Answer choice (E): The willingness of the Chinese to work for low wages was mentioned as a basis for discrimination (lines 12-13).

Passage #9 Analysis: Nutrition and Sodium

Paragraph One:

In the first paragraph, the author concedes that excessive intake of sugar is harmful, but rejects the view that sugar is itself toxic. In fact, the author regards our obsession with sugar as harmful in itself, because it detracts our attention from keeping track of our sodium intake. The last sentence of the first paragraph is critical, as it captures the main point of the passage.

Paragraph Two:

The second paragraph describes the deleterious effects of excessive sodium intake, which explains the position stated in the last sentence of the first paragraph: by focusing exclusively on our sugar intake, we fail to recognize the dangers inherent in consuming too much sodium.

Paragraph Three:

The third paragraph outlines yet another reason why low-carb diets can be harmful: not only do they distract us from monitoring our sodium intake (first paragraph), but they also inadvertently increase our consumption of sodium. The author draws an analogy between low-carb and low-fat diets, suggesting that each diet merely substitutes one harmful additive for an equally harmful one. The passage concludes by outlining an alternative nutritional approach: well-balanced diets that use natural ingredients to satisfy our needs.

VIEWSTAMP Analysis:

There are two **Viewpoints** outlined in this passage: the nutritional biologists' (lines 1-2) and the author's.

The **Structure** of the passage is as follows:

Paragraph One: Reject the view that sugar is toxic, and shift our attention to the importance of sodium intake.

Paragraph Two: Explain why excessive sodium intake can be harmful.

Paragraph Three: Describe the harmful nature of "fad diets" and suggest an alternative nutritional approach.

Although the **Tone** is predominantly descriptive, the author takes a clear stance against "fad diets," which adds a polemic touch to the tone of the passage. The author appears well-informed on the subject of nutrition.

The passage presents one central **Argument**, which is causal. Low-carb diets are potentially harmful, because (1) they detract our attention from monitoring our sodium intake, and (2) they are often tasteless, which increases the consumption of sodium. This position assumes that excessive sodium intake is undesirable, an assumption supported by evidence presented in the second paragraph of the passage.

The **Main Point** of the passage is to argue that low-carb diets lead to an increased consumption of sodium, and explain why this is potentially harmful. Even more broadly speaking, the purpose of the passage is to argue that a particular dietary trend is potentially harmful, and explain why this is so.

Question #1: GR, Must, P. The correct answer choice is (B)

The answer to this General Reference, Purpose question is prephrased in the VIEWSTAMP analysis above.

Answer choice (A) is attractive, but incorrect. The author clearly seeks to shift the reader's attention from sugar to sodium, arguing that the latter can be just as harmful when taken in excess. However, this answer choice fails the Fact Test, because there is no evidence suggesting that excessive consumption of sodium is *more* harmful than is excessive consumption of sugar. In fact, the author refers to added sodium as "equally harmful" (line 35), and believes that our obsession with sugar detracts from focusing on an "equally important part of any balanced diet: sodium" (lines 11-12).

Answer choice (B) is the correct answer choice, because the first and the third paragraphs assert that our obsession with sugar is harmful (line 10 and lines 30-32), whereas the second paragraph explains why it is so (it promotes the increased consumption of sodium—an undesirable dietary habit).

Answer choice (C) is incorrect, because it focuses exclusively on the content of the second paragraph, not of the passage as a whole. Furthermore, sodium intake itself is not undesirable; *excessive* sodium intake is.

Answer choice (D) is incorrect. While the author does reject the view that sugar is toxic (lines 5-6), this is not the main purpose of the passage.

Answer choice (E) is incorrect for a number of reasons. First, neither sugar nor sodium are "harmful nutritional substances." They are harmful as additives (line 35) when consumed in excess, but they are "otherwise benign nutritional substance[s]" (lines 7-8). Secondly, although the author does enumerate the harmful effects of consuming too much sugar (line 5) and salt (lines 20-27), the main purpose of the passage is not to compare and contrast these effects.

Question #2: SR, Must, P. The correct answer choice is (B)

This question asks us to examine why the author mentions the fact that low-carb diets are often tasteless (lines 32-33). Arriving at a suitable prephrase is key. The author remarks on the tasteless nature of low-carb diets in order to explain why they inadvertently increase the consumption of sodium (lines 30-31), which is unhealthy.

Answer choice (A) is incorrect, because the author does not intend to distinguish low-carb from low-fat diets; on the contrary—she draws an analogy between the two (lines 34-38).

Answer choice (B) is the correct answer choice. Since low-carb diets are tasteless, we try to make them tastier by consuming more salt, and in doing so substitute one harmful additive for another. In other words, the tasteless nature of low-carb diets indicates a way in which such diets promote unhealthy eating habits.

Answer choice (C) is incorrect, because the failure rate of low-carb diets was never discussed.

Answer choice (D) is attractive, but incorrect. While tastelessness is clearly a downside of low-carb diets, there is no evidence that it is *unique* to such diets. Furthermore, the purpose of this paragraph is not to illustrate the downsides of low-carb diets, but rather to explain the particular mechanism by which they promote increased consumption of sodium.

Answer choice (E) is incorrect, because no alternative dietary regimen is recommended.

Question #3: CR, Must. The correct answer choice is (A)

This Must Be True question concerns sodium intake. As always, passage organization is key: sodium intake is discussed primarily in the second paragraph, which can serve as a useful reference point in validating the correct answer choice.

Answer choice (A) is the correct answer choice, because "everyone needs sodium in his or her diet" (lines 15-16). Clearly, then, sodium intake is a necessary component of any diet.

Answer choice (B) is incorrect, because it describes the harmful effects of *excessive* sodium intake only, not of sodium intake in general.

Answer choice (C) is incorrect, because sodium is just as toxic as sugar only in sufficiently large quantities (lines 7-9).

Answer choice (D) is incorrect, because sodium intake itself does not necessarily represent a health risk. Excessive consumption of sodium does.

Answer choice (E) is incorrect, because it contains an exaggeration ("invariably"). While excessive consumption of sodium is indeed a risk factor for those suffering from hypertension (line 21), we cannot conclusively prove that it *invariably* makes hypertension worse.

Question #4: CR, Must, AP. The correct answer choice is (D)

This Author Perspective question tests our understanding of the author's attitude towards low-carb diets. The answer should be prephrased: the author considers them potentially harmful, because they may lead to an increased consumption of sodium (lines 30-32). The attitude is therefore negative, which helps eliminate answer choices (A) and (B). Remember: the general direction of your prephrase is more important than the precision with which you can predict the correct answer choice.

Answer choice (A) is incorrect, because the author does not necessarily regard low-carb diets as beneficial: the third paragraph clearly suggests that the costs of such diets might outweigh the benefits. This answer choice describes the viewpoint of the nutritional biologists mentioned in lines 1-5, which is not the author's viewpoint.

Answer choice (B) is incorrect, because the author has a somewhat negative view of low-carb diets. Although she regards sugar as potentially toxic, she does not necessarily believe that the benefits of low-carb diets outweigh the costs.

Answer choice (C) is incorrect. Although carbohydrates are indeed a macronutrient (line 43), the author never describes low-carb diets as *overly* restrictive of carbohydrates. Remember: the author views excessive consumption of sugar as harmful (first paragraph), and is likely to agree that sugar consumption should be somewhat restricted. Whether low-carb diets are *overly* restrictive of sugar is impossible to determine given the information provided in the passage.

Answer choice (D) is the correct answer choice. The third paragraph contrasts well-balanced diets to those that focus on a single nutritional additive (lines 39-45). Since low-carb diets exemplify the latter trend, it is reasonable to infer that the author would regard them as inconsistent with the tenets of a well-balanced diet.

Answer choice (E) is attractive, but incorrect. The author clearly sees low-carb diets as harmful, in part because they detract from focusing on sodium (lines 10-12), and also because they lead to an increased consumption of sodium (line 32). There is no evidence, however, that low-carb diets *require* us to consume more sodium. The author's argument is causal, not conditional.

Question #5: SR, Must, P. The correct answer choice is (C)

The answer to this Purpose question is prephrased in the VIEWSTAMP analysis above.

Answer choice (A) is incorrect, because the second paragraph only supports the author's central argument, which is suggested in the first and summarized in the third paragraphs.

Answer choice (B) is attractive, but incorrect. While the first paragraph certainly suggests that classifying sugar as a "toxin" is a misconception, the second paragraph makes no attempt of explaining why this misconception should be corrected, i.e. why sugar should *not* be classified as a toxin. The purpose of the second paragraph is to explain why a different nutritional additive—sodium—can be just as harmful when consumed in excess.

Answer choice (C) is the correct answer choice. The first paragraph describes our modern-day obsession with cutting sugar at the expense of sodium (i.e. an "outlook"). By describing the deleterious effects of excessive sodium intake, the second paragraph explains why this outlook is potentially harmful.

Answer choice (D) is incorrect, because the second paragraph does not undermine the argument presented in the first paragraph. On the contrary—it supports that argument by illustrating the harmful effects of excessive sodium intake.

Answer choice (E) is incorrect, because the author does not make any recommendations until the end of the passage. There is no course of action recommended in the first paragraph.

Question #6: SR, Must, Expansion. The correct answer choice is (A)

This Expansion question requires you to extrapolate ideas from the passage in order to determine what sentence or idea could follow it. The correct answer choice will be dependent upon the two or three sentences at the end of the passage, but the question is difficult because it asks you to infer the flow and direction of the passage from a somewhat limited set of rules.

Answer choice (A) is the correct answer choice. In the last paragraph, the author laments the practice of substituting one harmful additive for an equally harmful one, arguing for a more holistic approach to nutrition. This suggests that she would be critical of any dietary approach that judges food one component at a time.

Answer choice (B) is incorrect, because the author does not necessarily view all dietary regimens as harmful. Just because dietary regimens focusing on a single nutritional additive are harmful (lines 34-41) does not mean that *all* dietary regimens are potentially harmful.

Answer choice (C) is incorrect. Although our views on nutrition are clearly evolving, there is no evidence that these views are reflected in the dietary choices we make. Note that the author is critical of certain dietary choices (the so-called "fad diets").

Answer choice (D) is incorrect, because the author does not necessarily seek greater consistency in manufacturers' dietary recommendations. Such a consistency would only be preferable if these recommendations were warranted, which—according to the author—they are not. The passage is critical of manufacturers not because their recommendations are inconsistent, but because they merely substitute one harmful additive for an equally harmful one.

Answer choice (E) is incorrect, because the author does not necessarily believe that any food will ultimately be reported as *healthful*. She does not regard high-carb diets as particularly healthful, for instance. Rather, the author is critical of our obsession with specific nutritional additives as *unhealthy* (fat, sugar, etc.).

Passage #10 Analysis: Stanislavski

Paragraph One:

The passage begins by introducing Stanislavski and his Method of acting. The Method is described as "one of the most influential systematic approaches to training actors" (lines 3-4) and "foundational to most contemporary acting theories" (lines 7-8). Clearly, the author has the utmost respect for Stanislavski and his work, setting the tone for the remainder of the passage.

Paragraph Two:

This paragraph elaborates upon the principles and objectives that lay at the core of the Method: To develop realistic characters, actors are taught to draw upon their own emotional recall. However, they are also warned against blurring the boundaries between actor and spectator, character and self.

Paragraph Three:

This is the most theoretically dense portion of the passage, so it's worth taking the discussion down a notch: The author questions the positivistic assumptions upon which the Method is premised, arguing that the Method is so successful precisely because it blurs the boundaries between acting and living. In support of this theory, the author invokes the views of another scholar, Sharon Carnicke.

VIEWSTAMP Analysis:

The primary **Viewpoint** presented here is that of the author (lines 8-12, 26-49). Two additional viewpoints are suggested: Stanislavski's (lines 16-25 and 33), and Sharon Carnicke's (lines 36-39).

The **Structure** of the passage is as follows:

Paragraph One: Introduce Stanislavski's Method of acting.

Paragraph Two: Describe the central tenets of the Method.

Paragraph Three: Critically examine some of the assumptions upon which the Method is premised, and state the main point of the passage.

The author's **Tone** is respectful of the Stanislavski's Method, viewing it as successful in practice (line 47). At the same time, the author is critical of some of the theoretical assumptions upon which it is premised.

There are two central **Arguments** presented in the passage: Stanislavski believes that an actor must draw upon her own emotional recall to recreate a character, without ever blurring the boundary between character and self, actor and spectator, etc. The author's counterargument is that the Method cannot sustain the distinctions it assumes to exist. As evidence, the author critically examines Stanislavski's motto ("an actor does not act, but lives") and also introduces the viewpoint of another scholar, Sharon Carnicke.

The **Main Point** of the passage is that the Method cannot sustain the oppositions upon which it is premised, because it requires actors to draw upon their own emotional recall in recreating a role. The main point can be found in the third paragraph. The purpose of the passage is to discuss Stanislavski's Method of acting and offer a critical perspective on some of its central presuppositions.

Question #1: GR, Main Point. The correct answer choice is (B)

The answer to the Main Point question should always be prephrased. See VIEWSTAMP analysis above.

Answer choice (A) is incorrect, because it does not represent a summary of the passage. The claim that Stanislavski uses real-life emotions as a source of representational technique is stated as a fact, and no additional support is given for this claim.

Answer choice (B) is the correct answer choice. In the third paragraph, the author discusses how the central tenets of the Method unsettle the seemingly irreducible differences upon which it is premised. The first two paragraphs provide the contextual background for this argument, while the second part of the third paragraph supports it.

Answer choice (C) is incorrect, because it contains an exaggeration. In lines 16-17, the author clearly states that Stanislavski understood *better than anyone else* that acting is an inherently relational art. Just because Stanislavski may not recognize the full theoretical implications of his own theory does not mean that he misunderstood the relationship between the two.

Answer choice (D) is incorrect, because the author never suggested that the Method is imperfect. Furthermore, its importance to contemporary acting theories is merely alluded to in the first paragraph, and no support for that statement is given.

Answer choice (E) is incorrect, because the central focus of the Method is not the main point of the passage.

Question #2: CR, Must, AP. The correct answer choice is (B)

The author reveals her views of the Method primarily in the third paragraph of the passage. The Method presumed seemingly irreducible differences (lines 28-31) that are more complex than they appear at first. This view is reasserted at the very end of the passage.

Answer choice (A) is incorrect. The author is respectful of Stanislavski's Method and shows scholarly interest in it. However, she does not praise it as an impressive modern theoretical text.

Answer choice (B) is the correct answer choice. The Method is decidedly successful (lines 46-47), even though it cannot sustain some of its presuppositions (lines 28-32 and 42-46).

Answer choice (C) is incorrect, because the Method is not necessarily unique in its autobiographical and experiential origins: the first paragraph implies that other modern theoretical texts in the humanities may share a similar origin (lines 8-12).

Answer choice (D) is incorrect, because the author clearly regards the Method as valuable in both theory and practice (lines 1-8 and 46-47).

Answer choice (E) is incorrect, because it contains an exaggeration ("fundamentally misunderstood").

Question #3: GR, Must, O. The correct answer choice is (A)

Passage organization is prephrased in our VIEWSTAMP analysis above.

Answer choice (A) is the correct answer choice. A methodology is described in the first and second paragraphs, its theoretical presuppositions are scrutinized in the first half of the third paragraph, and a counterargument is made in the second half of that paragraph (lines 31-49).

Answer choice (B) is incorrect, because the author does not delve into a discussion contrasting the advantages and disadvantages of the Method.

Answer choice (C) is incorrect, because the conditions that brought about the Method of acting are neither mentioned nor alluded to.

Answer choice (D) is attractive, but incorrect. Although the author evaluates the Method and explains its central predicament (i.e. that it cannot sustain the boundaries it assumes to exist), no tentative resolution of the predicament is recommended.

Answer choice (E) is incorrect, because the historical relevance of the Method is never debated.

Question #4: CR, Parallel. The correct answer choice is (E)

To answer this Parallel question correctly, we need to attain a more abstract understanding of how actors prepare using the Method. From the second paragraph, we know that they draw upon their own emotional recall to recreate a character. Using the Test of Abstraction from Parallel Reasoning questions, we can formulate a suitable prephrase: the correct answer choice must describe someone who relies on her own subjective experience for artistic purposes.

Answer choice (A) is incorrect, because a physics professor questioning the central tenets of theoretical physics alludes to the *author's* attitude towards Stanislavski's Method, not to an *actor's* use of that Method.

Answer choice (B) is attractive, but incorrect. A painter making a faithful reproduction of an original painting does parallel the Method's objective to recreate realistic characters. However, the painter accomplishes her goal by studying Renaissance art. By contrast, Stanislavski's actor relies on her own emotional recall in recreating her character. Although the two objectives match, they are achieved in different ways.

Answer choice (C) is incorrect, because it has little in common with the central tenets of Stanislavski's Method. For instance, actors are never told to rehearse a more *difficult* role than the one they are supposed to master.

Answer choice (D) is incorrect, because improvisation is never mentioned as an element of the Method of acting.

Answer choice (E) is the correct answer choice. A photographer taking pictures of her own hometown is similar to an actor relying on her own subjective experience of an emotional state. Both seek to achieve a similar artistic purpose: an actor seeks to create a realistic character, whereas a photographer wants to convey a more vivid sense of nostalgia.

Question #5: SR, Must, P. The correct answer choice is (C)

The answer to the Purpose question should always be prephrased, and is directly related to your understanding of argumentation and viewpoints. See VIEWSTAMP analysis above.

Answer choice (A) is incorrect, because Carnicke discusses, rather than illustrates, a central tenet of the Method. Furthermore, the author mentions Carnicke in order to support an observation about the Method (that it has *already* placed life squarely on stage), which is not a tenet of the method.

Answer choice (B) is incorrect because the author's purpose in the last paragraph is not to *emphasize* the degree to which the Method demands emotional recall. The author takes for granted that such a demand exists, but does not emphasize this point.

Answer choice (C) is the correct answer choice. The author introduces Carnicke in order to substantiate the point that the Method has *already* placed life squarely on stage (lines 34-36), and also support the subsequent observation that the Method blurs the boundary between what is real and what is acted (lines 39-42).

Answer choice (D) is incorrect, because the theoretical value of the Method is never contrasted with its practical value.

Answer choice (E) is the Opposite answer. The author does not seek to *support* Stanislavski's understanding of the relationship between acting and living; instead, she seeks to undermine some of the assumptions upon which that understanding is premised.

Question #6: GR, Must, SP. The correct answer choice is (C)

To answer this Subject Perspective question, passage organization is key. Stanislavski's principles are discussed in the second paragraph, which is likely to be useful in proving the correct answer choice.

Answer choice (A) is incorrect, because this is Carnicke's interpretation of the Stanislavski's text, and not necessarily something that Stanislavski himself would agree with. Remember—his Method assumes that there is an "irreducible difference between actor and spectator, character and self, reality and fantasy" (lines 28-31).

Answer choice (B) is incorrect, because Stanislavski cautions actors to *avoid* self-consciousness at all costs (lines 23-24). Thus, he would probably disagree with the notion that actors must be aware of the emotional recall they are experiencing.

Answer choice (C) is the correct answer choice. Stanislavski urges actors to draw upon their own emotional recall to recreate a character (lines 18-19), suggesting that actors must have already experienced the emotional state they are attempting to recreate.

Answer choice (D) is incorrect, because Stanislavski believes that internal dialogue is *more* important than public appearance (lines 21-24). Thus, he would probably disagree with the notion that internal dialogue is antithetical to good acting.

Answer choice (E) is incorrect, because it alludes to the author's own position, not Stanislavski's. Remember—Stanislavski held that an actor should never blur the boundary between herself and her character (lines 20-21). It is the author who believes that the Method inadvertently blurs the boundary between the two.

Question #7: CR, Must, AP. The correct answer choice is (B)

To answer this Author's Perspective question, passage organization is once again key. The author's take on Stanislavski's Method is presented in the third paragraph, which is likely to be useful in proving the correct answer choice.

Answer choice (A) is incorrect, because Stanislavski did not necessarily fail to understand why actors must experience the emotions they perform on stage. The reasoning behind Stanislavski's recommendations is never discussed.

Answer choice (B) is the correct answer choice. According to the passage, Stanislavski *inadvertently* equates experiencing with acting (lines 36-39), unaware of the far more complex relationship between reality and fantasy (lines 31-32). Thus, the author would probably agree that Stanislavski was not fully aware of the complex relationship between experiencing and acting: the difference is *seemingly irreducible* (line 29), but in reality it is far more complex than Stanislavski assumed.

Answer choice (C) is incorrect, because Stanislavski was adamant about actors not blurring the difference between character and self.

Answer choice (D) is incorrect, because Stanislavski *inadvertently*, rather than intentionally, blurred the boundary between acting and living (line 38).

Answer choice (E) is incorrect, because Stanislavski clearly believes that there is an irreducible difference between actors and spectators (lines 29-30).

THE POWERSCORE LSAT READING COMPREHENSION BIBLE WORKBOOK

Chapter Three: PrepTest 69 Reading Comprehension Section

Chapter Three: PrepTest 69 Reading Comprehension Section

Chapter Notes ■■■■■■■■■

This chapter contains the complete PrepTest 69 Reading Comprehension section. We recommend taking the complete section as a 35-minute timed exercise. Then, check your work against the answer key and explanations that immediately follow the section.

To identify each Reading Comprehension section and the corresponding explanations, use the black sidebars as a reference. The sidebar will identify the PrepTest from which the section is drawn.

As you begin the section, remember to consider your overall time and pacing strategy, and keep in mind that you are not required to complete the passages in the order they are presented to you. Remember to apply the approaches outlined in *The Reading Comprehension Bible*, and good luck!

SECTION III
Time—35 minutes
27 Questions

Directions: Each set of questions in this section is based on a single passage or a pair of passages. The questions are to be answered on the basis of what is stated or implied in the passage or pair of passages. For some of the questions, more than one of the choices could conceivably answer the question. However, you are to choose the best answer; that is, the response that most accurately and completely answers the question, and blacken the corresponding space on your answer sheet.

The prevailing trend in agriculture toward massive and highly mechanized production, with its heavy dependence on debt and credit as a means of raising capital, has been linked to the growing problem
(5) of bankruptcy among small farms. African American horticulturalist Booker T. Whatley has proposed a comprehensive approach to small farming that runs counter to this trend. Whatley maintains that small farms can operate profitably despite these economic
(10) obstacles, and he provides guidelines that he believes will bring about such profitability when combined with smart management and hard work.

Whatley emphasizes that small farms must generate year-round cash flow. To this end, he
(15) recommends growing at least ten different crops, which would alleviate financial problems should one crop fail completely. To minimize the need to seek hard-to-obtain loans, the market for the farm products should be developed via a "clientele membership club"
(20) (CMC), whereby clients pay in advance for the right to go to the farm and harvest what they require. To help guarantee small farmers a market for all of their crops, Whatley encourages them to grow only crops that clients ask for, and to comply with client requests
(25) regarding the use of chemicals.

Whatley stresses that this "pick-your-own" farming is crucial for profitability because 50 percent of a farmer's production cost is tied up with harvesting, and using clients as harvesters allows the farmer to
(30) charge 60 percent of what supermarkets charge and still operate the farm at a profit. Whatley's plan also affords farmers the advantage of selling directly to consumers, thus eliminating distribution costs. To realize profits on a 25-acre farm, for example,
(35) Whatley suggests that a CMC of about 1,000 people is needed. The CMC would consist primarily of people from metropolitan areas who value fresh produce.

The success of this plan, Whatley cautions, depends in large part on a farm's location: the farm
(40) should be situated on a hard-surfaced road within 40 miles of a population center of at least 50,000 people, as studies suggest that people are less inclined to travel any greater distances for food. In this way, Whatley reverses the traditional view of hard-surfaced
(45) roads as farm-to-market roads, calling them instead "city-to-farm" roads. The farm should also have well-drained soil and a ready water source for irrigation, since inevitably certain preferred crops will not be drought resistant. Lastly, Whatley recommends
(50) carrying liability insurance upwards of $1 million to

cover anyone injured on the farm. Adhering to this plan, Whatley contends, will allow small farms to exist as a viable alternative to sprawling corporate farms while providing top-quality agricultural goods
(55) to consumers in most urban areas.

1. Which one of the following most accurately states the main point of the passage?

(A) In reaction to dominant trends in agriculture, Booker T. Whatley has advanced a set of recommendations he claims will enable small farms to thrive.

(B) Booker T. Whatley's approach to farming is sensitive to the demands of the consumer, unlike the dominant approach to farming that focuses on massive and efficient production and depends on debt and credit.

(C) As part of a general critique of the trend in agriculture toward massive production, Booker T. Whatley assesses the ability of small farms to compete against large corporate farms.

(D) While CMCs are not the only key to successful small farming, Booker T. Whatley shows that without them small farms risk failure even with a diversity of crops and a good location.

(E) The adoption of Booker T. Whatley's methods of small farming will eventually threaten the dominance of large-scale production and reliance on debt and credit that mark corporate farming.

GO ON TO THE NEXT PAGE.

2. Based on the information in the passage, which one of the following would Whatley be most likely to view as facilitating adherence to an aspect of his plan for operating a small farm?

(A) a farmer's planting a relatively unknown crop to test the market for that crop

(B) a farmer's leaving large lanes between plots of each crop to allow people easy access at harvest time

(C) a farmer's traveling into the city two afternoons a week to sell fresh produce at a farmer's market

(D) a farmer's using an honor system whereby produce is displayed on tables in view of the road and passersby can buy produce and leave their money in a box

(E) a farmer's deciding that for environmental reasons chemicals will no longer be used on the farm to increase yields

3. According to the passage, "pick-your-own" farming is seen by Whatley as necessary to the operation of small farms for which one of the following reasons?

(A) Customers are given the chance to experience firsthand where their produce comes from.

(B) It guarantees a substantial year-round cash flow for the farm.

(C) It allows farmers to maintain profits while charging less for produce than what supermarkets charge.

(D) Only those varieties of crops that have been specifically selected by clients within the CMC will be grown by the farmer.

(E) Consumers who are willing to drive to farms to harvest their own food comprise a strong potential market for farmers.

4. The author of the passage is primarily concerned with

(A) summarizing the main points of an innovative solution to a serious problem

(B) examining contemporary trends and isolating their strengths and weaknesses

(C) criticizing widely accepted practices within a key sector of the economy

(D) demonstrating the advantages and disadvantages of a new strategy within an industry

(E) analyzing the impact of a new idea on a tradition-driven industry

5. The passage provides the most support for inferring which one of the following statements?

(A) A corporate farm is more likely to need a loan than a small farm is.

(B) If small farms charged what supermarkets charge for produce that is fresher than that sold by supermarkets, then small farms would see higher profits in the long term.

(C) Consumers who live in rural areas are generally less inclined than those who live in metropolitan areas to join a CMC.

(D) If a CMC requests fewer than ten different crops to be grown, then at least one of Whatley's recommendations will not be followed.

(E) Distribution costs are accounted for in the budget of a small farm with a CMC and are paid directly by customers.

6. According to the passage, Whatley advocates which one of the following actions because it would help to guarantee that small farms have buyers for all of their produce?

(A) growing at least ten different crops

(B) charging 60 percent of what supermarkets charge for the same produce

(C) recruiting only clients who value fresh produce

(D) honoring the crop requests and chemical-use preferences of clients

(E) irrigating crops that are susceptible to drought

7. Which one of the following inferences is most supported by the information in the passage?

(A) The advance payment to the farmer by CMC members guarantees that members will get the produce they want.

(B) Hard-surfaced roads are traditionally the means by which some farmers transport their produce to their customers in cities.

(C) A typical population center of 50,000 should be able to support CMCs on at least fifty 25-acre farms.

(D) Consumers prefer hard-surfaced roads to other roads because the former cause less wear and tear on their vehicles.

(E) Most roads with hard surfaces were originally given these surfaces primarily for the sake of farmers.

GO ON TO THE NEXT PAGE.

When Jayne Hinds Bidaut saw her first tintype,
she was so struck by its rich creamy tones that she
could hardly believe this photographic process had
been abandoned. She set out to revive it. Bidaut had
(5)　been searching for a way to photograph insects from
her entomological collection, but paper prints simply
seemed too flat to her. The tintype, an image captured
on a thin, coated piece of iron (there is no tin in it),
provided the detail and dimensionality she wanted.
(10)　The image-containing emulsion can often create a
raised surface on the plate.

　　　For the photographer Dan Estabrook, old albumen
prints and tintypes inspired a fantasy. He imagines
planting the ones he makes in flea markets and antique
(15)　shops, to be discovered as "originals" from a bygone
time that never existed.

　　　On the verge of a filmless, digital revolution,
photography is moving forward into its past. In
addition to reviving the tintype process, photographers
(20)　are polishing daguerreotype plates, coating paper with
egg whites, making pinhole cameras, and mixing
emulsions from nineteenth-century recipes in order
to coax new expressive effects from old photographic
techniques. So diverse are the artists returning to
(25)　photography's roots that the movement is more like
a groundswell.

　　　The old techniques are heavily hands-on and
idiosyncratic. That is the source of their appeal. It is
also the prime reason for their eclipse. Most became
(30)　obsolete in a few decades, replaced by others that were
simpler, cheaper, faster, and more consistent in their
results. Only the tintype lasted as a curiosity into the
twentieth century. Today's artists quickly discover that
to exploit the past is to court the very uncertainty that
(35)　early innovators sought to banish. Such unpredictability
attracted Estabrook to old processes. His work embraces
accident and idiosyncrasy in order to foster the illusion
of antiquity. In his view, time leaches meaning from
every photograph and renders it a lost object, enabling
(40)　us to project onto it our sentiments and associations.
So while the stains and imperfections of prints made
from gum bichromate or albumen coatings would
probably have been cropped out by a nineteenth-
century photographer, Estabrook retains them to
(45)　heighten the sense of nostalgia.

　　　This preoccupation with contingency offers a
clue to the deeper motivations of many of the
antiquarian avant-gardists. The widely variable
outcome of old techniques virtually guarantees that
(50)　each production is one of a kind and bears, on some
level, the indelible mark of the artist's encounter with
a particular set of circumstances. At the same time,
old methods offer the possibility of recovering an
intimacy with photographic communication that
(55)　mass media have all but overwhelmed.

8.　In the context of the third paragraph, the function of the
phrase "on the verge of a filmless, digital revolution" (line
17) is to

(A)　highlight the circumstances that make the
renewed interest in early photographic processes
ironic
(B)　indicate that most photographers are wary of
advanced photographic techniques
(C)　reveal the author's skeptical views regarding
the trend toward the use of old photographic
techniques
(D)　suggest that most photographers who are artists
see little merit in the newest digital technology
(E)　imply that the groundswell of interest by
photographers in old processes will probably turn
out to be a passing fad

9.　Based on the passage, which one of the following most
accurately describes an attitude displayed by the author
toward artists' uses of old photographic techniques?

(A)　doubtful hesitation about the artistic value of
using old techniques
(B)　appreciative understanding of the artists' aesthetic
goals
(C)　ironic amusement at the continued use of
techniques that are obsolete
(D)　enthusiastic endorsement of their implicit critique
of modern photographic technology
(E)　whimsical curiosity about the ways in which the
processes work

10.　Information in the passage most helps to answer which
one of the following questions?

(A)　What are some nineteenth-century photographic
techniques that have not been revived?
(B)　What is the chemical makeup of the emulsion
applied to the iron plate in the tintype process?
(C)　What are the names of some contemporary
photographers who are using pinhole cameras?
(D)　What effect is produced when photographic paper
is coated with egg whites?
(E)　What were the perceived advantages of the
innovations that led to the obsolescence of many
early photographic techniques and processes?

GO ON TO THE NEXT PAGE.

11. Which one of the following most accurately describes the primary purpose of the passage?

(A) to make a case for the aesthetic value of certain old photographic processes
(B) to provide details of how certain old methods of photographic processing are used in producing artistic photographs
(C) to give an account of a surprising recent development in the photographic arts
(D) to explain the acclaim that photographers using old photographic techniques have received
(E) to contrast the approaches used by two contemporary photographers

12. Which one of the following is most analogous to the use of old photographic techniques for artistic purposes by late-twentieth-century artists, as described in the passage?

(A) A biomedical researcher in a pharmaceutical firm researches the potential of certain traditional herbal remedies for curing various skin conditions.
(B) An architect investigates ancient accounts of classical building styles in order to get inspiration for designing a high-rise office building.
(C) An engineer uses an early-twentieth-century design for a highly efficient turbocharger in preference to a new computer-aided design.
(D) A clothing designer uses fabrics woven on old-fashioned looms in order to produce the irregular texture of handwoven garments.
(E) An artist uses a computer graphics program to reproduce stylized figures from ancient paintings and insert them into a depiction of a modern city landscape.

13. Based on the information in the passage, it can be inferred that Estabrook believes that

(A) photography in the nineteenth century tended to focus on subjects that are especially striking and aesthetically interesting
(B) artists can relinquish control over significant aspects of the process of creating their work and still produce the aesthetic effects they desire
(C) photographs produced in the nineteenth and early twentieth centuries were generally intended to exploit artistically the unpredictability of photographic processing
(D) it is ethically questionable to produce works of art intended to deceive the viewer into believing that the works are older than they really are
(E) the aesthetic significance of a photograph depends primarily on factors that can be manipulated after the photograph has been taken

14. The reasoning by which, according to the passage, Estabrook justifies his choice of certain strategies in photographic processing would be most strengthened if which one of the following were true?

(A) When advanced modern photographic techniques are used to intentionally produce prints with imperfections resembling those in nineteenth-century prints, the resulting prints invariably betray the artifice involved.
(B) The various feelings evoked by a work of art are independent of the techniques used to produce the work and irrelevant to its artistic value.
(C) Most people who use photographs as a way of remembering or learning about the past value them almost exclusively for their ability to record their subjects accurately.
(D) People who are interested in artistic photography seldom see much artistic value in photographs that appear antique but are not really so.
(E) The latest photographic techniques can produce photographs that are almost completely free of blemishes and highly resistant to deterioration over time.

GO ON TO THE NEXT PAGE.

PT 69 RC

Passage A is from a 2007 article on the United States patent system; passage B is from a corporate statement.

Passage A

Theoretically, the patent office is only supposed to award patents for "nonobvious" inventions, and the concept of translating between an Internet address and a telephone number certainly seems obvious. Still,
(5) a court recently held that a technology company had infringed on patents covering computer servers that perform these translations.

In an ideal world, patents would be narrow enough that companies could "invent around" others'
(10) patents if licensing agreements cannot be reached. Unfortunately, the patent system has departed from this ideal. In recent decades, the courts have dramatically lowered the bar for obviousness. As a result, some patents being granted are so broad that
(15) inventing around them is practically impossible.

Large technology companies have responded to this proliferation of bad patents with the patent equivalent of nuclear stockpiling. By obtaining hundreds or even thousands of patents, a company
(20) can develop a credible deterrent against patent lawsuits: if someone sues it for patent infringement, it can find a patent the other company has infringed and countersue. Often, however, a fundamental mistake is made: not joining this arms race. As a result, a
(25) company can find itself defenseless against lawsuits.

Software patents are particularly ripe for abuse because software is assembled from modular components. If the patent system allows those components to be patented, it becomes almost
(30) impossible to develop a software product without infringing numerous patents. Moreover, because of the complexity of software, it is often prohibitively expensive to even find all the patents a given software product might in principle be infringing. So even a
(35) software maker that wanted to find and license all of the patents relevant to its products is unlikely to be able to do so.

Passage B

Software makers like ours have consistently taken the position that patents generally impede innovation
(40) in software development and are inconsistent with open-source/free software. We will continue to work to promote this position and are pleased to join our colleagues in the open-source/free software community, as well as those proprietary vendors who have publicly
(45) stated their opposition to software patents.

At the same time, we are forced to live in the world as it is, and that world currently permits software patents. A small number of very large companies have amassed large numbers of software
(50) patents. We believe such massive software patent portfolios are ripe for misuse because of the questionable nature of many software patents generally and because of the high cost of patent litigation.

One defense against such misuse is to develop a
(55) corresponding portfolio of software patents for defensive purposes. Many software makers, both open-source and proprietary, pursue this strategy. In the interests of our company and in an attempt to protect and promote the open-source community,
(60) we have elected to adopt this same stance. We do so reluctantly because of the perceived inconsistency with our stance against software patents; however, prudence dictates this position.

15. Which one of the following pairs would be most appropriate as titles for passage A and passage B, respectively?

(A) "The Use and Abuse of Patents"
"The Necessary Elimination of Software Patents"
(B) "Reforming Patent Laws"
"In Defense of Software Patents"
(C) "Patenting the Obvious"
"Patents: A Defensive Policy"
(D) "A Misunderstanding of Patent Policies"
"Keeping Software Free but Safe"
(E) "Developing a Credible Deterrent Against Patent Lawsuits"
"An Apology to Our Customers"

16. Which one of the following is mentioned in passage A but not in passage B?

(A) the amassing of patents by software companies
(B) the cost of finding all the patents a product may infringe
(C) the negative effect of patents on software development
(D) the high cost of patent litigation in general
(E) the dubious nature of many software patents

17. Which one of the following comes closest to capturing the meaning of the phrase "invent around" (line 9)?

(A) invent a product whose use is so obvious that no one can have a patent on it
(B) conceal the fact that a product infringes a patent
(C) implement a previously patented idea in a way other than that intended by the patent holder
(D) develop new products based on principles that are entirely different from those for products affected by competitors' patents
(E) devise something that serves the same function as the patented invention without violating the patent

GO ON TO THE NEXT PAGE.

18. Which one of the following most accurately describes the relationship between the two passages?

(A) Passage A objectively reports a set of events; passage B subjectively takes issue with aspects of the reported events.

(B) Passage A discusses a problem in an industry; passage B states the position of a party dealing with that problem.

(C) Passage A is highly critical of a defensive strategy used by an industry; passage B is a clarification of that strategy.

(D) Passage A describes an impasse within an industry; passage B suggests a way out of this impasse.

(E) Passage A lays out both sides of a dispute; passage B focuses on one of those sides.

19. The authors of the passages would be most likely to agree that software companies would be well advised to

(A) amass their own portfolios of software patents
(B) attempt to license software patented by other companies
(C) exploit patents already owned by competitors
(D) refrain from infringing on any patents held by other companies
(E) research the patents relevant to their products more thoroughly

20. In terms of what it alludes to, "this same stance" (line 60) is most closely related to which one of the following phrases in passage A?

(A) nonobvious (line 2)
(B) invent around (line 9)
(C) lowered the bar (line 13)
(D) credible deterrent (line 20)
(E) modular components (lines 27–28)

21. Which one of the following, if true, would cast doubt on the position concerning innovation in software development taken in the first paragraph of passage B?

(A) Most patents for software innovations have a duration of only 20 years or less.

(B) Software companies that do not patent software generally offer products that are more reliable than those that do.

(C) Some proprietary vendors oppose software patents for self-interested reasons.

(D) Software innovation would be less profitable if software could not be patented.

(E) The main beneficiaries of software innovations are large corporations rather than individual innovators.

GO ON TO THE NEXT PAGE.

PT 69 RC

Calvaria major is a rare but once-abundant tree found on the island of Mauritius, which was also home to the dodo, a large flightless bird that became extinct about three centuries ago. In 1977 Stanley Temple,
(5) an ecologist whose investigation of *Calvaria major* was a sidelight to his research on endangered birds of Mauritius, proposed that the population decline of *Calvaria major* was linked to the demise of the dodo, a hypothesis that subsequently gained considerable
(10) currency. Temple had found only thirteen *Calvaria major* trees on Mauritius, all overmature and dying, and all estimated by foresters at over 300 years old. These trees produced fruits that appeared fertile but that Temple assumed could no longer germinate,
(15) given his failure to find younger trees.

The temporal coincidence between the extinction of the dodo and what Temple considered the last evidence of natural germination of *Calvaria major* seeds led him to posit a causal connection. Specifically,
(20) he hypothesized that the fruit of *Calvaria major* had developed its extremely thick-walled pit as an evolutionary response to the dodo's habitual consumption of those fruits, a trait enabling the pits to withstand the abrasive forces exerted on them in
(25) the birds' digestive tracts. This defensive thickness, though, ultimately prevented the seeds within the pits from germinating without the thinning caused by abrasion in the dodo's gizzard. What had once been adaptive, Temple maintained, became a lethal
(30) imprisonment for the seeds after the dodo vanished.

Although direct proof was unattainable, Temple did offer some additional findings in support of his hypothesis, which lent his argument a semblance of rigor. From studies of other birds, he estimated the
(35) abrasive force generated within a dodo's gizzard. Based on this estimate and on test results determining the crush-resistant strength of *Calvaria major* pits, he concluded that the pits could probably have withstood a cycle through a dodo's gizzard. He also fed *Calvaria*
(40) *major* pits to turkeys, and though many of the pits were destroyed, ten emerged, abraded yet intact. Three of these sprouted when planted, which he saw as vindicating his hypothesis.

Though many scientists found this dramatic and
(45) intriguing hypothesis plausible, Temple's proposals have been strongly challenged by leading specialists in the field. Where Temple had found only thirteen specimens of *Calvaria major*, Wendy Strahm, the foremost expert on the plant ecology of Mauritius,
(50) has identified hundreds, many far younger than three centuries. So *Calvaria major* seeds have in fact germinated, and the tree's reproductive cycle has thus continued, since the dodo's disappearance. Additional counterevidence comes from horticultural
(55) research by Anthony Speke, which shows that while only a minority of unabraded *Calvaria major* seeds germinate, the number is still probably sufficient to keep this species from becoming extinct. The population decline, while clearly acute, could easily

(60) be due to other factors, including disease and damage done by certain nonindigenous animals introduced onto Mauritius in the past few centuries.

22. Which one of the following most accurately expresses the main point of the passage?

(A) *Calvaria major* germination, though rare, is probably adequate to avoid extinction of the species.

(B) The appeal of Temple's hypothesis notwithstanding, the scarcity of *Calvaria major* is probably not due to the extinction of the dodo.

(C) Temple's experimentation with *Calvaria major* pits, though methodologically unsound, nevertheless led to a probable solution to the mystery of the tree's decline.

(D) Temple's dramatic but speculative hypothesis, though presented without sufficient supporting research, may nevertheless be correct.

(E) Calvaria major would probably still be scarce today even if the dodo had not become extinct.

23. The author indicates that Temple's research on birds of the island of Mauritius

(A) was largely concerned with species facing the threat of extinction

(B) furnished him with the basis for his highly accurate estimates of the crush-resistant strength of *Calvaria major* pits

(C) provided experimental evidence that some modern birds' gizzards exert roughly the same amount of abrasive force on their contents as did dodo gizzards

(D) was comprehensive in scope and conducted with methodological precision

(E) was originally inspired by his observation that apparently fertile Calvaria major pits were nevertheless no longer able to germinate

GO ON TO THE NEXT PAGE.

PT 69 RC

24. In saying that Temple's supporting evidence lent his argument a "semblance of rigor" (lines 33–34), the author most likely intends to indicate that

(A) despite his attempts to use strict scientific methodology, Temple's experimental findings regarding *Calvaria major* pits were not carefully derived and thus merely appeared to support his hypothesis

(B) direct proof of a hypothesis of the sort Temple was investigating is virtually impossible to obtain, even with the most exact measurements and observations

(C) in contrast to Temple's secondhand information concerning the age of the thirteen overmature *Calvaria major* trees he found, his experiments with turkeys and other birds represented careful and accurate firsthand research

(D) in his experimentation on *Calvaria major* pits, Temple produced quantitative experimental results that superficially appeared to bolster the scientific credibility of his hypothesis

(E) although the consensus among experts is that Temple's overall conclusion is mistaken, the scientific precision and the creativity of Temple's experimentation remain admirable

25. The passage indicates which one of the following about the abrasion of *Calvaria major* pit walls?

(A) Thinning through abrasion is not necessary for germination of *Calvaria major* seeds.

(B) In Temple's experiment, the abrasion caused by the digestive tracts of turkeys always released *Calvaria major* seeds, undamaged, from their hard coverings.

(C) Temple was mistaken in believing that the abrasion caused by dodos would have been sufficient to thin the pit walls to any significant degree.

(D) Abrasion of *Calvaria major* pit walls by the digestive tracts of animals occurred commonly in past centuries but rarely occurs in nature today.

(E) Temple overlooked the fact that other natural environmental forces have been abrading *Calvaria major* pit walls since the dodo ceased to fulfill this role.

26. It can be most logically inferred from the passage that the author regards Temple's hypothesis that the extinction of the dodo was the cause of *Calvaria major*'s seeming loss of the ability to reproduce as which one of the following?

(A) essentially correct, but containing some inaccurate details

(B) initially implausible, but vindicated by his empirical findings

(C) an example of a valuable scientific achievement outside a researcher's primary area of expertise

(D) laudable for its precise formulation and its attention to historical detail

(E) an attempt to explain a state of affairs that did not in fact exist

27. Based on the passage, it can be inferred that the author would be likely to agree with each of the following statements about *Calvaria major* EXCEPT:

(A) The causes of the evolution of the tree's particularly durable pit wall have not been definitively identified by Temple's critics.

(B) The notion that the thickness of the pit wall in the tree's fruit has been a factor contributing to the decline of the tree has not been definitively discredited.

(C) In light of the current rate of germination of seeds of the species, it is surprising that the tree has not been abundant since the dodo's disappearance.

(D) There is good reason to believe that the tree is not threatened with imminent extinction.

(E) Calvaria major seeds can germinate even if they do not first pass through a bird's digestive system.

S T O P

IF YOU FINISH BEFORE TIME IS CALLED, YOU MAY CHECK YOUR WORK ON THIS SECTION ONLY.
DO NOT WORK ON ANY OTHER SECTION IN THE TEST.

PT 69 RC

June 2013 Section 3: Reading Comprehension

Overview: The higher-than-average difficulty of this section was hardly surprising. While neither of the first two passages was particularly dense, many of the questions that followed each passage required close reading and unusually high attention to detail (especially questions #5, #7, and #14). That, coupled with the high number of questions per passage (7), resulted in a relatively slow first half of the section. Unfortunately, the comparative passage (Nonobvious Inventions) was the wrong one to try and pick up speed on. The esoteric subject matter of patent law was only compounded by the rambling argument in passage A, requiring you to slow down instead of speeding up. Thankfully, awareness of passage similarities and differences was sufficient to answer most of the questions relatively quickly. The last passage (The Dodo Bird) was probably the easiest one to follow, because it followed a predictable structure for a Science passage. However, the passage severely penalized test takers who tried to save time by skimming at the end, because the main point was not explicitly stated until the end of the passage. Not coincidentally, half the questions hinged on your understanding of the last paragraph.

Passage #1: Small Farms

Paragraph One:

The passage opens with a rather common paradigm in Reading Comprehension passages: the author outlines a problem and immediately proposes a solution. The problem, in this case, involves the high rate of bankruptcy among small farms; the solution, proposed by Booker Whatley, suggests that small farms can thrive despite the prevailing trend toward massive agricultural production. The last sentence captures Whatley's main point, but does not delve into details about *how* small farms can become profitable. We can expect to learn more about that in the next paragraph.

Paragraph Two:

The second paragraph summarizes Whatley's guidelines for small farmers, and is key to understanding the passage. Each recommendation represents the means of achieving a particular objective:

Objective		Solution
1. Generate year-round cash flow	⟶	Grow at least 10 different crops
2. Avoid taking on loans	⟶	Clientele membership club (CMC)
3. Secure a market for all crops	⟶	Grow only crops that clients ask for

While you need not remember every single objective and the specific means to achieving it, it is critical to at least notate the solutions. Their specificity is incredibly helpful, adding some substance to a passage that would otherwise be quite vague.

Paragraph Three:

Compared to the second paragraph, the third one plays a supporting role. Here, the author explains *why* "pick-your-own" farming makes financial sense: by using clients as harvesters, Whatley argues that small farmers can save money, undercut supermarkets and still operate the farm at a profit. Who are these clients, you may ask? Well, according to Whatley, they would be city dwellers who value fresh produce enough to drive to farms in order to harvest their own food.

You are completely justified in having a strong reaction to this line of reasoning. In fact, you *should* have a reaction. You may think it's a great idea to pick your own kale, and that Whatley is awesome for advocating something you've been dying to do yourself. It is also OK if you see him as an absolute lunatic ("Me? On a farm?!"). Either way, having a strong reaction to the passage you read is tremendously helpful: it both reveals, and in turn promotes, an active, aggressive approach to Reading Comprehension that is critical to mastering this section. It also makes the whole sordid experience slightly more fun.

Paragraph Four:

The author concludes by outlining an additional set of recommendations for small farmers, and then restates Whatley's main point. Particularly important is the caveat mentioned in the beginning of the paragraph: the success of Whatley's plan depends on a farm's location, on hard-surfaced roads close to the city. Whatley calls these roads "city-to-farm" (rather than "farm-to-market"). Make sure to notate each additional recommendation, and be prepared to reference that section of the text should a question require you to do so.

VIEWSTAMP Analysis:

The primary **Viewpoint** presented here is that of Whatley, who argues that small farms can thrive by following certain guidelines. The farmers' own position are never overtly discussed.

The general **Structure** of the passage is as follows:

Paragraph One: Describe a problem affecting small farms, and introduce someone who has a solution (Booker T. Whatley).

Paragraph Two: Outline Whatley's guidelines for operating a small farm.

Paragraph Three: Explain why "pick-your-own" farming is crucial for operating a small farm.

Paragraph Four: Explain the importance of location and list additional recommendations to help small farmers adopt Whatley's solutions.

Strangely enough, Whatley's views are neither challenged nor defended. The author exhibits a **Tone** that is somewhat deferential towards the African American horticulturalist, but no overt judgment is made as to the merits of the proposed recommendations.

The only **Argument** presented is that of Whatley, who proposes a solution to the problems associated with small-scale farming. The feasibility of his recommendations is the main point of the passage, and is supported by various observations in the third and fourth paragraphs.

The **Main Point** is to describe Whatley's recommendations, the adoption of which is supposed to help small farms thrive despite the prevailing trends in agriculture.

Question #1: GR, Main Point. The correct answer choice is (A)

The answer to a Main Point question should always be prephrased. See VIEWSTAMP analysis above.

Answer choice (A): This is the correct answer choice. The main point of the passage is to present Whatley's position, which is summarized in the first paragraph and then restated at the end of the fourth.

Answer choice (B): While Whatley's approach to farming is indeed sensitive to the demands of the consumer, it is unclear whether the dominant trends in agriculture are different in this respect. Even if such a distinction can be made, it would certainly not be the main point of the passage.

Answer choice (C): His preference for small farms notwithstanding, Whatley never intended to provide a "general critique" of the prevailing trend in agriculture. Furthermore, Whatley does not merely "assess" the ability of small farms to compete; instead, he provides a set of recommendations to *help* them compete.

Answer choice (D): Hopefully, you were able to eliminate this answer choice relatively quickly, because CMCs are not the main point of the passage. Furthermore, it is unclear whether they are *necessary* for the success of small farming.

Answer choice (E): The author never explicitly discusses what effect, if any, the adoption of Whatley's methods would have on farming, let alone suggest that it would eventually threaten the dominance of large-scale production.

Question #2: CR, Must—PR, SP. The correct answer choice is (B)

To answer this Must Be True—Principle question correctly, you need to have a good handle on Whatley's plan for operating a small farm. The correct answer choice must describe a strategy that conforms to the core principles of that plan, thereby facilitating its implementation.

Answer choice (A): Whatley does not consider small farms to be a testing ground for new crops. This strategy carries a considerable risk, which Whatley clearly seeks to avoid.

Answer choice (B): This is the correct answer choice. One aspect of Whatley's plan involves selling directly to customers, who would travel to the farm to harvest their own produce ("pick your own farm"). If farmers designed their farms so as to allow people easier access at harvest time, this would help farmers implement Whatley's recommendations.

Answer choice (C): Whatley expects city dwellers to visit the farms, not the farmers to visit the city. This is a Reverse answer choice.

Answer choice (D): There is no indication that Whatley's plan would benefit from an honor system: if farm profitability is the ultimate objective, this strategy is unlikely to be particularly helpful.

Answer choice (E): Whatley's position regarding the use of chemicals can be found in lines 24-25: farmers should comply with *clients'* requests (rather than make that decision on their own). Moreover, there is little reason to expect that Whatley would sacrifice crop yields for environmental reasons alone.

Question #3: CR, Must, SP. The correct answer choice is (C)

To answer this Concept Reference question, you need to provide a reason why "pick-your-own" farming is a good idea. Once again, passage organization is key. Whatley's reasons for promoting a "pick-your-own" farming approach are discussed in the third paragraph: by using clients as harvesters, small farmers can save money, undercut supermarkets and operate their farms at a profit.

Answer choice (A): Customers may well enjoy experiencing firsthand where their produce comes from, but Whatley never mentions this as a reason why "pick-your-own" farming is crucial for profitability.

Answer choice (B): This answer choice contains an exaggeration ("substantial"). Moreover, while Whatley argues that small farms must generate year-round cash flow (lines 13-14), there is no evidence that "pick-your-own" farming *guarantees* such a cash flow. This is a Mistaken Reversal of the argument in lines 26-27, in which "pick-your-own" farming is seen as a necessary, not a sufficient, condition for profitability.

Answer choice (C): This is the correct answer choice: "pick-your-own" farming allows farmers to undercut supermarkets and still operate the farm at a profit (lines 26-31).

Answer choice (D): This is an attractive Shell Game answer choice, because it agrees with Whatley's recommendation that farmers grow only those crops specifically requested by their clients (lines 21-24). However, this answer choice is incorrect for two reasons: First, Whatley tells farmers to grow only the *crops* requested by their clients (if clients ask for apples, grow apples), not some specific *variety* of crops (Granny Smith vs. Fuji, for instance). More importantly, his advice is never advanced as a reason why "pick-your-own" farming is necessary for the operation of small farms. Rather, it is only seen as a strategy to help farmers guarantee a market for all their crops (line 22).

This is a great example of a trap you can easily avoid by focusing on passage structure: the author confines the discussion of *why* Whatley's plan is crucial for profitability to the third paragraph only. Any answer choice that mentions ideas brought up elsewhere in the passage is likely to be incorrect.

Answer choice (E): Whatley does not recommend "pick-your-own" farming because there is a strong market for it. Location is important to ensure a sizable market, but that was never advanced as a reason to adopt his plan. If you focused on the argument in the third paragraph, this answer choice would be relatively easy to eliminate.

Question #4: GR, Must, P. The correct answer choice is (A)

The answer to this Purpose question should be broad in scope, and is prephrased in the VIEWSTAMP analysis above.

Answer choice (A): This is the correct answer choice. The solution is clearly innovative, because Whatley's approach to small farming runs counter to the dominant trends in agriculture (lines 7-8). The problem is described as "growing" in line 4, so to call it "serious" would not be an exaggeration.

Answer choice (B): The author never isolated the strengths and weaknesses of any contemporary trends.

Answer choice (C): Even though Whatley may well be critical of the prevailing trends in agriculture and its "sprawling corporate farms" (lines 53-54), such criticism is subtly insinuated and not the main purpose of the passage.

Answer choice (D): There is no debate of the "pros-and-cons" regarding Whatley's approach to small farming: the author is never critical of his recommendations, making this answer choice relatively easy to eliminate.

Answer choice (E): This is an attractive answer choice, because Whatley clearly believes that adhering to his plan will have an impact on agriculture (lines 52-55). However, there is no indication that the *author* would agree with this prediction. Remember: the purpose of the passage is to describe Whatley's ideas, not analyze their impact.

Question #5: GR, Must. The correct answer choice is (D)

The general nature of the question makes it difficult to arrive at a more precise prephrase. Instead, try the process of elimination: any answer choice that cannot be proven by the passage will be incorrect.

Answer choice (A): Although corporate farming depends heavily on debt and credit as a means of raising capital (lines 3-4), no comparison is made between corporate and small farms in this respect.

Answer choice (B): Small farms can allegedly charge less than supermarkets and still operate at a profit (lines 29-31), but that does not mean that farmers' profits would rise if they charged the same. Such hypotheticals are impossible to prove with the information given.

Answer choice (C): No comparison is ever made between rural and urban consumers' inclination to join a CMC. Just because CMCs would consist primarily of people from metropolitan areas does not mean that rural folk are less *willing* to join them. The reason why small farms must be located close to urban centers is to guarantee a client base large enough to ensure profitability, not necessarily one that is more inclined to join a CMC.

Answer choice (D): This is the correct answer choice. It is tricky, and many students tend to dismiss it all too quickly. Recall that one of Whatley's recommendations involved growing at least ten different crops (line 15). Logically, then, if a CMC requests fewer than ten different crops, then at least one of Whatley's recommendations will not be followed.

The ability to answer this question correctly underscores the importance of knowing passage structure, along with the need to make a few simple notations while reading. The answer choice describes a situation whereby one of Whatley's recommendations is not being followed. As long as you know where these recommendations were discussed in the passage, you can easily return to that portion of the text and validate your choice. Better yet, observant test-takers would have notated each of the three main guidelines described in the second paragraph, and expect to be questioned on that list.

Answer choice (E): By selling directly to consumers, small farms with a CMC can *eliminate* distribution costs (lines 31-33). Such costs do not need to be accounted for, or paid for by customers.

Question #6: CR, Must, SP. The correct answer choice is (D)

This Concept Reference question asks us to identify an element of Whatley's plan that helps guarantee that small farms have buyers for all of their produce. If you notated the three main recommendations in the second paragraph, you should have no trouble proving the correct answer choice.

Answer choice (A): This Shell Game answer represents a common psychometric trick. The need to grow at least ten different crops appeared in the correct answer choice to the previous question, and is indeed one of the recommendations mentioned in the second paragraph. However, grouping multiple crops is not meant to help small famers secure buyers for all their produce (this would be somewhat counterintuitive). Instead, it aims to soften the financial blow should one crop fail completely (lines 16-17). This answer choice is incorrect.

Answer choice (B): This is another Shell Game answer. "Pick-your-own" farming enables farmers to charge 60 percent of what supermarkets charge for the same produce, but there is no evidence that undercutting supermarkets will in turn guarantee buyers for all crops.

Answer choice (C): CMCs are clearly geared towards clients who value fresh produce, but there is no evidence that *only* such clients will ever be recruited. Furthermore, the mere preference for fresh produce is unlikely to guarantee buyers for all of crops grown on the farm.

Answer choice (D): This is the correct answer choice. To guarantee a market for all their crops, Whatley encourages farmers to grow only crops that clients ask for, and also to comply with their wishes regarding chemical use (lines 21-25).

Answer choice (E): While irrigating crops is mentioned in the last paragraph, this is not a strategy that aims to guarantee buyers. Avoid picking an answer choice simply because you recall reading it in the passage, unless you can prove that it answers the specific question at hand.

Question #7: GR, Must. The correct answer choice is (B)

As with Question 5, the general nature of the question stem makes it difficult to arrive at a precise prephrase. Instead, try the process of elimination: any answer choice that cannot be proven by the passage will be incorrect.

Answer choice (A): Farmers are encouraged to grow only the crops requested by clients, but no guarantee is ever made that the clients will get the produce they want.

Answer choice (B): This is the correct answer choice. In the last paragraph, the author describes how Whatley reverses the traditional view of hard-surfaced roads as farm-to-market roads, calling them instead "city-to-farm" roads (lines 44-46). It is reasonable to conclude, then, that these roads are traditionally the means by which farmers transport their produce to the cities.

Answer choice (C): A typical 25-acre farm needs a CMC with 1,000 members, not a population center of 1,000 people. The author never suggested that a population center of 50,000 can support fifty farms with CMCs. Test makers are quite fond of "tricking" you with numbers: pay close attention to what they mean, and what they don't.

Answer choice (D): There are probably quite a few reasons why consumers would prefer hard-surfaced roads to other roads. No specific reason for their preference is mentioned in the passage.

Answer choice (E): While hard-surfaced roads are traditionally the means by which farmers transported their produce, the roads were not necessarily *intended* for farmers. Some might have been, but we have no way of proving that by relying solely on the information contained in the passage.

Passage #2: Tintype

Paragraph One:

In the first paragraph, the author introduces Jayne Hinds Bidaut, who revived the tintype technique in order to take pictures of insects. Just in case you do not know what a tintype is, its definition can be found in lines 7-8 and should be notated.

Paragraph Two:

The second paragraph introduces another photographer—Dan Estabrook—who imagines using old techniques to take photos that people would discover as "originals" in flea markets or antique shops.

Paragraph Three:

The third paragraph provides additional examples of obsolete photographic techniques that are suddenly *en vogue*. It is entirely unnecessary to remember every single one of them, so use a bracket to notate the examples (Ex.), and make a mental note to refer to that section of the passage when needed. There is no discernible point to this passage yet, but you should get a general sense of where it is going: old photographic techniques are being revived, and you should expect to find out why.

Paragraph Four:

In the fourth paragraph, the author outlines some of the motivations behind the contemporary revival of the old photographic processing. While its imperfections caused earlier photographers to seek more reliable replacements, these same imperfections are now exploited for artistic purposes. To exemplify this trend, the author mentions Estabrook: he embraced accident and unpredictability in photographic processing because they foster the illusion of antiquity.

Paragraph Five:

The last paragraph is rather vague, but its subtlety is key to understanding the author's attitude toward artists' uses of old photographic techniques. The author appreciates the fact that each photograph is a unique testament to the artist's encounter with the world, and clearly values the intimacy of our experience generated by such photographs.

VIEWSTAMP Analysis:

There are several **Viewpoints** expressed in this passage (Bidaut's, Estabrook's, the author's), but there are no meaningful differences between them.

The **Structure** of the passage is as follows:

Paragraph One: Introduce Bidaut and describe what a tintype is.

Paragraph Two: Describe Estabrook's penchant for planting fake antique photographs in flea markets.

Paragraph Three: Mention other photographic techniques that have recently been revived.

Paragraph Four: Explain the appeal of old photographic techniques to modern-day artists such as Estabrook.

Paragraph Five: Reveal the author's attitude toward the use of old photographic techniques.

The author's **Tone** is revealed primarily in the last paragraph. She appreciates the revival of old photographic techniques and understands their aesthetic appeal.

The primary **Argument** in the passage is that of the author, whose appreciation of old photographic techniques is supported by a series of observations regarding their modern use. It is important to recognize that the actual argument in defense of such techniques is not made until the last paragraph of the passage. The other argument to note is Estabrook's, a photographer who embraces the imperfections of old photographic processes in order to achieve certain aesthetic effects. The two arguments are in agreement, and neither of them is challenged by a third party.

The **Main Point** is to account for the revival of various old photographic techniques and explain their aesthetic significance to modern artists.

Question #8: SR, Must, P. The correct answer choice is (A)

This Specific Reference/Purpose question asks us to explain why the author highlights the fact that we are "on the verge of a filmless, digital revolution" in line 17. Such questions almost always require a more thorough understanding of the context in which the quoted reference appears, and their answers should always be prephrased.

Answer choice (A): This is the correct answer choice. The first three paragraphs describe the peculiar revival of old photographic techniques. Highlighting our advanced technological age makes this revival seem even more striking, unusual, and ironic.

Answer choice (B): While some photographers seem to eschew new technology in favor of old-fashioned ones, there is no reason to suspect that *most* photographers are wary of using advanced photographic techniques. This answer choice contains an exaggeration and is incorrect.

Answer choice (C): The author is not skeptical toward the trend of using old photographic techniques; on the contrary, she seems quite fond of it. This answer choice can easily be eliminated if you kept awareness of passage tone.

Answer choice (D): Just because some photographers have rediscovered old processes does not mean that *most* photographers now see little merit in the newest digital technology. As with answer choice (B), this one contains an exaggeration.

Answer choice (E): As someone who appreciates the recent interest in old photographic techniques, the author is unlikely to suggest that it will turn out to be a passing fad. Such a prediction implies skepticism regarding this trend, for which there is no basis. As with answer choice (C), you can easily eliminate this answer choice if you paid attention to the tone of the passage.

Question #9: CR, Must, Tone. The correct answer choice is (B)

To determine the author's attitude toward the use of old photographic techniques, we need to evaluate the language used in the last paragraph and formulate a suitable prephrase. Such is provided in the VIEWSTAMP analysis above.

Answer choice (A): This answer choice is incorrect, because the author is neither hesitant nor skeptical toward the value of using old techniques. Her attitude is overwhelmingly positive.

Answer choice (B): This is the correct answer choice. In the last paragraph of the passage, the use of old photographic techniques is said to reveal "the deeper motivations" of the artists (line 47), ensuring that each production is "one of a kind" (line 50). This language reveals a decidedly positive attitude, respectful of the artists' aesthetic objectives.

Answer choice (C): We have no reason to believe that the author finds the continued use of old techniques to be ironic or amusing. (Just because you may feel this way does not mean the author shares your views.)

Answer choice (D): This answer choice may seem attractive, but is out of scope. While the author clearly sees the use of old techniques in a positive light, her endorsement is not intended to critique modern photographic technology.

Answer choice (E): This is another attractive, but incorrect, answer choice. The author describes how some of the processes work, but her descriptions are brief and to the point. There is nothing "whimsical" about them. Furthermore, the author shows less curiosity about the *ways* in which the processes work than about their overall aesthetic value.

Question #10: GR, Must. The correct answer choice is (E)

To identify a question whose answer can be found in the passage, try the process of elimination. The general nature of the question stem makes it difficult to arrive at a precise prephrase.

Answer choice (A): The passage only provides information regarding techniques that *have* been revived. This answer choice is incorrect.

Answer choice (B): This is a tricky question, requiring us to return to the passage and verify the information provided. Passage organization is key: the first paragraph describes the tintype in some detail, alluding to an image-containing emulsion applied to the iron plate (lines 7-11). The chemical composition of that emulsion, however, is never discussed, making this answer choice incorrect.

Answer choice (C): Pinhole cameras are mentioned on line 21, but the photographers using them are never discussed by name.

Answer choice (D): Coating paper with egg whites is mentioned in lines 20-21, but the resulting photographic effect is never described.

Answer choice (E): This is the correct answer choice. In the fourth paragraph, the author describes the modern techniques as being "simpler, cheaper, faster, and more consistent in their results" (lines 31-32), qualities that led to the obsolescence of earlier photographic processes.

Question #11: GR, Must, P. The correct answer choice is (C)

The answer to this Purpose question should be broad in scope, and is prephrased in the VIEWSTAMP analysis above.

Answer choice (A): This answer choice can seem attractive, because the author clearly sees the aesthetic value of using old photographic techniques. However, for the most part her tone is descriptive rather than polemic, so it is somewhat misleading to describe the entire passage as "making a case" for anything. Indeed, the author's own beliefs do not become apparent until the last paragraph. Keep in mind that your job is to determine the primary purpose of the passage *as a whole*: just because the author seems convinced of something does not mean that the *purpose of the passage* is to convince us of that same thing.

Answer choice (B): This answer choice is the polar opposite of answer choice (A), and is also incorrect. Details about the modern uses of old photographic techniques are provided in the first three paragraphs only; the fourth and the fifth paragraphs explain why such processes are aesthetically valuable. The primary purpose of the passage is not to delve into specifics.

Answer choice (C): This is the correct answer choice. The phrase "give an account" is general enough to capture both the provision of detail in the first three paragraphs, and the expository content of the last two. The development in photographic arts is clearly recent, and can easily be described as "surprising" given our advanced technological age. Note also that the adjective "surprising" is synonymous to "ironic," which—not coincidentally—was key in answering question 8.

Answer choice (D): This answer choice can be eliminated relatively quickly, because there is no evidence that the photographers received popular acclaim.

Answer choice (E): The author describes the approaches used by two contemporary photographers, but no explicit comparison is made between them. This answer choice is incorrect.

Question #12: CR, Parallel. The correct answer choice is (D)

To answer this Parallel question correctly, we need to attain a more abstract understanding of the ways in which contemporary photographers use old processes. Using the Test of Abstraction from Parallel Reasoning questions, we can formulate a suitable prephrase: The correct answer choice must describe a contemporary use of an obsolete technique, the product of which contains certain highly desirable imperfections.

Answer choice (A): The medicinal use of traditional herbal remedies bears some resemblance to the revival of obsolete photographic techniques, but the remedies are not sought out because of their imperfections. Rather, the researcher is interested in their potential for curing various skin conditions. This answer choice is incorrect.

Answer choice (B): Unlike an architect investigating classical buildings to get inspiration for a modern project, the photographers described in the passage are not necessarily *inspired* by the use of old techniques. Furthermore, the photographs are deliberately left imperfect in order to foster the illusion of antiquity; there is no evidence of similar imperfections in the design of the high-rise office buildings (or so we hope). This answer choice is incorrect.

Answer choice (C): The engineer's preference for an earlier, highly efficient design bears no resemblance to the use of less efficient photographic techniques. This answer choice is incorrect.

Answer choice (D): This is the correct answer choice. Just as the artistic photographs are made using obsolete techniques, so are the fabrics woven on old-fashioned looms. In either case, the final product contains desirable imperfections, making this answer choice a perfect match.

Answer choice (E): Hopefully you were able to eliminate this answer choice relatively quickly, because computer graphics modeling is not an obsolete technique.

Question #13: CR, Must, SP. The correct answer choice is (B)

This Must Be True question concerns Estabrook's beliefs. As always, passage organization is key: Estabrook's penchant for planting fake antique photographs in flea markets is described in the second paragraph, and his artistic motivations are discussed in the fourth. Either paragraph can serve as a useful reference point in validating the correct answer choice.

Answer choice (A): It is the photographic *processes* of the nineteenth century, not their subject matter, that Estabrook found especially striking and interesting. This answer choice is incorrect.

Answer choice (B): This is the correct answer choice. In the fourth paragraph, Estabrook is described as an artist who is attracted to the unpredictability of old processes (lines 35-36): instead of cropping out the imperfections they produce, he retained them in order to foster the illusion of antiquity. Clearly, Estabrook must believe that artists like himself can relinquish control over the creative process and still produce the aesthetic effects they desire.

Answer choice (C): This answer choice describes how *modern-day* photographers are using obsolete techniques, not how their predecessors used them in the past. Earlier photographers tried to edit out the imperfections resulting from the use of unpredictable processing (line 41-45). This answer choice is incorrect.

Answer choice (D): Clearly, Estabrook does not see his own methods as ethically questionable. (Just because you may see them this way does not mean that Estabrook shares your views). This answer choice is incorrect.

Answer choice (E): Estabrook does not manipulate the photographs he takes: he retains their imperfections so that they appear old and antiquated. We have no reason to suspect that he would view the aesthetic significance of a photograph as contingent upon factors that can be manipulated. This answer choice is incorrect.

Question #14: CR, Strengthen, SP. The correct answer choice is (A)

This is a relatively challenging question, in which we are asked to strengthen the reasoning by which Estabrook justifies his choice of artistic techniques. From the fourth paragraph, we know that he embraces their imperfections in order to achieve certain aesthetic effects. The correct answer choice must defend this view.

Answer choice (A): This is the correct answer choice. If advanced photographic techniques cannot faithfully reproduce the desired imperfections in nineteenth-century prints, it would be reasonable for Estabrook to resort to older processes in order to make more faithful reproductions. This answer choice helps justify Estabrook's choice of strategy by eliminating an alternative strategy for achieving his artistic objectives.

Answer choice (B): This is the Opposite answer. If the feelings evoked by a work of art were irrelevant to its artistic value, there would be little reason to produce prints that evoke sentiments such as nostalgia. This answer choice would undermine Estabrook's artistic objectives.

Answer choice (C): The ability of photographs to record subjects accurately has no bearing on Estabrook's artistic objectives. To convey the experience of nostalgia, Estabrook embraces accident and idiosyncrasy, not accuracy. This answer choice is incorrect.

Answer choice (D): This is another Opposite answer, because it undermines Estabrook's decision to create fake antique photographs. If such prints were of little artistic value, his choice of strategy would be seriously compromised.

Answer choice (E): The ability of modern techniques to produce *perfect* photographs has no bearing on Estabrook's decision to use outdated techniques, because his goal is to create artistic prints that are *im*perfect. This answer choice is incorrect.

Passage #3: Nonobvious Inventions

Passage A

The author of passage A describes how patenting obvious inventions has resulted in patent abuse.

Paragraph One:

The first paragraph clarifies the distinction between "obvious" and "nonobvious" inventions, and describes how the patent system should work in theory: patents should only be awarded for inventions that are not obvious. Unfortunately, obvious inventions are also being patented—and herein lies the problem.

Pay attention to examples that illustrate abstract or convoluted concepts. Translating between an Internet address and a telephone number is said to be an example of an obvious invention, but if you find this example confusing, think of something more familiar. Imagine patenting "riding a bike": this would result in a patent that is so broad that it would be impossible to circumvent. "Biking" is an obvious invention that should not be patented. On the other hand, patenting a "folding bike"—one you can take on the subway, for instance—is probably OK. Why? Because the patent would be much narrower, and the invention—not so "obvious."

Paragraph Two:

The second paragraph summarizes the problem in the patent system: the definition of what constitutes a "nonobvious" invention has become too broad, and as a result patents are being awarded too facilely for obvious inventions. This is clearly a problem, because patenting obvious inventions results in patents that are too broad to "invent around" or circumvent.

Paragraph Three:

The third paragraph describes how companies have responded to the proliferation of "bad patents": they accumulate large portfolios of patents in order to create a credible deterrent against lawsuits. That way, if company A sues company B for patent infringement, company B can always find some patent that company A has infringed upon, and countersue. The author regrets this state of affairs, but also suggests that not joining the "arms race" would be a mistake.

Paragraph Four:

The fourth paragraph focuses on software patents and explains why they are especially vulnerable to patent abuse.

Passage B

The author of passage B is a software maker dealing with the problem of patent abuse described in passage A. The business strategy adopted is identical to the one described in passage A.

Paragraph One:

The first paragraph explains why the author opposes software patents: they impede innovation.

Paragraph Two:

The second paragraph shows why the author's principled opposition to software patents cannot be put into practice. The problem, as in passage A, involves the practice of companies stockpiling massive patent portfolios. The author regrets having to play by the rules, adding the high cost of litigation as yet another downside to this practice.

Paragraph Three:

The final paragraph describes the software maker's response to the misuse of software patents. To avoid finding itself defenseless against lawsuits, the company chooses to develop their own portfolio of software patents in what passage A called "joining the arms race."

Passage Similarities and Differences

The two passages share similar views toward the patent system, which is criticized for allowing the proliferation of bad patents. Both authors lament the defensive strategy of amassing large portfolios of patents, and both consider such a solution regrettable yet necessary. The two passages are similar in scope, although passage B focuses exclusively on software patents; in passage A, software is just an example of an industry that is affected by patent abuse.

While substantively similar, the two passages approach the problem of patent abuse from different angles. Passage A provides the conceptual framework for understanding the misuse of patents, whereas passage B describes the position of someone dealing with that problem. Compared to passage B, passage A is a much denser read, describing the blurred boundaries between two key terms in patent law ("obvious" and "nonobvious" inventions). Both passages take issue with the patent system, but passage B outlines the position of someone directly affected by it.

Question #15: GR, Must. The correct answer choice is (C)

This question asks us to determine the most appropriate title for passage A and passage B. To do so, we need to evaluate the scope of the two passages, and determine a title that is neither overly restrictive nor too broad for each one. While it may be difficult to arrive at an exact prephrase, knowing the main point and purpose of each passage would be tremendously helpful in eliminating the four incorrect answer choices.

Answer choice (A): "The Use and Abuse of Patents" would not be a terrible title for passage A; however, "use" is somewhat misleading as the author only focuses on the *abuse* of patents, not their general use. More importantly, the second title is outside the scope of passage B. Although its author is clearly opposed to software patents (lines 38-41), the primary purpose of that passage is to describe a software maker's response to the abuse of patents, not argue in favor of their elimination. This answer choice is incorrect.

Answer choice (B): This Opposite answer choice can be immediately eliminated, because the author of passage B opposes, rather than defends, the use of software patents.

Answer choice (C): This is the correct answer choice. "Patenting the Obvious" is an appropriate title for passage A, which describes how patenting obvious inventions has resulted in the abuse of patents. Passage B is also appropriately titled "Patents: A Defensive Policy," because the primary purpose of the second passage is to describe the defensive policy adopted by a software maker in response to patent abuse.

Answer choice (D): Neither title is appropriate for either passage. Passage A does not attribute the problems in the patent system to some "misunderstanding" of patent policies. Likewise, keeping software "free but safe" may sound attractive in the real world, but it has nothing to do with the argument in passage B. This answer choice is incorrect.

Answer choice (E): There is no apology in passage B, making this answer choice easy to eliminate.

Question #16: GR, Must. The correct answer choice is (B)

This question asks about information contained in only one of the two passages. You are supposed to exclude passage B from consideration: the correct answer choice can be proven *only* by reference to passage A. Instead of attempting to formulate a precise prephrase, eliminate any answer choice containing an item that appears in both passages, or in neither of them, or in passage B only.

Answer choice (A): This answer choice is incorrect, because the accumulation of patents by software companies is mentioned in both passages.

Answer choice (B): This is the correct answer choice, because the cost of finding all the patents a product may infringe upon is mentioned in passage A (lines 31-34), but not in passage B. Passage B only mentions the high cost of litigation (line 53), which is a different issue altogether.

Answer choice (C): The negative effect of patents on software development is mentioned in both passages; in fact, it is a central idea in passage B. This answer choice is incorrect.

Answer choice (D): This is the Reverse answer choice, as the high cost of patent litigation is mentioned in passage B (line 53), but not in passage A.

Answer choice (E): This is another Reverse answer choice, because the "questionable" nature of software patents is discussed in passage B (line 51) but not in passage A.

Question #17: SR, Purpose. The correct answer choice is (E)

This question asks us to determine the meaning of the term "invent around," as it is used in passage A. In the second paragraph, the author explains why patents should be narrow enough to "invent around," and laments the practice of issuing patents that are "so broad that inventing around them is practically impossible" (lines 14-15). Specific Reference/Purpose questions require contextual awareness of the referenced text, and are best approached with an active prephrase.

Answer choice (A): This is the Reverse answer choice. Inventing around existing patents requires "nonobvious" inventions that *can* be patented, rather than "obvious" inventions that *cannot* be patented.

Answer choice (B): Concealing a patent infringement sounds unwise, and is never discussed in either passage. This answer choice is incorrect.

Answer choice (C): This answer choice may sound attractive, because one could argue that using a patented invention in a novel way is tantamount to "inventing around" that patent. While this may be a hotly debated issue in patent law, it is not the *author's* argument. Beware of introducing outside information to the passage when answering Must Be True questions.

Answer choice (D): While "inventing around" does require developing new products, there is no reason to believe that the principles upon which such inventions are based must be "entirely different" from those for products affected by competitors' patents. This answer choice contains an exaggeration and is incorrect.

Answer choice (E): This is the correct answer choice. From the discussion in the second paragraph of passage A, we know that "inventing around" existing patents requires such patents to be narrow enough that companies can circumvent them, i.e. devise products that are functionally similar to the ones patented, but different enough to avoid patent infringement.

Question #18: GR, Must. The correct answer choice is (B)

This question asks us to identify the abstract relationship between the two passages. While understanding Passage Similarities and Differences is key, pay close attention to the general purpose behind each passage.

Answer choice (A): Although the author of passage A is not directly affected by the problem of patent abuse, she makes no effort to *objectively* report it, and is clearly critical of the patent system (lines 11-12). This answer choice is incorrect.

Answer choice (B): This is the correct answer choice. Both passages discuss the problem of patent abuse; however, as a software maker, the author of passage B is directly affected by it.

Answer choice (C): Although the author of passage A has clear reservations about the strategy of accumulating large patent portfolios, she is not "highly critical" of it. In fact, the author (reluctantly) urges companies to adopt it in order to avoid a "fundamental mistake" (lines 23-24). This answer choice is incorrect.

Answer choice (D): Just because passage A outlines a problem does not mean the problem can be properly described as an "impasse" (i.e. a standoff or a stalemate). Also, the defensive strategy adopted in passage B is not a solution to the problem, let alone a "way out of this impasse." This answer choice is incorrect.

Answer choice (E): The two passages adopt a similar stance toward patent abuse, and neither of them considers *both* sides of the dispute. This answer choice is incorrect.

Question #19: CR, Must. The correct answer choice is (A)

This question asks us to determine what strategy the two authors would recommend to software companies, based on the arguments presented in *both* passages. Use the discussion of Passage Similarities above to arrive at a suitable prephrase, and keep in mind that the correct answer choice must contain a recommendation with which *both* authors would agree.

Answer choice (A): This is the correct answer choice. Both authors agree that companies need to adopt a defensive strategy of amassing large portfolios of patents (lines 18-21 and 54-56). Just because their agreement is reluctant does not make their recommendation any less valid, or true.

Answer choice (B): The strategy of licensing software patented by other companies was deemed prohibitively expensive in passage A (lines 32-37), and was not discussed in passage B. This answer choice is incorrect.

Answer choice (C): The strategy of *exploiting* patents owned by other companies was not discussed in either passage. This answer choice is incorrect.

Answer choice (D): Although refraining from patent infringement seems like a sensible idea, passage A argues that it is almost impossible to avoid infringement due to the high number and complexity of patents (lines 29-31). This answer choice is incorrect.

Answer choice (E): Passage B never mentions the idea of researching relevant patents, while passage A rejects it as "prohibitively expensive" (lines 31-34). This answer choice is incorrect.

Question #20: SR, Must. The correct answer choice is (D)

This question asks us to determine what phrase in passage A is most analogous to the phrase "this same stance," as it is used in passage B (line 60). The abstract nature of such questions presents a considerable challenge to some test takers, so it is important to adopt a step-by-step approach.

First, examine how the phrase "this same stance" is used in passage B (line 60). Looking back at the last paragraph of that passage, it becomes clear that the "stance" in question is referring to the author's reluctant decision to develop a portfolio of software patents. In the third paragraph of Passage A, the author describes this same defensive strategy by using a variety of metaphors that date back to the Cold War: "nuclear stockpiling," "credible deterrent," "arms race." Any of these phrases would be appropriate reference points in answering the question.

Answer choice (A): The phrase "nonobvious" in passage A does not refer to the strategy of amassing a portfolio of patents. This answer choice is incorrect.

Answer choice (B): The phrase "invent around" in passage A refers to the practice of circumventing properly issued patents, not to the strategy of dealing with patent abuse. This answer choice is incorrect.

Answer choice (C): The phrase "lower the bar" refers to the legal standard for "obviousness." This answer choice is incorrect.

Answer choice (D): This is the correct answer choice, as prephrased in the discussion above.

Answer choice (E): The phrase "modular components" in passage A describes some of the reasons *why* software patents are ripe for abuse, not *how* software makers respond to that abuse. This answer choice is incorrect.

Question #21: CR, Weaken. The correct answer choice is (D)

Approach this Weaken question as you would any similar Logical Reasoning question: the correct answer choice must undermine the conclusion of the argument outlined in the first paragraph of passage B. The author explains her opposition to software patents, arguing that such patents impede innovation:

<u>Cause</u>   <u>Effect</u>

Software patents ⟶ Inno~~v~~ation

The correct answer choice would weaken this conclusion by showing that software patents do not necessarily impede, and might actually promote, innovation.

Answer choice (A): This is an attractive answer choice, because if software patents expire after 20 years, their negative effects would not persist interminably. However, just because the effects are limited in time does not make them any less severe. Inhibiting innovation for 20 years may still present an astronomical opportunity cost. This answer choice is incorrect.

Answer choice (B): This is the Opposite answer. If open-source software were more reliable than patented software, this would strengthen the author's opposition to software patents.

Answer choice (C): Just because some companies oppose software patents for self-interested reasons does not make their argument any less credible. This is a classic Source Argument flaw: we cannot weaken an argument by questioning the character or motivations of those making the argument. This answer choice is incorrect.

Answer choice (D): This is the correct answer choice. If innovation becomes less profitable as a result of *not* patenting software, vendors would have little incentive to continue innovating. Innovation would be inhibited not by software patents (as the author suggests), but rather by the *absence* of patents. This would weaken the author's argument, and challenge the defense of open-source software outlined in the first paragraph of passage.

Answer choice (E): Who benefits from software innovations has no bearing on whether patented software impedes innovation. This answer choice is incorrect.

Passage #4: The Dodo Bird

Paragraph One:

Most science passages begin by outlining some unexplained phenomenon or unresolved question, and this one is no exception. Here, the question is why the *Calvaria major*, a once-abundant tree found on the island of Mauritius, is now almost extinct. One ecologist, Stanley Temple, blames the dodo bird. He points to the unusual coincidence between the time the dodo bird became extinct and the age of the only surviving *Calvaria major* trees today, arguing that the extinction of the dodo bird prevented the tree from reproducing.

Paragraph Two:

The second paragraph elaborates on Temple's hypothesis by describing exactly how the extinction of the dodo led to the scarcity of *Calvaria major* trees. His logic goes like this: The dodo used to eat the fruits of *Calvaria major,* as a result of which their pits evolved a thick wall meant to withstand the abrasive forces in the bird's digestive tract. The seeds inside the pit could still germinate upon exit, because the abrasion caused thinning of the pit wall, but with the dodo now extinct these seeds get trapped inside the thick-walled pit. As a result, the seeds can no longer germinate.

Paragraph Three:

The third paragraph presents additional findings in support of Temple's theory, but suggests that their credibility is somewhat suspect. Temple used other birds such as turkeys to determine whether the pits of the *Calvaria major* could have withstood the dodo's digestive system, and found some evidence supporting his position. Nevertheless, the author describes Temple's hypothesis as having only a "semblance of rigor" (lines 33-34), suggesting that a critique will follow in the next paragraph.

Paragraph Four:

The fourth paragraph indicates that Temple's proposal is disputed by "leading specialists in the field" (lines 46-47), and introduces several arguments against it. One ecologist (Strahm) found evidence suggesting that *Calvaria major* seeds can germinate without the dodo's help. Another expert (Speke) speculated that *Calvaria major* germination, though rare, is probably adequate enough to prevent the species from becoming extinct. The author accepts these findings as evidence that the population decline of the *Calvaria major* tree could have easily resulted from factors other than the extinction of the dodo bird. The last sentence of this paragraph summarizes the main point of the passage.

VIEWSTAMP Analysis:

There are three **Viewpoints** outlined in this passage: those of Temple, the leading specialists'—including Strahm and Speke—and the author's. The bulk of this passage discusses Temple's hypothesis, which the leading specialists challenge in the fourth paragraph. The author implicitly agrees with the specialists' position that the dodo was not necessary for the survival of *Calvaria major*, but her views are not explicitly stated until the fourth paragraph.

The **Structure** of the passage is as follows:

Paragraph One: Introduce Stanley Temple and his theory.

Paragraph Two: Elaborate on the causal reasoning underlying Temple's hypothesis.

Paragraph Three: Describe additional findings supporting Temple's position, but suggest that his argument may not be rigorous enough.

Paragraph Four: Attack Temple's hypothesis and summarize the main point of the passage.

The author's **Tone** can most accurately be described as skeptical: she regards Temple's hypothesis as initially plausible (line 45), but ultimately unconvincing (lines 46-62).

The passage presents two central **Arguments**. One of them is Temple's, which attributes the present-day scarcity of *Calvaria major* trees to the disappearance of the dodo bird:

<u>Cause</u>   <u>Effect</u>

V_{Temple}: Dodo extinction ⟶ Decline of Calvaria major

The counterargument is that of the author, who challenges Temple's hypothesis by describing the recent findings of various experts in the field. Due to their explanatory potential, both Temple's and the author's arguments are inherently causal, as they present competing causes for the same effect.

The **Main Point** of the passage is that the scarcity of *Calvaria major* is probably due to factors other than the disappearance of the dodo bird, in spite of Temple's claims to the contrary. The author alludes to her suspicion that Temple's hypothesis is not credible in the third paragraph, but does not explicitly reject it until the very end of the passage. This passage structure severely penalizes test-takers who try to save time by skimming at the end, and is quite common in Reading Comprehension passages.

Question #22: GR, Main Point. The correct answer choice is (B)

The main point of the passage is prephrased in the VIEWSTAMP analysis above.

Answer choice (A): This answer choice summarizes Speke's position (lines 54-58), not the main point of the passage. This answer choice is incorrect.

Answer choice (B): This is the correct answer choice: the scarcity of *Calvaria major* is probably due to factors other than the disappearance of the dodo bird. The main point is not explicitly stated until the fourth paragraph, which underscores the importance of actively engaging the passage until the very end.

Answer choice (C): This answer choice is incorrect, because Temple's experimentation with *Calvaria major* pits did not solve the mystery of the tree's decline.

Answer choice (D): The author does not leave open the possibility that Temple's hypothesis may be correct. The last paragraph discredits much of the evidence Temple used in his defense. This answer choice is incorrect.

Answer choice (E): Given the author's refusal to accept Temple's hypothesis, she would probably agree that *Calvaria major* would still be scarce today even if the dodo had not become extinct. However, our job is to identify the main point of the passage, not a hypothetical implication of that point. This answer choice is incorrect.

Question #23: CR, Must. The correct answer choice is (A)

The scope of Temple's research was outlined in the first paragraph, and additional mention of his experiments with birds was made in the third paragraph. Either paragraph would serve as a useful reference point in validating the correct answer choice.

Answer choice (A): This is the correct answer choice. Recall that Temple's investigation of *Calvaria major* was peripheral to his research on endangered birds (lines 6-8). We can safely conclude that his research on birds was largely concerned with species facing the threat of extinction.

Answer choice (B): There is no reason to believe that Temple's estimates of the crush-resistant strength of *Calvaria major* pits was highly accurate. This answer choice contains an exaggeration and is incorrect.

Answer choice (C): Temple *assumed* that some modern birds' digestive tracts exert similar abrasive pressure as those of the dodo bird, but no "experimental evidence" was furnished to support his assumption. This answer choice is incorrect.

Answer choice (D): Given the overt skepticism exhibited in the third and fourth paragraphs, the author is unlikely to describe Temple's research on birds as "comprehensive in scope and conducted with methodological precision." Temple's argument is said to have only a "*semblance* of rigor" (lines 33-34). This answer choice is incorrect.

Answer choice (E): This answer choice is quite attractive, because in his quest to explain why apparently fertile *Calvaria major* pits were no longer able to germinate, Temple studied birds whose digestive tracts resembled those of the dodo. However, the bulk of Temple's research on birds did not seek to validate the dodo theory: his investigation of *Calvaria major* was peripheral ("a sidelight") to his research on endangered birds (lines 5-8). Furthermore, we cannot prove that it was specifically the fertile *Calvaria major* pits that gave Temple the idea to study dodo-like birds. The causal relationship between the two is merely speculative and cannot be proven with the information provided.

Question #24: SR, Must, P. The correct answer choice is (D)

Purpose questions introducing a Specific Reference usually require a more complete understanding of the context in which the referenced text appears, and are best approached with an active prephrase.

This question asks us to evaluate the function of the phrase "semblance of rigor" (lines 33-34), as it is used in the third paragraph. The phrase exhibits skepticism toward Temple's hypothesis, implying that his experimental findings only *appear* to support it (but may not adequately do so).

Answer choice (A): This answer choice may seem attractive, because it agrees with our prephrase that Temple's findings "merely appeared" to support his hypothesis. However, we have no evidence that they were "not carefully derived": nowhere in the third paragraph is the *manner* in which Temple derived his results overtly criticized. This answer choice is incorrect.

Answer choice (B): This is a Shell Game answer. Direct proof of Temple's hypothesis is indeed "unattainable" (line 31), but this has nothing to do with the meaning of the phrase in question. Just because some remark appears in the same sentence as the referenced text does not mean that it would automatically provide a suitable answer.

Answer choice (C): Hopefully, you were able to eliminate this answer choice relatively quickly, because the author does not seek to differentiate between Temple's firsthand and secondhand research. It is unclear how the phrase "semblance of rigor" would relate to such an evaluation.

Answer choice (D): This is the correct answer choice. Indeed, the experimental results obtained by Temple can properly be described as quantitative, as they estimate quantifiable characteristics such as the abrasive forces within the dodo's gizzard. The term "semblance" clearly suggests that these results only *appear* to bolster the credibility of Temple's hypothesis.

Answer choice (E): The author never attempts to defend the scientific precision and creativity of Temple's experimentation, and no such purpose can be inferred from the phrase "semblance of rigor." This answer choice is incorrect.

Question #25: CR, Must. The correct answer choice is (A)

Use the Fact Test to prove the correct answer choice to this Concept Reference question. While arriving at a precise prephrase may be challenging, note that the question is not about what Temple *believed* to be true about the abrasion of *Calvaria major* pit walls, but about what the *passage* indicates to be true. Use the VIEWSTAMP method to distinguish between Temple's perspective and that of the author: this question is about the latter, not the former. The distinction between fact and opinion is crucial on the LSAT, and key to answering this question correctly.

Answer choice (A): This is the correct answer choice. In the fourth paragraph, the author describes Strahm's finding of multiple *Calvaria major* specimens, "many far younger than three centuries" (lines 50-51). From this discovery the author concludes that "seeds have *in fact* germinated […] since the dodo's disappearance" (lines 51-53), suggesting that thinning through abrasion is not necessary for germination.

Answer choice (B): This answer choice is factually incorrect, because in Temple's experiment with turkeys, only *some* of the pits emerged abraded but intact (lines 40-41).

Answer choice (C): The author does not question the dodo's ability to thin the *Calvaria major* pit walls. The issue is whether the dodo was *necessary* to thin the walls and ensure germination, not whether it was *sufficient* for that process to occur. This answer choice is incorrect.

Answer choice (D): There is no evidence to support the observation that abrasion of *Calvaria major* pit walls was more common in the past than it is today. This might have been true if, as Temple claims, the dodo bird had played a role in the germination of *Calvaria major* seeds; however, the author finds this theory doubtful.

Answer choice (E): Temple overlooked other possible explanations for the population decline of *Calvaria major*. The passage says nothing about other forces that could have abraded the *Calvaria major* seeds. This answer choice is incorrect.

Question #26: Must, AP The correct answer choice is (E)

The answer to this Author Perspective question is already prephrased in our VIEWSTAMP analysis above, and represents the main point of the passage. The author regards Temple's hypothesis as initially plausible (line 45) but ultimately unconvincing, suggesting that the scarcity of *Calvaria major* could have been caused by factors other than the disappearance of the dodo bird (58-62).

Answer choice (A): As shown in the last paragraph, the author does not regard Temple's views as essentially correct. On the contrary: she agrees with the leading experts in the field that the population decline of *Calvaria major* could be due to factors other than the disappearance of the dodo bird. This answer choice is incorrect.

Answer choice (B): While Temple saw his empirical findings as vindicating his hypothesis (lines 42-43), the author remains skeptical, holding that they only lent his argument "a semblance of rigor" (lines 33-34). This answer choice is incorrect.

Answer choice (C): The author does not praise Temple's hypothesis as an example of a valuable scientific achievement, making this answer choice easy to eliminate.

Answer choice (D): As with answer choice (C), there is no evidence that the author regards Temple's theory as laudable or praiseworthy. Its formulation only *appears* precise ("semblance of rigor").

Answer choice (E): This is the correct answer choice. In the last paragraph, the author rejects the belief that the scarcity of *Calvaria major* was necessarily caused by the disappearance of the dodo bird. Temple's hypothesis, in other words, is seen as an attempt to explain a state of affairs that did not in fact exist.

Question #27: CR, MustX. The correct answer choice is (C)

To answer this Must Be True/EXCEPT question, proceed by the process of elimination: four of the answer choices will contain statements with which the author is likely to agree, and will be incorrect. Questions of this type are usually time-consuming, because the correct answer choice must be the one we *cannot* prove by referring to information contained in the passage.

Answer choice (A): This answer choice is incorrect, because the author is likely to agree with it (even if she does not explicitly say so in the passage). Think of it this way: if Temple's critics had definitively identified the reasons for *Calvaria major*'s durable pit wall, the author would surely have brought that up, because such a finding would have been directly relevant to the main point of the passage. The failure of the author to specify what actually caused the evolution of the pit wall is an omission suggesting that the cause is still unknown.

Answer choice (B): This answer choice contains a double negative and should be simplified: it holds that the durable nature of the pit walls *could* have hurt the tree's survival. The author is likely to agree with this claim. Recall Speke's observation that "only a minority of unabraded *Calvaria major* seeds germinate" (lines 55-56), suggesting that the thickness of the pit wall has been a contributing factor in the tree's decline. The author implicitly agrees with the viewpoints of the experts described in the fourth paragraph, and Speke's observation is no exception.

Answer choice (C): This is the correct answer choice, because the author does not appear particularly surprised by the population decline of *Calvaria major*. Such a decline is quite normal given the difficulty of getting *Calvaria major* seeds to germinate; in fact, the author herself proposes several factors that could have plausibly caused it (lines 58-62). Just because the precise cause for a particular phenomenon is yet to be identified does not mean that the phenomenon is unexpected or surprising.

Answer choice (D): This answer choice is incorrect, because the author does not seem to fear the immediate extinction of *Calvaria major*. In the fourth paragraph, she cites a research study showing that the number of germinating seeds is "probably sufficient to keep this species from becoming extinct" (lines 57-58). The author implicitly agrees with the leading experts in the field, suggesting that she would also agree with this claim.

Answer choice (E): This answer choice is incorrect, because the author is likely to agree that abrasion is not necessary for *Calvaria major* seeds to germinate. In the fourth paragraph, she describes Strahm's finding of multiple *Calvaria major* specimens, "many far younger than three centuries" (lines 50-51). From this discovery the author concludes that "seeds have *in fact* germinated [...] since the dodo's disappearance" (lines 51-53), suggesting that thinning through abrasion is not necessary for germination.

THE POWERSCORE LSAT READING COMPREHENSION BIBLE WORKBOOK

Chapter Four:
PrepTest 70
Reading
Comprehension
Section

4

Chapter Four: PrepTest 70 Reading Comprehension Section

Chapter Notes ████████████████

This chapter contains the complete PrepTest 70 Reading Comprehension section. We recommend taking the complete section as a 35-minute timed exercise. Then, check your work against the answer key and explanations that immediately follow the section.

To identify each Reading Comprehension section and the corresponding explanations, use the black sidebars as a reference. The sidebar will identify the PrepTest from which the section is drawn.

As you begin the section, remember to consider your overall time and pacing strategy, and keep in mind that you are not required to complete the passages in the order they are presented to you. Remember to apply the approaches outlined in *The Reading Comprehension Bible*, and good luck!

Directions: Each set of questions in this section is based on a single passage or a pair of passages. The questions are to be answered on the basis of what is <u>stated</u> or <u>implied</u> in the passage or pair of passages. For some of the questions, more than one of the choices could conceivably answer the question. However, you are to choose the <u>best</u> answer; that is, the response that most accurately and completely answers the question, and blacken the corresponding space on your answer sheet.

An organism is considered to have an infection when a disease-causing agent, called a pathogen, establishes a viable presence in the organism. This can occur only if the pathogenic agent is able to reproduce
(5) itself in the host organism. The only agents believed until recently to be responsible for infections—viruses, bacteria, fungi, and parasites—reproduce and regulate their other life processes by means of genetic material, composed of nucleic acid (DNA or RNA). It was thus
(10) widely assumed that all pathogens contain such genetic material in their cellular structure.

This assumption has been challenged, however, by scientists seeking to identify the pathogen that causes Creutzfeldt-Jakob disease (CJD), a degenerative
(15) form of dementia in humans. CJD causes the brain to become riddled with tiny holes, like a sponge (evidence of extensive nerve cell death). Its symptoms include impaired muscle control, loss of mental acuity, memory loss, and chronic insomnia. Extensive experiments
(20) aimed at identifying the pathogen responsible for CJD have led surprisingly to the isolation of a disease agent lacking nucleic acid and consisting mainly, if not exclusively, of protein. Researchers coined the term "prion" for this new type of protein pathogen.

(25) Upon further study, scientists discovered that prions normally exist as harmless cellular proteins in many of the body's tissues, including white blood cells and nerve cells in the brain; however, they possess the capability of converting their structures into a
(30) dangerous abnormal shape. Prions exhibiting this abnormal conformation were found to have infectious properties and the ability to reproduce themselves in an unexpected way, by initiating a chain reaction that induces normally shaped prions to transform
(35) themselves on contact, one after another, into the abnormal, pathogenic conformation. This cascade of transformations produces a plaque, consisting of thread-like structures, that collects in the brain and ultimately destroys nerve cells. Because prions, unlike
(40) other pathogens, occur naturally in the body as proteins, the body does not produce an immune response when they are present. And in the absence of any effective therapy for preventing the cascade process by which affected prions reproduce
(45) themselves, CJD is inevitably fatal, though there are wide variations in pre-symptomatic incubation times and in how aggressively the disease progresses.

Although the discovery of the link between prions and CJD was initially received with great skepticism
(50) in the scientific community, subsequent research has supported the conclusion that prions are an entirely new class of infectious pathogens. Furthermore, it is

now believed that a similar process of protein malformation may be involved in other, more
(55) common degenerative neurological conditions such as Alzheimer's disease and Parkinson's disease. This possibility has yet to be fully explored, however, and the exact mechanisms by which prions reproduce themselves and cause cellular destruction have yet to
(60) be completely understood.

1. Which one of the following most accurately expresses the main point of the passage?

(A) Although most organisms are known to produce several kinds of proteins, the mechanism by which isolated protein molecules such as prions reproduce themselves is not yet known in detail.

(B) Research into the cause of CJD has uncovered a deadly class of protein pathogens uniquely capable of reproducing themselves without genetic material.

(C) Recent research suggests that prions may be responsible not only for CJD, but for most other degenerative neurological conditions as well.

(D) The assertion that prions cause CJD has been received with great skepticism in the scientific community because it undermines a firmly entrenched view about the nature of pathogens.

(E) Even though prions contain no genetic material, it has become clear that they are somehow capable of reproducing themselves.

GO ON TO THE NEXT PAGE.

2. Which one of the following is most strongly supported by the passage?

   (A) Understanding the cause of CJD has required scientists to reconsider their traditional beliefs about the causes of infection.
   (B) CJD is contagious, though not highly so.
   (C) The prevention of CJD would be most efficiently achieved by the prevention of certain genetic abnormalities.
   (D) Although patients with CJD exhibit different incubation times, the disease progresses at about the same rate in all patients once symptoms are manifested.
   (E) The prion theory of infection has weak support within the scientific community.

3. If the hypothesis that CJD is caused by prions is correct, finding the answer to which one of the following questions would tend most to help a physician in deciding whether a patient has CJD?

   (A) Has the patient suffered a severe blow to the skull recently?
   (B) Does the patient experience occasional bouts of insomnia?
   (C) Has the patient been exposed to any forms of radiation that have a known tendency to cause certain kinds of genetic damage?
   (D) Has any member of the patient's immediate family ever had a brain disease?
   (E) Does the patient's brain tissue exhibit the presence of any abnormal thread-like structures?

4. Which one of the following is most strongly supported by the passage?

   (A) The only way in which CJD can be transmitted is through the injection of abnormally shaped prions from an infected individual into an uninfected individual.
   (B) Most infectious diseases previously thought to be caused by other pathogens are now thought to be caused by prions.
   (C) If they were unable to reproduce themselves, abnormally shaped prions would not cause CJD.
   (D) Alzheimer's disease and Parkinson's disease are caused by different conformations of the same prion pathogen that causes CJD.
   (E) Prion diseases generally progress more aggressively than diseases caused by other known pathogens.

5. It can be inferred from the passage that the author would be LEAST likely to agree with which one of the following?

   (A) The presence of certain abnormally shaped prions in brain tissue is a sign of neurological disease.
   (B) Some patients currently infected with CJD will recover from the disease.
   (C) Prions do not require nucleic acid for their reproduction.
   (D) The body has no natural defense against CJD.
   (E) Scientists have only a partial understanding of the mechanism by which prions reproduce.

6. Given the manner in which the term "pathogen" is used in the passage, and assuming that the prion theory of infection is correct, which one of the following statements must be false?

   (A) Nothing that lacks nucleic acid is a pathogen.
   (B) Prions are a relatively newly discovered type of pathogen.
   (C) All pathogens can cause infection.
   (D) Pathogens contribute in some manner to the occurrence of CJD.
   (E) There are other pathogens besides viruses, bacteria, fungi, and parasites.

7. Which one of the following, if true, would most undermine the claim that prions cause CJD?

   (A) Several symptoms closely resembling those of CJD have been experienced by patients known to have a specific viral infection.
   (B) None of the therapies currently available for treating neurological diseases is designed to block the chain reaction by which abnormal prions are believed to reproduce.
   (C) Research undertaken subsequent to the studies on CJD has linked prions to degenerative conditions not affecting the brain or the central nervous system.
   (D) Epidemiological studies carried out on a large population have failed to show any hereditary predisposition to CJD.
   (E) A newly developed antibacterial drug currently undergoing clinical trials is proving to be effective in reversing the onset of CJD.

GO ON TO THE NEXT PAGE.

One of the more striking developments in modern North American dance was African American choreographer Katherine Dunham's introduction of a technique known as dance-isolation, in which one part
(5) of the body moves in one rhythm while other parts are kept stationary or are moved in different rhythms. The incorporation of this technique into North American and European choreography is relatively recent, although various forms of the technique have long
(10) been essential to traditional dances of certain African, Caribbean, and Pacific-island cultures. Dunham's success in bringing dance-isolation and other traditional techniques from those cultures into the mainstream of modern North American dance is due
(15) in no small part to her training in both anthropological research and choreography.

As an anthropologist in the 1930s, Dunham was one of the pioneers in the field of dance ethnology. Previously, dance had been neglected as an area of
(20) social research, primarily because most social scientists gravitated toward areas likely to be recognized by their peers as befitting scientifically rigorous, and therefore legitimate, modes of inquiry. Moreover, no other social scientist at that time was sufficiently
(25) trained in dance to be able to understand dance techniques, while experts in dance were not trained in the methods of social research.

Starting in 1935, Dunham conducted a series of research projects into traditional Caribbean dance
(30) forms, with special interest in their origins in African culture. Especially critical to her success was her approach to research, which diverged radically from the methodology that prevailed at the time. Colleagues in anthropology advised her not to become too closely
(35) involved in the dances she was observing, both because of the extreme physical demands of the dances, and because they subscribed to the long-standing view, now fortunately recognized as unrealistic, that effective data gathering can and must be conducted
(40) from a position of complete detachment. But because of her interest and her skill as a performer, she generally eschewed such caution and participated in the dances herself. Through prolonged immersion of this kind, Dunham was able not only to comprehend
(45) various dances as complex cultural practices, but also to learn the techniques well enough to teach them to others and incorporate them into new forms of ballet.

Between 1937 and 1945, Dunham developed a research-to-performance method that she used to adapt
(50) Caribbean dance forms for use in theatrical performance, combining them with modern dance styles she learned in Chicago. The ballets she created in this fashion were among the first North American dances to rectify the exclusion of African American themes from the
(55) medium of modern dance. Her work was thus crucial in establishing African American dance as an art form in its own right, making possible future companies such as Arthur Mitchell's Dance Theater of Harlem.

8. Which one of the following most accurately expresses the main point of the passage?

(A) Katherine Dunham transformed the field of anthropology by developing innovative research methodologies for studying Caribbean and other traditional dance styles and connecting them with African American dance.

(B) Katherine Dunham's ballets were distinct from others produced in North America in that they incorporated authentic dance techniques from traditional cultures.

(C) Katherine Dunham's expertise as an anthropologist allowed her to use Caribbean and African dance traditions to express the aesthetic and political concerns of African American dancers and choreographers.

(D) The innovative research methods of Katherine Dunham made possible her discovery that the dance traditions of the Caribbean were derived from earlier African dance traditions.

(E) Katherine Dunham's anthropological and choreographic expertise enabled her to make contributions that altered the landscape of modern dance in North America.

9. According to the passage, Dunham's work in anthropology differed from that of most other anthropologists in the 1930s in that Dunham

(A) performed fieldwork for a very extended time period

(B) related the traditions she studied to those of her own culture

(C) employed a participative approach in performing research

(D) attached a high degree of political significance to her research

(E) had prior familiarity with the cultural practices of the peoples she set out to study

GO ON TO THE NEXT PAGE.

10. The passage suggests that the "peers" mentioned in line 22 would have been most likely to agree with which one of the following statements about the study of dance?

(A) Most social scientists who have attempted to study dance as a cultural phenomenon have misinterpreted it.

(B) Social scientists need not be well versed in dance traditions in order to obtain reliable data about them.

(C) Research into dance as a cultural form cannot be conducted with a high degree of scientific precision.

(D) Most experts in the field of dance are too preoccupied to conduct studies in the field of dance ethnology.

(E) Dance forms are too variable across cultures to permit rigorous means of data collection.

11. In the last sentence of the second paragraph, the author mentions "experts in dance" primarily in order to

(A) suggest why a group of social scientists did not embrace the study of a particular cultural form

(B) suggest that a certain group was more qualified to study a particular cultural form than was another group

(C) identify an additional factor that motivated a particular social scientist to pursue a specific new line of research

(D) contribute to an explanation of why a particular field of research was not previously pursued

(E) indicate an additional possible reason for the tension between the members of two distinct fields of research

12. According to the passage, which one of the following was true of the dance forms that Dunham began studying in 1935?

(A) They were more similar to dance forms used in Pacific-island cultures than to any other known dance forms.

(B) They represented the first use of the technique of dance-isolation within a culture outside of Africa.

(C) They shared certain rhythmic characteristics with the dance forms employed in North American ballets.

(D) They had already influenced certain popular dances in North America.

(E) They were influenced by the traditions of non-Caribbean cultures.

13. Which one of the following is most analogous to Dunham's work in anthropology and choreography as that work is described in the passage?

(A) A French archaeologist with training in musicology researches instruments used in seventeenth century France, and her findings become the basis for a Korean engineer's designs for devices to simulate the sounds those instruments most likely made.

(B) An Australian medical researcher with training in botany analyzes the chemical composition of plants that other researchers have collected in the Philippines, and then an Australian pharmaceutical company uses her findings to develop successful new medicines.

(C) A Canadian surgeon uses her skill in drawing to collaborate with a Vietnamese surgeon to develop a manual containing detailed illustrations of the proper techniques for certain types of reconstructive surgery performed in both countries.

(D) A Brazilian teacher with training in social psychology conducts a detailed study of teaching procedures while working with teachers in several Asian countries, then introduces the most effective of those procedures to teachers in his own country.

(E) An Italian fashion designer researches the social significance of clothing design in several cultures and then presents his research in a highly acclaimed book directed toward his colleagues in fashion design.

14. The passage suggests that the author would be most likely to agree with which one of the following statements about the colleagues mentioned in line 33?

(A) They were partly correct in recommending that Dunham change her methods of data collection, since injury sustained during fieldwork might have compromised her research.

(B) They were partly correct in advising Dunham to exercise initial caution in participating in the Caribbean dances, since her skill in performing them improved with experience.

(C) They were incorrect in advising Dunham to increase the degree of her detachment, since extensive personal investment in fieldwork generally enhances scientific rigor.

(D) They were incorrect in assuming that researchers in the social sciences are able to gather data in an entirely objective manner.

(E) They were incorrect in assuming that dance could be studied with the same degree of scientific rigor possible in other areas of ethnology.

GO ON TO THE NEXT PAGE.

Passage A

Research concerning happiness and wealth reveals a paradox: at any one time richer people report higher levels of happiness than poorer people in the same society report, and yet over time advanced societies
(5) have not grown happier as they have grown richer. Apparently, people are comparing their income with some norm, and that norm must be rising along with actual income. Two phenomena—habituation and rivalry—push up the norm.
(10) When our living standards increase, we love it initially but then we adjust and it makes little difference. For example, if we ask people with different incomes what income they consider sufficient, the "required income" correlates strongly with their actual income:
(15) a rise in actual income causes a roughly equivalent rise in required income. We can also look at reported happiness over time. Job satisfaction depends little on the absolute level of wages but rises if wages rapidly increase.
(20) We do not have the same experience with other aspects of our lives. We do not foresee how we adjust to material possessions, so we overinvest in acquiring them, at the expense of leisure.

Now consider the phenomenon of rivalry. In a
(25) study conducted by Solnick and Hemenway, people were asked to choose between two options, with all prices held constant:

A. You earn $50,000 a year while everyone else earns $25,000;
(30) B. You earn $100,000 a year while others make $200,000.

The majority chose the first. They were happy to be poorer, provided their relative position improved. And indeed, how people compare to their "reference
(35) group"—those most like them—is crucial for happiness. In East Germany, for example, living standards have soared since 1990, but the level of happiness has plummeted because people now compare themselves with West Germans, rather than with people in other
(40) Soviet bloc countries.

Passage B

Does the Solnick and Hemenway study mean that we care most about one-upmanship? Perhaps out of our primeval past comes the urge to demonstrate our superiority in order to help ensure mating prospects,
(45) keeping our genetic lines going. Still programmed like this, we get unexplainable pleasure from having a bigger house than our neighbors.

This theory may sound good and is commonly heard, but it is not the explanation best supported by
(50) the evidence. Rather, the data show that earning more makes people happier because relative prosperity makes them feel that they are successful, that they have created value.

If two people feel equally successful, they will be
(55) equally happy even if their incomes differ greatly. Of course, people who earn more generally view themselves as successful. But it is the success—not the money per se—that provides the happiness. We use

material wealth to show not just that we are
(60) prosperous, but that we are prosperous because we create value.

What scholars often portray as an ignoble tendency—wanting to have more than others— is really evidence of a desire to create value. Wanting
(65) to create value benefits society. It is a bonus that it also brings happiness.

15. Both passages are primarily concerned with explaining which one of the following?

(A) the human desire to create value
(B) the relationship between income and happiness
(C) the biological basis of people's attitudes toward wealth
(D) the human propensity to become habituated to wealth
(E) the concept of "required income"

16. The author of passage B would be most likely to agree with which one of the following statements?

(A) The desire to demonstrate that one is wealthier than others is a remnant of human beings' primeval past.
(B) Very few people would be willing to accept a lower standard of living in return for greater relative wealth.
(C) Being wealthier than other people would not make one happier if one believed that one's wealth was due merely to luck.
(D) Gradual increases in employees' wages do not increase their job satisfaction.
(E) The overall level of happiness in a society usually increases as the society becomes wealthier.

17. The author of passage B would be most likely to regard the conclusion that the Solnick and Hemenway study points to the existence of a "phenomenon of rivalry" (line 24) as

(A) ungenerous in its view of human nature and mistaken in its interpretation of the evidence
(B) flattering in its implications about human nature but only weakly supported by the available evidence
(C) plausible in its account of human nature but based largely upon ambiguous evidence
(D) unflattering in its implications about human nature but more or less valid in the conclusions drawn from the evidence
(E) accurate concerning human nature and strongly supported by the evidence

GO ON TO THE NEXT PAGE.

18. Which one of the following pairs most accurately describes why the authors of passage A and passage B, respectively, mention the study by Solnick and Hemenway?

(A) to present a view that will be argued against to present a view for which additional evidence will be provided

(B) to present a view that will be argued against to provide evidence for one explanation of a phenomenon

(C) to provide evidence for one explanation of a phenomenon to present a view for which additional evidence will be provided

(D) to provide evidence for one explanation of a phenomenon to introduce the main topic to be discussed

(E) to introduce the main topic to be discussed to present a view that will be argued against

19. Which one of the following pairs of terms would most likely be used by the authors of passage A and passage B, respectively, to describe a person who wants to make more money than his or her neighbors?

(A) insular, cosmopolitan
(B) altruistic, egocentric
(C) happy, miserable
(D) misguided, admirable
(E) lucky, primitive

20. In arguing for their respective positions, the author of passage A and the author of passage B both do which one of the following?

(A) explain a phenomenon by pointing to its biological origins
(B) endorse a claim simply because it is widely believed
(C) accept a claim for the sake of argument
(D) attempt to resolve an apparent paradox
(E) assert that their positions are supported by data

GO ON TO THE NEXT PAGE.

It is generally believed that while in some cases government should intervene to protect people from risk—by imposing air safety standards, for example—in other cases, such as mountain climbing, the onus
(5) should be on the individual to protect himself or herself. In the eyes of the public at large, the demarcation between the two kinds of cases has mainly to do with whether the risk in question is incurred voluntarily. This distinction between voluntary and involuntary
(10) risk may in fact be the chief difference between lay and expert judgments about risk. Policy experts tend to focus on aggregate lives at stake; laypeople care a great deal whether a risk is undertaken voluntarily. However, judgments about whether a risk is
(15) "involuntary" often stem from confusion and selective attention, and the real reason for such judgments frequently lies in an antecedent judgment of some other kind. They are thus of little utility in guiding policy decisions.

(20)   First, it is not easy to determine when a risk is voluntarily incurred. Although voluntariness may be entirely absent in the case of an unforeseeable collision with an asteroid, with most environmental, occupational, and other social risks, it is not an all-or-
(25) nothing matter, but rather one of degree. Risks incurred by airline passengers are typically thought to be involuntary, since passengers have no control over whether a plane is going to crash. But they can choose airlines on the basis of safety records or choose not to
(30) fly. In characterizing the risks as involuntary, people focus on a small part of a complex interaction, not the decision to fly, but the accident when it occurs.

     Second, people often characterize risks as "voluntary" when they do not approve of the purpose
(35) for which people run the risks. It is unlikely that people would want to pour enormous taxpayer resources into lowering the risks associated with skydiving, even if the ratio of dollars spent to lives saved were quite good. By contrast, people would
(40) probably not object to spending enormous resources on improving the safety of firefighters, even though the decision to become a firefighter is voluntary. In short, there is no special magic in notions like "voluntary" and "involuntary." Therefore, regulatory
(45) policy should be guided by a better understanding of the factors that underlie judgments about voluntariness.

     In general, the government should attempt to save as many lives as it can, subject to the limited public and private resources devoted to risk reduction.
(50) Departures from this principle should be justified not by invoking the allegedly voluntary or involuntary nature of a particular risk, but rather by identifying the more specific considerations for which notions of voluntariness serve as proxies.

21. Which one of the following most accurately expresses the main point of the passage?

(A)   In general, whether people characterize a risk as voluntary or involuntary depends on whether they approve of the purpose for which the risk is taken.

(B)   Decisions about government intervention to protect people from risks should be based primarily on how many lives can be saved rather than on whether the risks are considered voluntary.

(C)   Though laypeople may object, experts should be the ones to determine whether the risk incurred in a particular action is voluntary or involuntary.

(D)   Public-policy decisions related to the protection of society against risk are difficult to make because of the difficulty of distinguishing risks incurred voluntarily from those incurred involuntarily.

(E)   People who make judgments about the voluntary or involuntary character of a risk are usually unaware of the complicated motivations that lead people to take risks.

22. The passage indicates that which one of the following is usually a significant factor in laypeople's willingness to support public funding for specific risk-reduction measures?

(A)   an expectation about the ratio of dollars spent to lives saved

(B)   deference to expert judgments concerning whether the government should intervene

(C)   a belief as to whether the risk is incurred voluntarily or involuntarily

(D)   a judgment as to whether the risk puts a great number of lives at stake

(E)   a consideration of the total resources available for risk reduction

23. According to the passage, which one of the following do laypeople generally consider to involve risk that is not freely assumed?

(A)   traveling in outer space
(B)   participating in skydiving
(C)   serving as a firefighter
(D)   traveling in airplanes
(E)   climbing mountains

GO ON TO THE NEXT PAGE.

24. It can be inferred from the passage that the author would be most likely to agree with which one of the following statements?

(A) People should generally not be protected against the risks incurred through activities, such as skydiving, that are dangerous and serve no socially useful purpose.

(B) The fact that plane crash victims chose to fly would usually be deemed by policy experts to be largely irrelevant to decisions about the government's role in regulating air safety.

(C) Both the probability of occurrence and the probability of resulting death or injury are higher for plane crashes than for any other kind of risk incurred by airline passengers.

(D) For public-policy purposes, a risk should be deemed voluntarily incurred if people are not subject to that risk unless they make a particular choice.

(E) The main category of risk that is usually incurred completely involuntarily is the risk of natural disaster.

25. The author's use of the phrase "no special magic" (line 43) is most likely meant primarily to convey that notions like "voluntary" and "involuntary"

(A) do not exhaustively characterize the risks that people commonly face

(B) have been used to intentionally conceal the factors motivating government efforts to protect people from risks

(C) have no meaning beyond their literal, dictionary definitions

(D) are mistakenly believed to be characteristics that inform people's understanding of the consequences of risk

(E) provide a flawed mechanism for making public policy decisions relating to risk reduction

26. The passage most strongly supports the inference that the author believes which one of the following?

(A) Whenever an activity involves the risk of loss of human life, the government should intervene to reduce the degree of risk incurred.

(B) Some environmental risks are voluntary to a greater degree than others are.

(C) Policy experts are more likely than laypeople to form an accurate judgment about the voluntariness or involuntariness of an activity.

(D) The government should increase the quantity of resources devoted to protecting people from risk.

(E) Government policies intended to reduce risk are not justified unless they comport with most people's beliefs.

27. Which one of the following most accurately describes the author's attitude in the passage?

(A) chagrin at the rampant misunderstanding of the relative risks associated with various activities

(B) concern that policy guided mainly by laypeople's emphasis on the voluntariness of risk would lead to excessive government regulation

(C) skepticism about the reliability of laypeople's intuitions as a general guide to deciding government risk-management policy

(D) conviction that the sole criterion that can justify government intervention to reduce risk is the saving of human lives

(E) eagerness to persuade the reader that policy experts' analysis of risk is distorted by subtle biases

S T O P

IF YOU FINISH BEFORE TIME IS CALLED, YOU MAY CHECK YOUR WORK ON THIS SECTION ONLY.
DO NOT WORK ON ANY OTHER SECTION IN THE TEST.

October 2013 Section 2: Reading Comprehension

Overview: Many test takers found the Reading Comprehension section of this test to be reasonably challenging, as has been common in recent LSAT reading sections. The wording chosen by the authors in this section was not overly complex, but there were quite a few challenging questions, as well as an apparent effort on the part of the test makers to get away from the standard mix of Reading Comprehension questions. The first passage, for example, was followed by back-to-back Cannot Be True questions, as well as an Evaluate the Argument question—a type that is not entirely uncommon in Logical Reasoning, but made its first appearance ever in an LSAT Reading Comprehension section.

Opening the section was a Science passage that dealt with a new type of infectious agent (prions, which normally exist innocuously as non-pathogenic cellular proteins, but were recently found to cause Creutzfeldt-Jakob disease). Technical and scientific terms tend to throw off many test takers, but those who were able to get past the jargon found a fairly straightforward passage. The author of the second passage in the section discussed Katherine Dunham's technique, "dance isolation," which she brought to North American dance, thanks largely to her dual specialties of choreography and anthropological research. Some students found the language and content of this passage challenging, as well as the Parallel Reasoning, Subject Perspective, and Author's Perspective questions that were included among the questions that followed the passage. Next came Social Science, in the Comparative Reading Passages, both of which discussed a study by researchers Solnick and Hemenway that dealt with the issues of wealth and happiness. The language used in the Comparative Reading passage set was not overly sophisticated, but to do well on the questions that followed, it was vital (as is usually the case) to retain a solid grasp on the similarities and differences between the two passages. In the final passage in the section, the author explored the issues of the determination of risk, both voluntary and involuntary, and protective government intervention. Much of the difficulty associated with this passage appeared in the questions; given that they included three Author's Perspective questions and a Purpose question, students needed a full understanding of the author's tone and perspective in order to do well on the questions that followed.

Passage 1: Pathogens

Paragraph One:

The author opens the first passage with the definition of an infection: when a pathogen, or disease causing agent, acquires the ability to reproduce inside an organism (i.e. creates a "viable presence"). "Until recently," the author provides, it was believed that only four agents could cause infection: 1) viruses; 2) bacteria; 3) fungi; and 4) parasites, all of which reproduce and live using genetic material made up of nucleic acid, specifically either DNA or RNA. As such, the corresponding belief was that all pathogens have such genetic material.

Paragraph Two:

If the previous paragraph discussed a "recently held" belief, we can expect that this belief would be eventually challenged. Which it is here. The Creutzfeldt-Jakob disease, or CJD, is a type of degenerative dementia which creates tiny holes in the brain, suggesting the death of a significant number of nerve cells. Four symptoms of the disease are listed: loss of muscle control, mental sharpness, and memory, as well as chronic insomnia. The pathogen that causes CJD appears to be comprised primarily of protein rather than nucleic acid, unlike the disease-causing agents discussed in the first paragraph. Researchers named the protein pathogen "prion."

Paragraph Three:

The author continues the discussion of the prions, which normally appear in many body tissues as harmless protein cells but are able to transform into a dangerous shape, changing normal prions into pathogenic ones on contact. The pathogenic prions create a thread-like plaque that eventually destroys nerve cells as it collects in the brain. Further, the body's immune system does not react to prions as it does to other pathogens, because prions are proteins that are normally present in the body. Since there is no effective way to fight the prion reproductive chain reaction, CJD is always fatal, although the disorder varies both in degree of aggressiveness and incubation time.

Paragraph Four:

After initial skepticism regarding the link between prions and CJD, research has provided support for the characterization of prions as a new class of pathogen. While prions' processes of reproduction and destruction are not completely understood, similar protein malformation is thought to be involved in more common conditions such as Alzheimer's and Parkinson's.

VIEWSTAMP Analysis:

The only **Viewpoints** presented in this passage are those of the author, who simply presents the facts, and of the general scientific community.

The **Structure** of the passage is as follows:

Paragraph One: Define "infection," provide a list of four infectious agents that was previously believed to be exhaustive.

Paragraph Two: Introduce the example of Creutzfeldt-Jakob disease and the concept of the prion, a recently discovered protein pathogen.

Paragraph Three: Elaborate on the topic of prions and explain their pathogenic effects.

Paragraph Four: Affirm the status of prions as a new class of pathogen, and suggest that other conditions may be attributable to similar protein malformations.

The **Tone** of the passage is well-reasoned and somewhat academic; the author provides a scholarly presentation of recent scientific pathogen research.

The author's **Main Point** is to discuss the prion, a recently discovered, self-reproducing protein pathogen that has now been added to the other four previously known pathogenic agents.

Question #1: GR, Main Point. The correct answer choice is (B)

The answer to this Main Point question is prephrased in our VIEWSTAMP analysis above.

Answer choice (A): Although it is accurate to say that the mechanism by which prions reproduce themselves is not yet completely understood, how many types of protein most organisms produce is unknown. Furthermore, this answer choice is too narrow in scope to represent the main point of the passage.

Answer choice (B): This is the correct answer choice. As discussed above, the author's main point is to discuss prions, a new kind of pathogen made up, surprisingly, of protein rather than standard DNA or RNA associated with the four previously known infection-causing agents.

Answer choice (C): In the last paragraph, the author mentions that similar protein malformation might take place in other conditions, but does not go so far as to assert that this applies to "most" other neurological conditions. Since this choice doesn't even pass the Fact Test, it cannot be the correct answer choice to this Main Point question.

Answer choice (D): At the beginning of the last paragraph, the author states that the scientific community was initially skeptical regarding the link between prions and CJD, subsequent research has supported the notion that prions are a new class of pathogen. This answer choice implies that the controversy over prions and CJD continues to this day, which is unwarranted. And even if it did, this would not be the main point of the passage.

Answer choice (E): The passage does describe the prions' general approach to reproduction, and the author mentions that they lack nucleic acid, but this is not the main point of the passage, so it cannot be the correct response to this Main Point question.

Question #2: GR, Must. The correct answer choice is (A)

Since this is a Global Reference question, there is not much prephrasing to be done; the correct answer choice will be the one that passes the Fact Test, and can thus be confirmed by the information provided in the stimulus.

Answer choice (A): This is the correct answer choice. At the beginning of the last paragraph, the author provides that after initial skepticism from the scientific community, subsequent research has confirmed that prions are indeed a pathogen to be added to the list of four infection-causing agents previously believed to be complete. Thus, it is reasonable to infer that scientists had to reconsider their traditional beliefs about the causes of infection in order to understand CJD, which is caused by prions.

Answer choice (B): CJD is caused by prions, which occur naturally, and then malform and reproduce. The author does not mention whether the disease is contagious (let alone how much so) so this choice is not supported by the passage.

Answer choice (C): The author does not discuss CJD prevention, so this choice should be ruled out of contention.

Answer choice (D): This is an Opposite answer. At the end of the third paragraph, the author explicitly states that wide variations exist in both incubation times and the aggressiveness of the disease, directly contradicting this answer choice.

Answer choice (E): Although the author does mention that prions were initially received with skepticism from the scientific community, it is clear that recent research has led to broader acceptance.

Question #3: CR, Evaluate the Argument. The correct answer choice is (E)

As mentioned in the section overview, this question marks the very first appearance of an Evaluate the Argument question on a Reading Comprehension section. Since it is an Evaluate question, the correct answer choice will provide the inquiry most helpful in determining the presence of CJD. The correct answer choice will likely deal with either the presence of prions or that of an accompanying symptom.

Answer choice (A): The passage mentions nothing about how a blow to the skull might affect the likelihood of CJD, so there is no reason to believe that the answer to this question would be helpful to a physician attempting to make a diagnosis of CJD. As such, it cannot be the right answer to this Evaluate question.

Answer choice (B): Insomnia is not mentioned as a symptom associated with the presence of CJD, and so answering this question is unlikely to help a physician decide whether a patient has CJD.

Answer choice (C): Neither radiation nor genetic damage is mentioned as having any association with CJD; Consequently, whether the patient has been exposed to radiation would be irrelevant to a CJD diagnosis.

Answer choice (D): The author does not mention whether a family history of brain disease would have any effect on the likelihood of developing CJD, so this cannot be the answer to this Evaluate question.

Answer choice (E): This is the correct answer choice. In the middle of the third paragraph, the author mentions that CJD leads to the formation of a plaque, consisting of thread-like structures (lines 37-38). Thus, whether the patient's brain tissue exhibits the presence of such structures would clearly be relevant to a proper diagnosis.

Question #4: GR, Must. The correct answer choice is (C)

To answer this Global Reference, Must Be True question, apply the Fact Test and proceed by the process of elimination: any answer choice that cannot be proven by reference to information contained in the passage will be incorrect.

Answer choice (A): The passage provides that prions occur naturally in cell tissues, and that they possess the capability to, on their own, transform themselves into abnormal shapes. This choice discusses the *transmission* of CJD from an infected individual to an uninfected one, about which we know absolutely nothing.

Answer choice (B): If you found this answer choice appealing, that is, of course, by design; the author does mention in the final paragraph that other neurological disorders are now thought to be caused by similar processes, but this choice goes much farther than that, claiming that *most* infectious diseases are now thought to be caused by prions. This is entirely unsupported by the passage, so it should be ruled out of contention.

Answer choice (C): This is the correct answer choice. In the third paragraph, the author mentions that prions are able to reproduce in an unexpected way, helping to create the pathogenic conformation(lines 30-36). Clearly, then, if prions were unable to reproduce themselves, they would not cause CJD.

Answer choice (D): Although these neurological disorders are thought to result from processes similar to those that cause CJD, we do not know if they are caused by different conformations of the same prion pathogen that causes CJD.

Answer choice (E): The author never makes the assertion presented in this answer choice, nor does the passage even provide such a comparison.

Question #5: GR, Cannot, AP. The correct answer choice is (B)

Four of the five answer choices to this Cannot Be True, Author's Perspective question will state claims with which the author is likely to agree. By contrast, the correct answer choice will state a claim with which the author is unlikely to agree (and may, in fact, disagree).

Answer choice (A): Based on the discussion in lines 34-36, we can infer that the presence of abnormally shaped prions in the brain is a sign of a neurological disorder. Since the author is likely to agree with this statement, answer choice (A) is incorrect.

Answer choice (B): This is the correct answer choice. In line 45, the author specifies that CJD is inevitably fatal. Thus, the author would clearly disagree with the statement that some of those afflicted with the condition eventually recover, confirming this as the right answer to this Cannot Be True question.

Answer choice (C): We know from the second paragraph that a prion is a disease agent lacking nucleic acid (lines 19-24). Thus, they clearly do not require nucleic acid for reproduction.

Answer choice (D): From the discussion in lines 41-42, we know that the body has no natural defence against CJD. Since the author is likely to agree with this statement, answer choice (D) is incorrect.

Answer choice (E): The author closes the last paragraph saying that prions' exact mechanisms are not yet understood. Since the author would clearly agree with this choice, it should be ruled out of contention for this Cannot Be True question.

Question #6: CR, Cannot. The correct answer choice is (A)

To answer yet another Cannot Be True question, we need to identify an answer choice that is directly disproven by the passage. Specifically, we are instructed to assume that 1) the author's use of the term "pathogen" is correct; and 2) the prion theory of infection is also correct.

Answer choice (A): This is the correct answer choice. First, simplify the double negative here: "nothing that lacks nucleic acid is a pathogen" is a convoluted way of saying, "if something does not have nucleic acid, it is not a pathogen." But, is the prion not a pathogen lacking nucleic acid (lines 19-24)? Clearly, this answer choice cannot be true given the prion theory of infection, validating it as the correct answer choice to this Cannot Be True question.

Answer choice (B): The accuracy of this answer choice is confirmed by the author in the second paragraph, and this is a central point of the passage as well; this therefore cannot be the right answer to this Cannot Be True question.

Answer choice (C): The passage provides that a pathogen is a disease-causing agent, and that infections can only take place when the pathogenic agent is able to reproduce and create a viable presence in the organism. Since the choice is not refuted by the passage, it can be ruled out of contention in response to this Cannot Be True question.

Answer choice (D): If the prion theory of infection is correct, and prions are pathogens, then clearly pathogens do contribute in some manner to the occurrence of CJD. This answer choice is proven, not disproven, by the passage.

Answer choice (E): Yes, there are other pathogens besides the four listed: researchers coined the term "prion" for this new type of protein pathogen (lines 23-24). This answer choice states a provable claim and is therefore incorrect.

Question #7: CR, Weaken. The correct answer choice is (E)

The correct answer to this Weaken question will undermine the causal connection between prions and CJD. As we know from discussing causality in Logical Reasoning, the correct answer choice will likely present an alternative cause for the occurrence of CJD, or else provide counterexamples in which the cause occurs without the effect (or vice versa).

Answer choice (A): The fact that viral infections may in some cases bring about the same symptoms as CJD would not undermine the claim that prions cause CJD, so this cannot be the right answer to this Weaken question.

Answer choice (B): This choice is consistent with the claim that prions cause CJD, and that the disease is inevitably fatal, so this cannot be the right answer to this Weaken question.

Answer choice (C): Even if, as this choice provides, prions can cause other types of conditions, that would not weaken the claim that they cause CJD.

Answer choice (D): The presence or absence of heredity factors would have no effect on the claim that CJD is caused by prions, so this cannot be the right answer to this Weaken question.

Answer choice (E): This is the correct answer choice. If an antibacterial drug were effective in reversing CJD, that would suggest that CJD is caused by bacteria, one of the four previously known pathogens, rather than caused by prions. This answer choice suggests an alternate cause (bacteria) for the observed effect (CJD), weakening the argument that the prions and CJD are causally related.

Passage 2: Katherine Dunham's Dance

<u>Paragraph One</u>:

At the beginning of the opening paragraph, the author presents the subject of the passage: Katherine Dunham, an African American choreographer who was also an anthropologist—complementary fields of expertise which facilitate her introduction of "dance isolation" to modern North American dance. The technique, which isolates a given rhythm to a particular part of the body, has long been an important part of African, Caribbean, and Pacific-island cultures.

<u>Paragraph Two</u>:

In the early 1930s, Dunham helped to pioneer dance ethnology. Up until that point, field had not been studied by social scientists, who tended instead to focus on areas considered by their peers to be scientifically rigorous, and thus "legitimate." Further, beyond Dunham there were no others whose expertise included an overlap of dance and social science.

<u>Paragraph Three</u>:

In 1935, Dunham began a series of research projects dealing with Caribbean dance, focusing on its African origins. She was advised by colleagues in anthropology not to participate in the dancing itself, based on the prevailing view at the time that the proper approach to research was from a detached perspective. However, according to the author, Dunham's participation was crucial to her success: it allowed her to master the technique and then teach it while she incorporated it into new types of ballet.

<u>Paragraph Four</u>:

During the period from 1937 to 1945, Dunham used her "research-to-performance" method, combining Caribbean and modern dance learned in Chicago for theatrical performances, which were among the first to include African American themes in modern dance (note that the author phrases this as rectifying the exclusion of African American themes, taking a very supportive stance). The author closes the passage by pointing out that Dunham's work was vital to the establishment of African American dance as an art form, which made future dance companies, such as Arthur Mitchell's Dance Theater of Harlem, possible.

VIEWSTAMP Analysis:

The primary **Viewpoint** presented in this passage is that of the author. Two secondary viewpoints are alluded to in the second and third paragraphs: in the 1930s, Dunham's "peers" (line 22) focused on what they perceived as more "legitimate" modes of inquiry, whereas her "colleagues in anthropology" advised her to remain detached from dancing (lines 33-40). These viewpoints are complementary, and at odds with the position held by the author who regards them as "fortunately [...] unrealistic (line 38)".

The **Structure** of the passage is as follows:

Paragraph One: Introduce Katherine Dunham and the dance isolation technique that she introduced to modern dance in North America.

Paragraph Two: Discuss how Dunham's crossover expertise in both dance and social science allowed her to pioneer dance ethnology.

Paragraph Three: Focus on the mid-1930s: Dunham started researching Caribbean dance and its African roots. Despite some advice to the contrary, she participated in the dances herself.

Paragraph Four: Evaluate Dunham's contributions to modern dance in North America, and to the establishment of African American dance as a distinct art form.

The author's **Tone** is a positive one, clearly impressed by the multi-talented Dunham and her significant accomplishments.

The **Main Point** of the passage is that Katherine Dunham used her varied expertise to study, master, and spread themes from African, Caribbean, and Pacific-island dance, mixing them with modern North American dance, while helping to establish African American dance as an art form.

Question #8: GR, Main Point. The correct answer choice is (E)

The answer to this Main Point question is prephrased in the passage discussion above.

Answer choice (A): The author does mention that Dunham developed a research-to-performance method, but as discussed above that is not the main point of the passage, so this cannot be the right answer choice.

Answer choice (B): Dunham's works were distinct, but they might not have been the only ones that incorporated authentic dance techniques. In any case, this is certainly not the main point of the passage, so this choice should be ruled out of contention.

Answer choice (C): The author does not mention the expression of aesthetic or political concerns of African American dancers and choreographers. Since this choice doesn't even pass the Fact Test, it cannot possibly be the main point of the passage.

Answer choice (D): Although Dunham did focus on the African roots of Caribbean dance, the author does not claim that she discovered those roots.

Answer choice (E): This is the correct answer choice. As discussed, Dunham's crossover expertise allowed her to change North American modern dance.

Question #9: CR, Must. The correct answer choice is (C)

To answer this Concept Reference question, Structure and Viewpoint identification are both key. As previously mentioned, the viewpoint of "other anthropologists" is discussed primarily in the third paragraph: Dunham's colleagues advised her to remain detached from the object of her inquiry (lines 33-40), an advice she ultimately ignored by participating in the dances herself (lines 42-43). This section of the passage should be sufficient to validate one of the five answer choices.

Answer choice (A): The author does not compare the length of time that Dunham spent performing fieldwork to that of her colleagues.

Answer choice (B): Although Dunham was able to comprehend dancing as a complex cultural practice (lines 44-45), this is not described as a point of distinction between her work in anthropology and that of most other anthropologists in the 1930s.

Answer choice (C): This is the correct answer choice. As prephrased above, Dunham participated in the dances that she researched, in contrast to most other anthropologists who cautioned against such approach.

Answer choice (D): The passage does not mention whether or not Dunham attached political significance to her work, nor whether other social scientists of the time did, so this is not the right answer choice.

Answer choice (E): The author provides no basis for the claim that most other anthropologists didn't have such prior familiarity, and this is not the distinction referred to by this question.

Question #10: SR, Must, SP. The correct answer choice is (C)

This question refers to views expressed in the second paragraph. As prephrased in the Viewpoints discussion above, most social scientists of the time neglected dance, more interested in areas recognized by their peers as scientifically rigorous and thus legitimate. The implication is that the peers considered dance less legitimate, and not quite so scientifically rigorous.

Answer choice (A): There is no basis for the claim that Dunham's peers misinterpreted dance, so this cannot be the right answer choice.

Answer choice (B): Since Dunham's peers were not particularly interested in studying dance to begin with, this answer choice can be eliminated.

Answer choice (C): This is the correct answer choice. As prephrased above, Dunham's peers did not consider dance to be scientifically rigorous which matches the perspective referenced here.

Answer choice (D): Dunham's peers did not comment on whether or not dance experts can conduct research in dance ethnology. This is something that the author discussed at the end of the second paragraph, but it is not a view with which her peers would necessarily agree.

Answer choice (E): Precisely why Dunham's peers believed that dance cannot be studied with the requisite level of scientific rigor remains unknown.

Question #11: SR, Must, P. The correct answer choice is (D)

To answer this Specific Reference, Purpose question, it is critical to understand the context of the referenced claim and formulate a suitable prephrase. The author remarks that "experts in dance were not trained in the methods of social research" (lines 26-27) in order to explain her previous claim that dance had been neglected as an area of social research (lines 19-20). As usual, the key to identifying the function of a specific citation is to understand the context in which it appears, which may involve reading a few lines above or below the referenced material.

Answer choice (A): The author does not mention "the experts in dance" in order to explain why a group of scientists did not embrace the study of a particular cultural art form.

Answer choice (B): The proposition that one group was more qualified to study dance than another is neither asserted nor alluded to.

Answer choice (C): While it is true that the aforementioned experts were not trained in the method of social research, this only explains why the field of dance had been neglected, not why Dunham herself decided to pursue research into that field. The two are obviously related, but the second paragraph does not seek to explain Dunham's motivations. Its only purpose is to show that she was a pioneer in the field of dance ethnology.

Answer choice (D): This is the correct answer choice, as it agrees with our prephrase above.

Answer choice (E): The author does not say that there was any tension between the two fields of research, but merely that there was little overlap in expertise between them.

Question #12: CR, Must. The correct answer choice is (E)

Once again, passage Structure is key: the dance forms that Dunham began studying in 1935 are discussed in the third paragraph, which should be the obvious reference point for this question.

Answer choice (A): The passage provides no such comparison, so this cannot be the right answer choice.

Answer choice (B): The author specifically mentions that the technique had long been a part of the traditional dances of certain Caribbean and Pacific-island cultures as well, so this choice fails the Fact Test and should be ruled out of contention.

Answer choice (C): It was Dunham who helped to bring the technique to North American modern dance. The author doesn't mention any other shared characteristics.

Answer choice (D): Dunham brought the technique to North America; the dance forms that she studied had no prior influence on popular North American dance.

Answer choice (E): This is the correct answer choice. The Caribbean dance forms she studied were influenced by African culture (lines 30-31) and it was this influence on which Dunham focused.

Question #13: CR, Parallel. The correct answer choice (D)

To approach this Parallel question correctly, recall that Dunham used her expertise in both social science and choreography to incorporate the techniques of traditional Caribbean dance forms into new forms of ballet and theater (lines 43-50). Before you approach the answers, use the Test of Abstraction from Parallel Reasoning questions in the Logical Reasoning section of the test: the correct answer choice must describe an expert who 1) has training in another discipline and 2) introduces findings from another culture into her home country.

Answer choice (A): Although the French archaeologist has training in two disciplines (archeology and musicology), her similarity to Dunham stops here. Unlike Dunham, who studies Caribbean dance techniques and incorporates them into North American modern dance, the French archaeologist studies French musical instruments without incorporating her findings into another cultural milieu. Instead, here a Korean engineer takes advantage of these findings - a proposition that does not parallel Dunham's work.

Answer choice (B): Like Dunham, the Australian researcher has training in two fields (medicine and botany). What makes this answer choice even more attractive is that the subject of the researcher's work is foreign (plans from the Philippines).

Unlike Dunham, however, the Australian medical researcher relies on someone else to develop her findings into a useful product. By contrast, Dunham herself developed the research-to-performance method that she used to adapt Caribbean dance forms for use in theatrical performance (lines 48-50). This is a significant point of distinction, making answer choice (B) incorrect.

Answer choice (C): This answer choice describes a collaboration between two different scientists, which is not analogous to Dunham's work. Dunham herself had dual expertise in anthropology and choreography; she did not rely on someone else to collaborate with.

Answer choice (D): This is the correct answer choice as it matches the Test of Abstraction described above: The Brazilian teacher blends two types of expertise to conduct immersive research into other cultures, which he then shares with teachers in his own country.

Answer choice (E): Although the Italian fashion designer conducted research into other cultures, he did not have the requisite expertise in two different fields of academic inquiry, as Dunham did.

Question #14: SR, Must, AP. The correct answer choice is (D)

This is the third question in this Passage that deals with competing Viewpoints, making our VIEWSTAMP analysis that much more helpful. As discussed earlier, Dunham's "colleagues in anthropology" advised her to remain detached from dance (lines 33-40), which is at odds with the position held by the author. In line 38, the author refers to their viewpoint as "fortunately [...] unrealistic."

Answer choice (A): The author does not concede that Dunham's colleagues were "partly correct" about anything. This answer choice can be immediately eliminated.

Answer choice (B): As with answer choice (A), this one can be eliminated relatively quickly because the author does not concede that Dunham's colleagues were "partly correct" about anything.

Answer choice (C): Many test takers found this choice appealing based on the first half of the answer: The author would agree that Dunham's colleagues were incorrect in their recommendations. However, there is no reason to believe that the author would make a broad statement that personal investment enhances scientific rigor as a general rule. This answer choice contains an exaggeration and is therefore incorrect.

Answer choice (D): This is the correct answer choice. If it is "unrealistic" (lines 38) to conduct research from the position of complete detachment, then gathering data in the social sciences is not an entirely objective process. Dunham's colleagues clearly assumed that it is, an assumption that the author believes is incorrect. This answer choice properly reflects the Author's Perspective toward the viewpoint expressed in lines 33-40.

Answer choice (E): Dunham's peers did not assume that dancing could be studied with the same degree of scientific rigor possible in other areas of ethnology. If they had made such an assumption, the author would not have disagreed with it.

Passage 3: Happiness and Wealth

Passage A

This passage opens with an interesting paradox about wealth and happiness: While the wealthy are happier than the poor at any given time, advanced societies have not grown happier as they have grown richer. The author identifies two factors that might explain this paradox: habituation and rivalry.

The discussion in the second paragraph focuses on habituation. People initially love an increase in their standard of living but soon adjust their expectations, so that their requirements increase along with their income. Similarly, job satisfaction increases when wages rapidly increase, but doesn't seem to depend on absolute wages. Since we do not have the foresight to recognize how quickly we'll adjust to our newly acquired possessions, we keep buying more possessions instead of investing in something else, such as leisure.

Next, the discussion shifts to rivalry. The author presents a study done by Solnick and Hemenway in which people chose from two options: either earn $50,000 per year while everyone else earns $25,000, or earn $100,000 per year while all others make $200,000. Most chose the first option, meaning that they did not mind making less as long as they were doing better than everyone else.

People's income relative to others like them (their "reference group") is critical. The author closes the passage with the example of East Germany, where living standards have increased but happiness has plummeted. The author explains this paradox by observing that East Germans now compare themselves to West Germans, rather than to people in other Soviet bloc countries.

Passage B

The second passage opens with a possible explanation to the Solnick and Hemenway study (evolutionary one-upmanship), which is quickly dismissed in the second paragraph. Apparently, data show that earning more increases happiness because it leads to a feeling of greater success, and of having created value. The author argues that it is success success and added value, not money per se, that causes people to feel happier.

The closing paragraph reveals an optimistic perspective on our tendency to "want more than others": we do so because we want to create value, which benefits society. Happiness is just an added "bonus."

Passage Similarities and Differences

Passage A and B are both concerned with explaining the relationship between happiness and wealth. The author of passage A observes that the two correlate only to an extent, and argues that habituation and rivalry limit the extent to which wealth provides happiness. The author of passage B takes issue with the notion of "rivalry," arguing that a third factor—the desire to create value and feel successful—explains why earning more appears to provide happiness. The two are correlated, but both are the result of another cause.

Both passages exhibit an academic, well-informed tone, although the views expressed in passage B reveal an optimistic attitude that is somewhat lacking in passage A. The latter takes a rather pessimistic view of human nature, believing that we easily succumb to habit and rivalry (which is not terribly flattering).

Question #15: GR, Must, P. The correct answer choice is (B)

The first question asks for the primary purpose of both passages: both are primarily concerned with examining wealth and happiness.

Answer choice (A): Only the second author mentions the desire to create value as being the root of the feelings of success that bring happiness. Since this is not a central concern of both authors, it cannot be the right answer choice.

Answer choice (B): This is the correct answer choice. As prephrased, both authors are mainly interested in the relationship between income and happiness. This choice thus passes the Fact Test, confirming it as the right answer choice.

Answer choice (C): Only the author of passage B mentions the biological basis for the "one-upsmanship" drive, but this is not the primary focus of either passage.

Answer choice (D): The phenomenon of habituation is only discussed in the first passage, and its explanation is not the primary concern of the author.

Answer choice (E): The concept of "required income" is only discussed in the first passage, as it relates to the phenomenon of habituation. Since this is not the primary focus of either passage, it should be ruled out of contention in response to this Must Be True question.

Question #16: GR, Must, AP. The correct answer choice is (C)

To respond to this Global Reference question, it is critical to understand the perspective outlined in Passage B: relative prosperity makes people happier not because of "one-upsmanship," but rather because it gives them a feeling of success, and of having created value.

Answer choice (A): The evolutionary theory of one-upmanship is discussed in the first paragraph of passage B, but it is subsequently rejected (lines 48-50).

Answer choice (B): The author of passage B concedes that there is a natural drive for relative prosperity, as is reflected in the results of the Solnick and Hemenway study. This choice fails the Fact Test and cannot be the right answer to this Must Be True question.

Answer choice (C): This is the correct answer choice. If one believed that one's wealth was entirely attributable to luck, then that person would lack the satisfaction of having created value, which is, according to the second author, central to the correlation between happiness and wealth.

Answer choice (D): Although the central argument in passage B is that money per se does not provide happiness, it is entirely possible that a gradual increase in employees' wages could increase their job satisfaction, provided that the employees view themselves as valuable and successful.

Answer choice (E): The author of passage B does not view money and happiness as perfectly correlated; on the contrary, he accepts the results of the Solnick and Hemenway study, which shows that they are not (people are happy to be poorer, provided their relative position is improved).

Question #17: SR, Must, AP. The correct answer choice is (A)

To answer this Author's Perspective question, consider how the author of passage B would regard the "phenomenon of rivalry" mentioned in line 24 of passage A. As discussed in Passage Similarities and Differences above, passage B takes issue with the view that our quest for relative prosperity is based on a need to one-up our neighbors. Clearly, its author rejects the notion that the "phenomenon of rivalry" has any explanatory power in this case. This prephrase alone can help eliminate answer choices (C), (D), and (E).

Answer choice (A): This is the correct answer choice. As prephrased above, the second author disagrees with the rivalry interpretation, arguing that the desire for more is based on the intention to create value, not one-up our neighbor. The author of passage B also regards the rivalry interpretation as primeval (line 43), which is not terribly flattering.

Answer choice (B): The rivalry theory is certainly not flattering, so this choice should be quickly ruled out of contention.

Answer choice (C): The author of passage B does not regard the phenomenon of rivalry as particularly plausible (lines 48-53), and clearly has a rather optimistic view of human nature (lines 62-66).

Answer choice (D): The author of passage B would agree with the first part of this choice but disagree with the second part; the rivalry explanation is rather unflattering, but the author would not agree that it is more or less valid.

Answer choice (E): This is an Opposite Answer, because the author of the second passage sees the rivalry explanation as neither accurate nor strongly supported by the evidence.

Question #18: GR, Must, P. The correct answer choice is (D)

To answer this question correctly, you need to explain why each author mentions the study of Solnick and Hemenway. In passage A, this study was used as evidence that rivalry plays a role in improving our relative position. The author of passage B mentions the study in order to refute this theory and offer an alternative interpretation instead.

Answer choice (A): This answer choice is wrong on both counts: the first author does not argue against a view entailed by the study, nor does the second author provide additional evidence in support of that view.

Answer choice (B): This is the Reverse Answer; it is the second author who presents the study in order to argue against a position; meanwhile, it is the first author who presents it as evidence in support of that position.

Answer choice (C): The first part of this choice is accurate, as discussed above, but the second is not, as no additional evidence for the view is provided by the second author.

Answer choice (D): This is the correct answer choice, as it agrees with our prephrase above.

Answer choice (E): Many students found this choice appealing, because it captures well the function of the study in passage B. However, passage A does not mention the study in order to introduce the main topic to be discussed. The study is only used as supporting evidence of the rivalry phenomenon, which is not the main point of the passage.

Question #19: CR, Must, AP, Tone. The correct answer choice is (D)

To answer this question correctly, you need to understand each author's attitude toward the pursuit of relative prosperity. This comparative analysis was provided in our discussion of Passage Similarities and Differences above. However, given the range of possible adjectives that test makers can use to describe each attitude, it may be best to proceed by the process of elimination.

Answer choice (A): While "insular" has the negative connotation we are looking for, we have no reason to suspect that the author of passage A would regard the pursuit of material wealth as particularly "insular." Myopic, maybe, but not necessarily insular. Similarly, the term "cosmopolitan" has the positive connotation we have come to expect from passage B, but it falls entirely outside the scope of that passage.

Answer choice (B): The first author does not regard the pursuit of comparative wealth as "altruistic," nor does the second author regard it as "egocentric." Both terms are squarely at odds with the attitudes expressed in the passages.

Answer choice (C): As with answer choice (B), both terms in this answer choice conflict with the attitudes expressed in the passages. According to the first author, a person who wants to make more money than her neighbor would only be "happy" if her neighbor ends up making less. Even then, that person's happiness would be fleeting, because she would quickly adjust to her increased standard of living.

Would the author of passage B regard such a person as "miserable"? Not at all: the second author sees nothing wrong with the pursuit of material wealth, as long as it accomplishes a socially valuable objective.

Answer choice (D): This is the correct answer choice. As previously mentioned, the author of passage A views the pursuit of relative prosperity in a negative light: we remain ignorant of how we adjust to material possessions, so we overinvest in acquiring them (lines 20-23). It is entirely plausible that this author would describe someone trying to earn more money than her neighbor as "misguided."

Meanwhile, the views expressed in passage B reveal an optimistic, affirmative attitude toward human nature: there is nothing wrong with wealth accumulation, as long as it is done in pursuit of prosperity and value. "Admirable" seems on point here, though it probably overstates the author's attitude a tiny bit. Nevertheless, this pair of terms best reflects the difference in attitude between the two authors, making answer choice (D) correct.

Answer choice (E): There is nothing in the first passage to support the notion that the author would characterize a person who wants greater relative prosperity as "lucky." Furthermore, while the second author does mention the theory regarding an underlying biological drive, that author would not describe such a person as "primitive": in fact, this view was flatly rejected in the second paragraph of passage B.

Question #20: GR, Must, P. The correct answer choice is (E)

Approach this Purpose question by the process of elimination: the correct answer choice must provide a description that is consistent with each passage individually. Focus on what each author does, not on what she says.

Answer choice (A): Only the second author mentions biological origins, so this choice should be ruled out of contention.

Answer choice (B): Neither author endorses a claim just because it is widely believed, so this cannot be the right answer choice.

Answer choice (C): The second author considers a claim for the sake of argument (the claim that a biological component may explain the drive to have more than our neighbors), but the first author does not.

Answer choice (D): This might have been a tempting answer choice, because the author of passage A does attempt to resolve an apparent paradox (lines 1-5). However, the author of passage B has an entirely different objective, namely, to refute the rivalry hypothesis from passage A and provide an alternative interpretation of the available evidence. The Solnick and Hemenway study is perceived as neither paradoxical nor puzzling, just in need of a better explanation.

Answer choice (E): This is the correct answer choice, because both authors believe that the Solnick and Hemenway study supports their respective positions. Just because they have conflicting interpretations of this data does not mean that their methods of reasoning differ.

Passage 4: Risk Reduction

Paragraph One:

The author begins this final passage of the section by pointing out that some types of risks are generally believed to call for government intervention, while others are not; the government should be involved in guaranteeing air safety, for example, while it is largely up to a mountain climber to look out for his or her own safety. The author says that the difference in perception between the two scenarios comes down to whether or not the risks were taken on voluntarily. This "voluntary" factor, the author asserts, might be the main point of distinction between laypeople, who are more focused on whether an act was taken on voluntarily, and experts, who tend to concentrate on the total number of lives put at risk. According to the author, however, the layperson's focus on the voluntary vs. involuntary distinction is often confused or misguided, and in reality such judgments are often based on different underlying considerations, so this distinction is not particularly useful in the area of policy decisions.

Paragraph Two:

The author begins the second paragraph by pointing out that while a collision with an asteroid exemplifies an entirely involuntary act, in most situations the distinction between voluntary and involuntary is not quite so clear. The author provides the example of airline passengers, whose risks are generally considered involuntary based on their lack of control over the plane's course, in spite of the fact that such passengers could choose safer airlines or other modes of travel.

Paragraph Three:

Here the author points out that the characterization of an act as voluntary or involuntary can often involve other judgments as well, such as the degree to which we approve of the act whose risk is being assessed. Few would support significant government expenditures to protect skydivers, for example, but most would support such spending to protect firefighters, who, the author points out, also take on risks voluntarily. Since such factors can be the real reason for characterizations of risks as voluntary or involuntary, the author asserts that policies should be based on a clearer perspective regarding the basis for such judgments.

Paragraph Four:

In the concluding paragraph, the author recommends that the government use whatever limited public and private resources are devoted to risk reduction in an effort to save as many lives as possible. Doing otherwise, the author asserts, should be justified not by questionable characterizations of risk as voluntary or involuntary, but by the actual, specific, underlying considerations that guide such judgments.

<u>VIEWSTAMP</u> Analysis:

The primary **Viewpoint** presented here is that of the author, who discusses common misconceptions regarding the proper assignment of risk protection intervention. Two additional viewpoints are alluded to: those of policy experts (lines 11-12) and of laypeople (lines 12-15 and 30-42), whose misconceptions about "voluntary" and "involuntary" assumption of risk are extensively discussed.

The **Structure** of the passage is as follows:

<u>Paragraph One:</u>	Introduce the distinction between voluntary and involuntary risk, and suggest that such a distinction is of little utility in guiding policy decisions regarding risk prevention.
<u>Paragraph Two:</u>	Support the position in the first paragraph by suggesting that the assumption of risk is not always an entirely voluntary or an entirely involuntary act (see, e.g. flying).
<u>Paragraph Three:</u>	Show how our judgments about voluntariness often reflect subjective approval of purpose (e.g., skydivers vs. firefighters), and suggest that such judgments should not guide regulatory policy relating to risk reduction.
<u>Paragraph Four:</u>	Reiterate the position that judgments about voluntariness provide an inadequate basis for policy decisions relating to risk reduction, and propose an alternative policy relating to such decisions: save as many lives as possible. This is also the Main Point of the passage.

The **Tone** of the passage is convicted and prescriptive, critical of our rationale for determining which risks justify government intervention and which ones do not.

The primary **Argument** presented in the stimulus is also the author's **Main Point**: As a risk prevention policy, the government should save as many lives as possible with the limited resources it has, rather than invoke the allegedly voluntary or involuntary nature of the risk.

Question #21: GR, Main Point. The correct answer choice is (B)

The answer to this Main Point question should be prephrased, as shown in the VIEWSTAMP analysis above.

Answer choice (A): This answer choice deals with the author's discussion from the third paragraph about how people characterize acts as voluntary or involuntary based on whether they approve of a given act. While undeniably true, this observation merely supports the position that we should not base policy decisions on whether a risk can be characterized as voluntary or not. Because it does not capture the main point of the passage as a whole, this answer choice is incorrect.

Answer choice (B): This is the correct answer choice, restating the main point as discussed above. Government intervention in risky undertakings should not be based on a supposed distinction between voluntary and involuntary categories of risk, but instead on the general guiding principle provided by the author: maximize the number of lives saved, given the resources dedicated to risk prevention.

Answer choice (C): Just because the distinction between voluntary and involuntary risk is arbitrary, subjective, or problematic does not mean that it should be left to the experts. Such a recommendation is neither suggested nor alluded to.

Answer choice (D): As with answer choice (A), this answer choice states a provable claim: indeed, it is sometimes difficult to determine when a risk is voluntarily incurred (lines 20-21). However, this difficulty is not the main point of the passage; rather, it merely supports the claim that we should not base policy decisions on whether the risks are considered voluntary.

Answer choice (E): The passage does not specify whether or not people who make such judgments are aware of such complicated motivations, so this choice doesn't even pass the Fact Test, let alone provide the main point of the passage.

Question #22: CR, Must, SP. The correct answer choice is (C)

To answer this Concept Reference question, Passage Structure and Viewpoint identification are both key. In the third paragraph, the author observes that our willingness to spend resources on risk reduction depends, at least in part, on whether we consider the risk to be incurred voluntarily or not. Additionally, such characterizations are often based on whether we approve of the purpose for which people run the risks (lines 33-35). Either factor would represent a suitable prephrase to this question.

Answer choice (A): This answer choice would be attractive only if you misunderstood the perspective you are being asked about. It is the author, not laypeople, who considers the ratio of dollars spent to lives saved as a significant factor in deciding how to fund risk-reduction measures. Laypeople, on the other hand, do not take such factors into consideration, as evidenced by their unwillingness to spend money on lowering the risks associated with skydiving (lines 35-39).

Answer choice (B): The author does not suggest that laypeople tend to defer to experts, but rather that they have their own inclinations regarding acceptable types of risk reduction expenditures, so this choice is not accurate according to the information presented in the passage and thus cannot be the right answer.

Answer choice (C): This is the correct answer choice, ss discussed above.

Answer choice (D): As with answer choice (A), this is a factor that informs the *author's* support for risk-prevention measures, not laypeople's willingness to do the same.

Answer choice (E): The total resources available for risk reduction is a factor that the *author*, not laypeople, is willing to take into account (lines 47-49). This answer choice is incorrect for the same reason answer choices (A) and (D) are incorrect: all three conflate the Author's Perspective with a Subject Perspective.

Question #23: CR, Must, SP. The correct answer choice is (D)

This is the second Concept Reference, Subject Perspective question in a row, and, yet again, Viewpoint identification and Passage Structure are key. This question asks us to identify a risk that is generally considered by laypeople to be involuntarily assumed. The author provided the examples of an asteroid impact and a plane crash, so one of these examples will likely be found in the correct answer choice.

Answer choice (A): Traveling in outer space is not mentioned in the passage, so this cannot be the right answer.

Answer choice (B): This is an Opposite answer, as the author provides skydiving as a specific example of risk that is undertaken *voluntarily*.

Answer choice (C): This is another Opposite answer choice, as the decision to become a firefighter is described as voluntary (line 42). People support firefighters because of the purpose for which the risk is incurred, not because the risk is incurred voluntarily.

Answer choice (D): This is the correct answer choice. In the second paragraph, the author discusses airplane travel as a risk laypeople generally consider to be involuntary, i.e. not freely assumed (lines 25-28). The fact that the author find such a characterization problematic has no bearing on question at hand.

Answer choice (E): This is an Opposite Answer, as mountain climbing is presented as an example of an activity in which participants *voluntarily* take on risk (line 4), so this choice can be confidently ruled out of contention.

Question #24: GR, Must, AP. The correct answer choice is (B)

After being presented with two Subject Perspective questions, now we need to answer a broad, Author's Perspective question. Due to the lack of any Specific or Concept Reference here, prephrasing the correct answer choice would be quite challenging. Instead, use your understanding of Argumentation and Main Point to narrow down the range of possible contenders. And remember: the correct answer choice must pass the Fact Test, i.e. it must be provable using the information contained in the passage.

Answer choice (A): This is a judgment likely to be made by a layperson (lines 35-39), not by the author. Read carefully and know whose viewpoint you are being asked about!

Answer choice (B): This is the correct answer choice. In lines 25-32, the author describes the common belief that the risk incurred by flying is involuntary, because passengers have no control over whether a plane is going to crash. The fact that people can choose not to fly has no bearing on how we characterize the risk of flying. Thus, our ability to choose whether to fly is likely to be deemed irrelevant to decisions about the government's role in regulating air safety.

Answer choice (C): The author neither makes nor provides basis for such a comparison, so this choice fails the Fact Test.

Answer choice (D): The author veers clear of proposing a strict definition of what constitutes a voluntarily or involuntarily incurred risk. The voluntariness is "not an all-or-nothing matter, but rather one of degree" (lines 24-25).

Answer choice (E): The author mentions asteroids as an example of involuntary risk but does not say that natural disasters are the main type of involuntary risk.

Question #25: SR, Must, P. The correct answer choice is (E)

The answer to a Specific Reference, Purpose question should generally be prephrased. Here, the author uses the phrase "no special magic" to indicate that the distinction between voluntary and involuntary is generally arbitrary, and that such distinctions are actually based on underlying value judgements. As such, the author asserts, such distinctions should not advise policy decisions in this area.

Answer choice (A): Notions like "voluntary" and "involuntary" may not be exhaustive, but this is not what the author meant by saying that there is "no special magic" to such notions. For this to be the correct answer, the discussion in the third paragraph would need to explain what other characteristics should be taken into account when analyzing risk. It does not.

Answer choice (B): The author does not assert that the terms "voluntary" and "involuntary" have been used to *intentionally* conceal the real reasons why the government tries to protect people from risks, so this cannot be the right answer choice to this Must Be True question.

Answer choice (C): Whether the meaning of the terms in question extends beyond their dictionary definitions is never addressed. The problem with these terms is that they are used subjectively, not that they are used figuratively.

Answer choice (D): This is a classic Half-Right, Half-Wrong answer choice. Notions like "voluntary" and "involuntary" serve as proxies (line 54) for developing a regulatory policy regarding risk management. In other words, they are mistakenly believed to be characteristics that inform policy decisions, not our understanding of the consequences of risk. The two have little in common.

Answer choice (E): This is the correct answer choice. As prephrased above, the distinction between voluntary and involuntary should not, according to the author, be used as a basis to diverge from basic public policy directives.

Question #26: GR, Must, AP. The correct answer choice is (B)

This is another question whose answer can be difficult to prephrase, since it is a Global Reference question. As always, it will be important to have a good grasp on the author's tone to confidently attack a Must Be True, Author's Perspective question.

Answer choice (A): The author says that the proper policy is to try to save as many lives as possible given the resources available. The license to intervene is therefore limited, contrary to what this answer choice suggests.

Answer choice (B): This is the correct answer choice. In lines 23-25, the author states that most environmental (and other) risks are a matter of degree.

Answer choice (C): The author does not compare these two groups' judgements regarding voluntariness, so there is no way that this can be the right answer to this Must Be True, Author's Perspective question.

Answer choice (D): The author makes no recommendation to increase the quantity of available resources devoted to risk prevention measures.

Answer choice (E): The author does not assert that every risk reduction policy must comport with most people's beliefs, but instead says that divergences from the general policy (of maximizing the number of lives saved) should be based on an understanding of people's judgments regarding specific risk prevention measures. Deference to popular opinion is rarely something we see on the LSAT. Understanding this bias should help you eliminate this answer choice relatively quickly.

Question #27: GR, Must, AP, T. The correct answer choice is (C)

The answer to this Author's Perspective, Tone question is prephrased in our VIEWSTAMP analysis above.

Answer choice (A): This answer choice contains extreme language ("chagrin at the rampant misunderstanding") that does not reflect the author's seemingly well-reasoned position.

Answer choice (B): Although the author is critical of policy guided mainly by laypeople's emphasis on the voluntariness of risk, there is no indication that this rationale would lead to excessive government regulation. In fact, we already know that it could make certain activities, such as skydiving, insufficiently regulated.

Answer choice (C): This is the correct answer choice. As discussed earlier, the author is critical of our rationale for determining which risks justify government intervention. In other words, she is skeptical about the reliability of our intuitions (about voluntariness) that serve as a general guide to deciding government risk-management policy.

Answer choice (D): This answer choice can easily be eliminated, because it contains an exaggeration ("sole criterion"). Just because the saving of human lives is a prerogative does not mean that it is the only criterion that can justify government intervention.

Answer choice (E): The author does not appear eager to persuade the reader that subtle biases distort the policy experts' risk analysis; rather, the point is that some distinctions that are characterized as being based on voluntariness are actually based on other considerations, such as approval of the act in question. The biases in question distort *laypeople's* analysis of risk, not policy experts'.

Glossary

Additional Premise:

Additional premises are premises that may be central to the argument or they may be secondary. To determine the importance of the premise, examine the remainder of the argument.

Argument:

A set of statements wherein one statement is claimed to follow from or be derived from the others. An argument requires a conclusion.

Assumption

An assumption is an unstated premise of an argument. Assumptions are an integral component of the argument that the author takes for granted and leaves unsaid.

Best (in Question Stems):

In order to maintain test integrity the test makers need to make sure their credited answer choice is as airtight and defensible as possible. Imagine what would occur if a question stem, let us say a Weaken question, did not include a "most" or "best" qualifier: any answer choice that weakened the argument, even if only very slightly, could then be argued to meet the criteria of the question stem. A situation like this would make constructing the test exceedingly difficult because any given problem might have multiple correct answer choices. To eliminate this predicament, the test makers insert "most" into the question stem, and then they can always claim there is one and only one correct answer choice.

Cannot Be True Questions:

Ask you to identify the answer choice that cannot be true or is most weakened based on the information in the passage. Question stem example:

"If the statements in the passage are true, which one of the following CANNOT be true?"

Cause (C):

The event that makes another event occur.

Cause and Effect (CE):

When one event is said to make another occur. The cause is the event that makes the other occur; the effect is the event that follows from the cause. By definition, the cause must occur before the effect, and the cause is the "activator" or "ignitor" in the relationship. The effect always happens at some point in time after the cause.

CE: See Cause and Effect.

Comparative Reading:

Starting with the June 2007 LSAT, the makers of the test introduced the dual passage format to the exam, and every LSAT now features one dual passage set per section. The dual passage set can appear anywhere within the section (first, second, third, or last), and, as with single passages, the number of questions varies from five to eight.

Complex Argument:

Arguments that contain more than one conclusion. In these instances, one of the conclusions is the main conclusion, and the other conclusions are subsidiary conclusions (also known as sub-conclusions). In basic terms, a complex argument makes an initial conclusion based on a premise. The author then uses that conclusion as the foundation (or premise) for another conclusion, thus building a chain with several levels.

Concept Reference (CR):

In Reading Comprehension, these questions refer to a specific concept discussed in the passage without reference to the location of the relevant discussion.

Conclusion:

A statement or judgment that follows from one or more reasons. Conclusions, as summary statements, are supposed to be drawn from and rest on the premises.

Conclusion/Premise Indicator Form:

The test makers will sometimes arrange premise and conclusion indicators in a way that is designed to be confusing. One of their favorite forms places a conclusion indicator and premise indicator back-to-back, separated by a comma, as in the following examples:

"Therefore, since..."
"Thus, because..."
"Hence, due to..."

Conditional Reasoning:

The broad name given to logical relationships composed of sufficient and necessary conditions. Any conditional statement consists of at least one sufficient condition and at least one necessary condition. In everyday use, conditional statements are often brought up using the "if...then" construction. Conditional reasoning can occur in any question type.

Contender:

An answer choice that appears somewhat attractive, interesting, or even confusing. Basically, any answer choice that you cannot immediately identify as incorrect.

Counter-argument:

A statement that actually contains an idea that is counter to the author's main argument. Counter-arguments bring up points of opposition or comparison.

CR: See Concept Reference

Effect:

The event that follows from the cause.

Exaggerated Answer:

Exaggerated Answers take information from the passage and then stretch that information to make a broader statement that is not supported by the passage.

Except:

When "except" is placed in a question it negates the logical quality of the answer choice you seek. Literally, it turns the intent of the question stem upside down.

Expansion (E):

Expansion questions require you to extrapolate ideas from the passage to determine one of three elements: where the passage was drawn from or how it could be titled, what sentence or idea could come before the passage, and what sentence or idea could follow the passage.

Fact Test™:

The correct answer to a Must Be True question can always be proven by referring to the facts stated in the passage. An answer choice that cannot be substantiated by proof in the passage is incorrect.

Global Reference (GR):

In Reading Comprehension, Global Reference questions ask about information without specifying a location or concept within the passage (for example, "According to the statements in the passage which one of the following must be true?")

GR: See Global Reference

I

Inference

In logic, an inference can be defined as something that must be true. If you are asked to identify an inference of the argument, you must find an item that must be true based on the information presented in the argument.

J

Justify the Conclusion Questions:

Justify the Conclusion questions ask you to supply a piece of information that, when added to the premises, proves the conclusion. These questions appear very rarely in the Reading Comprehension section. Question stem example:

"Which one of the following, if assumed, allows the conclusion above to be properly drawn?"

L

Least:

When "least" appears in a question stem you should treat it exactly the same as "except." Note: this advice holds true only when this word appears in the question stem! If you see the word "least" elsewhere on the LSAT, consider it to have its usual meaning of "in the lowest or smallest degree."

Loser:

An answer choice which strikes you as clearly incorrect.

M

Main Point:

The central idea, or ultimate conclusion, that the author is attempting to prove.

Main Point Questions (MP):

Main Point questions are a variant of Must Be True questions. As you might expect, a Main Point question asks you to find the primary conclusion made by the author. Question stem example:

"Which one of the following most accurately expresses the main point of the passage?"

Method of Reasoning

The way in which a passage forms its argument.

Most (in Question Stems):

In order to maintain test integrity the test makers need to make sure their credited answer choice is as airtight and defensible as possible. Imagine what would occur if a question stem, let us say a Weaken question, did not include a "most" qualifier: any answer choice that weakened the argument, even if only very slightly, could then be argued to meet the criteria of the question stem. A situation like this would make constructing the test exceedingly difficult because any given problem might have multiple correct answer choices. To eliminate this predicament, the test makers insert "most" into the question stem, and then they can always claim there is one and only one correct answer choice.

MP: See Main Point.

Most Supported: See Must Be True.

Must Be True:

Must Be True questions ask you to identify the answer choice that is best proven by the information in the passage. Question stem examples:

"If the statements above are true, which one of the following must also be true?"
"Which one of the following can be properly inferred from the passage?"

N

N: See Necessary Condition.

Necessary Condition (N):

An event or circumstance whose occurrence is required in order for a sufficient condition to occur.

New Information:

Information that is not mentioned explicitly in the passage, or does not follow as a consequence of the information in the passage.

Not Necessarily True:

The logical opposite of "Must be true." When an answer choice is not proven by the information in the passage.

O

O: See Organization.

Opposite Answer:

Provides an answer that is completely opposite of the stated facts of the passage. Opposite Answers are very attractive to students who are reading too quickly or carelessly and quite frequently appear in Strengthen and Weaken questions.

Organization (O):

These Reading Comprehension questions ask you to describe a characteristic of the overall structure of the passage. For example, "The second paragraph serves primarily to...," or "Which one of the following best describes the organization of the passage." These questions are similar to the Method of Reasoning questions in the Logical Reasoning section, but are generally broader.

P

P: See Purpose

Parallel Reasoning:

In the Reading Comprehension section, these questions are usually broader in scope, asking you to find the scenario most analogous to an action in the passage. There is less of a focus on identifying premises and conclusions than in the Logical Reasoning section.

Passage:

The Reading Comprehension section is composed of three long reading passages, each approximately 450 words in length, and two shorter comparative reading passages. The passage topics are drawn from a variety of subjects, and each passage is followed by a series of five to eight questions that ask you to determine viewpoints in the passage, analyze organizational traits, evaluate specific sections of the passage, or compare facets of two different passages.

Premise:

A fact, proposition, or statement from which a conclusion is made. Literally, the premises give the reasons why the conclusion should be accepted.

Principle (PR):

A broad rule that specifies what actions or judgments are correct in certain situations. These are not a separate question type but are instead an "overlay" that appears in a variety of question types and the presence of the Principle indicator serves to broaden the scope of the question.

PR: See Principle.

Purpose (P):

These Reading Comprehension questions ask why the author referred to a particular word, phrase, or idea. This is essentially an extended Method of Reasoning question, requiring you to go beyond simply identifying the argument structure, and asking you the reasons behind the author's use of words or ideas.

Question Stem:

Follows the passage and poses a question directed at the passage. Make sure to read the question stem very carefully. Some stems direct you to focus on certain aspects of the passage and if you miss these clues you make the problem much more difficult.

Resolve the Paradox Questions:

Every Resolve the Paradox stimulus contains a discrepancy or seeming contradiction. You must find the answer choice that best explains the situation. Question stem example:

"Which one of the following, if true, would most effectively resolve the apparent paradox in the passage?"

Reverse Answer:

Occurs when an answer choice contains familiar elements from the passage, but rearranges those elements to create a new, unsupported statement.

S: See Sufficient Condition

Scope:

The range to which the premises and conclusion encompass certain ideas. An argument with a narrow scope is definite in its statements, whereas a wide scope argument is less definite and allows for a greater range of possibility.

Shell Game:

An idea or concept is raised in the passage, and then a very similar idea appears in the answer choice, but the idea is changed just enough to be incorrect but still attractive. This trick is called the Shell Game because it abstractly resembles those street corner gambling games where a person hides a small object underneath one of three shells, and then scrambles them on a flat surface while a bettor tries to guess which shell the object is under.

SN:

Abbreviation for Sufficient and Necessary Conditions. May be seen separately in diagramming as "S" and "N." See also Sufficient Condition and Necessary Condition.

Specific Reference (SR):

These Reading Comprehension questions provide you with a specific line reference or a reference to an easily found word or phrase within the passage. To attack the questions, refer to the line reference in the question and then begin reading about 5 lines above the reference.

SR: See Specific Reference.

Strengthen/Support Questions:

These questions ask you to select the answer choice that provides support for the author's argument or strengthens it in some way. Question stem examples:

"Which one of the following, if true, most strengthens the argument?"
"Which one of the following, if true, most strongly supports the statement above?"

Structure:

The order in which things are presented in the passage.

Sub-conclusion:

A conclusion that is then used as a premise to support another conclusion. This is also known as a secondary or subsidiary conclusion.

Sufficient Condition (S):

An event or circumstance whose occurrence indicates that a necessary condition must also occur. The sufficient condition does not make the necessary condition occur; it is simply an indicator.

T

Tone/Attitude:

Identifying the tone or attitude of each group can sometimes be more challenging. Attitude is the state of mind or feeling that each group takes to the subject matter at hand, and for our purposes, "attitude" and "tone" will be used interchangeably. In most passages, LSAT authors tend not to be extreme in their opinions.

V

VIEWSTAMP:

This acronym helps you remember the five critical elements to track in Reading Comprehension passages:

VIEW =	the different **VIEW**points in the passage	
S	=	the **S**tructure of the passage
T	=	the **T**one of the passage
A	=	the **A**rguments in the passage
MP	=	the **M**ain **P**oint

Viewpoint:

A viewpoint is the position or approach taken by a person or group. On the LSAT, Reading Comprehension passages typically contain anywhere from one to six different viewpoints. These viewpoints can be the author's or those of groups discussed by the author.

W

Weaken Questions:

Weaken questions ask you to attack or undermine the author's argument. Question stem example:

"Which one of the following, if true, most seriously weakens the argument?"

---

④M   T W Y   6max   ②M

Ø consec or same quarter

	1	2	3	4
✗	Y	MW	T	MY
	M	YW	MY	M/
[	M	W	M	WY
	M	TW	M	YT
	M	W	M Y	MY/T
	MM	W	M	Y I
	M	W	M	Y/WY
MTY		W	M/	M/WY
T/Y	MW	T/Y	WMM
M		W	MTY	
M	M	TWY	W	
MTY		W	MY	
				T
T		W		
Y	TW		Y	M
T	MW			

M   T/Y

M   T/YW
    T

E L M O P S Y ⑦

M → ØY   Y → ØM   M → ØY → L/O (Øboth) → F+S
F → ØP   P → ØF   5max   L+O → ⇢Y → ØM
ØY → L/O or smiler L+O → Y
Øboth L+O → F+S   ØF+S → both L+O

IN	OUT
✗ F L S Y	MOP
✗ L O Y F/P	M S F/P
LO Y	FM
P L O Y S/	FM S/
P O/	L Y F Ø/
Y FS O/	L M P O/
L/O	ØFØ FL
LØ	L O Y P
F S M	

FL or FP both out
P/S or both out

cbf

Smax

L+O → Y → ØM → ØS
S → M   ØM → ØS